MAT
MEMORIES

★ ★

To David
Best Wishes Always

J. L. Curry

95/250

JOHN "ALEXANDER" AREZZI
AND GREG OLIVER

MAT MEMORIES

MY WILD LIFE IN
PRO WRESTLING,
COUNTRY MUSIC, AND
WITH THE METS

WITH FOREWORDS BY
MICK FOLEY, JOHN GIBBONS,
AND SUZANNE ALEXANDER

Published by ECW Press
665 Gerrard Street East
Toronto, Ontario, Canada M4M 1Y2
416-694-3348 / info@ecwpress.com

Editor for the Press: Michael Holmes
Cover design: David Drummond
Cover photographs from the author's personal collection

To the best of his abilities, the author has related experiences, places, people, and organizations from his memories of them. In order to protect the privacy of others, he has, in some instances, changed the names of certain people and details of events and places.

LIBRARY AND ARCHIVES CANADA CATALOGUING IN PUBLICATION

Title: Mat memories : my wild life in pro wrestling, country music and with the Mets / John "Alexander" Arezzi and Greg Oliver ; with forewords by Mick Foley, John Gibbons, and Suzanne Alexander.

Names: Arezzi, John, 1957- author. | Oliver, Greg, author. | Foley, Mick, writer of foreword. | Gibbons, John, 1962- writer of foreword. | Alexander, Suzanne (Radio producer), writer of foreword.

Identifiers: Canadiana (print) 20200392077 | Canadiana (ebook) 20200392220

ISBN 978-1-77041-564-5 (softcover)
ISBN 978-1-77305-693-7 (EPUB)
ISBN 978-1-77305-694-4 (PDF)
ISBN 978-1-77305-695-1 (Kindle)

Subjects: LCSH: Arezzi, John, 1957- | LCSH: Wrestling promoters—United States—Biography. | LCSH: Sports personnel—United States—Biography. | LCSH: Concert agents—United States—Biography. | LCSH: Wrestling—United States—History. | LCSH: Country music—United States—History and criticism. | LCSH: New York Mets (Baseball team)—History. | LCGFT: Autobiographies.

Classification: LCC GV1196.A74 A3 2021 | DDC 796.812092—dc23

PRINTED AND BOUND IN CANADA

PRINTING: MARQUIS   5   4   3   2   1

*For my nephew, godson,
and best friend, Dominic.*

★ ★ ★ ★ ★ ★ ★ ★ ★ ★ ★ ★ ★ ★ ★ ★ ★ ★ ★ ★

MY NEPHEW, DOMINIC, AND ME AT
A METS PRESEASON GAME IN PORT
ST. LUCIE, FLORIDA, IN 2016. WE'VE
GONE TO SPRING TRAINING EVERY YEAR
SINCE 2007 (EXCEPT IN 2020 WHEN
COVID-19 HIT AND CANCELED OUR
ANNUAL SABBATICAL).

TABLE OF CONTENTS

WRESTLING FOREWORD

BY MICK FOLEY

I may be a grizzled veteran of the pro wrestling business, but I still enjoy watching today's product. But I find that some of today's wrestlers, talented as they may be, are sometimes missing that stamp of authenticity when it comes to their promo skills. It's not necessarily their fault; many of today's superstars simply lack a place to get their repetitions in, a necessary process that makes those promo skills part of muscle memory.

When I met John Arezzi in 1989, my wrestling career was at a crossroads. I was working as an independent wrestler, unaffiliated with any

WHY AM I USING A PEN TO INTERVIEW MICK FOLEY IN 1992?

★ IX ★

major wrestling organization. I had a vision for the type of character I wanted Cactus Jack to become. But I had been given little chance to work on my promo skills in the Memphis, Continental, and World Class territories, and even less with my first run in WCW.

Enter John Arezzi's *Pro Wrestling Spotlight* radio show—a cutting-edge program that somehow seamlessly blended an insider's look at the business, with an enthusiastic ability to promote current storylines. While it would seem odd and very much out of place for a wrestler to be in character for an extended amount of time on a modern show, John somehow made it work.

While I would be very hesitant to go back and listen to an episode featuring two hours of my voice, in character as Cactus Jack, it did wonders for my confidence, and I believe that my appearances on *Pro Wrestling Spotlight* were a major contributor to my vastly improved microphone skills as my career progressed. John's show is where I got a lot of my reps in, where cutting promos started to become part of that muscle-memory process.

John even played a small role in getting my foot back in the WCW door, as I was part of a *Pro Wrestling Spotlight* fan excursion to Baltimore, to watch the 1991 Great American Bash. It was on this outing that I had my first meeting with a legend, "The American Dream" Dusty Rhodes, who was booking WCW at the time.

From his humble origins as the president of Fred Blassie's fan club, to ringside photographer, to radio host, to investigative journalist, to promoter, to fan convention pioneer, to his own short-lived wrestling career (two matches), there is not much that John Arezzi has not done in professional wrestling.

This book is a very enjoyable account of a most interesting man, who played a pivotal role in the way the pro wrestling business was perceived. I give it a very enthusiastic Foley thumbs-up!

BASEBALL FOREWORD

BY JOHN GIBBONS

Life can be funny.

In 1981, while playing Class A baseball in the New York Mets organization, I shared a house in Shelby, North Carolina, with three guys, all different and unique in their own ways. What a mix, with J.P. Ricciardi from Boston, Mike Hennessy from New Jersey, John Arezzi from Long Island, and then me, a Texas-raised boy. Those boys never lacked for confidence, let's say that.

WHEN JOHN GIBBONS FINALLY MADE THE MAJOR LEAGUE ROSTER WITH THE NEW YORK METS IN 1984, I WAS THERE TO SEE HIM.

Since it was his rental, John had one bedroom, and J.P., Mike, and I took turns with the other bedroom. The other nights were rotated between the couch and the floor.

We weren't the cleanest of roommates. When we hit the road for games, we'd often leave a mess behind, and since John didn't travel with the team, he was the one that faced the pile of dishes and the mice scurrying across the counter. His Italian temper surfaced a few times, but we just laughed at him!

Out of the blue, John left baseball to get into music, after seeing Patty Loveless perform in a rock 'n' roll band. We thought he was crazy, but he was a hard-headed, brash New Yorker and did what he wanted.

As our career paths went different ways, we didn't see each other much. When I could help him with tickets for a baseball game, I would. That love of baseball—an obsession really—never left John. If he had stayed in the game, he would probably have succeeded.

His life is fascinating to me. One minute he's working for a baseball team. Then he becomes a manager in the music business. Then he's getting body slammed in the wrestling business!

Fast-forward to recent times, and my daughter, Jordan, developed a desire to get into country music, and who do I call? My old pal, John, who has connections in Nashville, and did his part to open doors for her and provide her with opportunities. That's a good friend stepping up. Johnny is a good buddy of mine, a good man.

Then he told me he was writing a book about his life.

I was honest with him: "I won't buy it, but good for you!"

COUNTRY FOREWORD

BY SUZANNE ALEXANDER

With a friendship that has lasted over 25 years, I have witnessed John's intense passion for music, wrestling, and baseball.

It's his sense of humor that drew me in and it's that humor that I still love to this day. But he's a man with a mission, always thinking and creating. There's never a time when he isn't inspiring someone to chase their dreams as he has chased his.

SUZANNE ALEXANDER
AND SARAH DARLING
IN THE GREAT
AMERICAN COUNTRY
STUDIO IN 2012.

It was his connections that started me on my career path in country music television and for that I will always be grateful.

As you read this book you can almost feel John thinking of his next move. His recall and storytelling make you feel like you're in the room for every big moment, and there are many.

I'll be the first to buy my ticket when his life story becomes a movie.

1.

INTRODUCTION

When my alarm clock goes off, and I eventually drag myself out of bed, I always take a moment to consider who I will be today.

Am I John Arezzi, the pioneering pro wrestling radio journalist, who hosted an influential show, *Pro Wrestling Spotlight*, in New York City from the late 1980s until the mid-'90s? The one who promoted wrestling shows across the U.S., and in southeast Asia and South America,

WHAT A LONG, STRANGE TRIP IT'S BEEN, AS JOHN AREZZI, JOHN ANTHONY, AND JOHN ALEXANDER.

featuring lucha libre stars before it was trendy? The one who was hated by Vince McMahon for my outspoken crusade for details of WWF's steroid issues and sex scandals? I'm also the one who helped Vince Russo get into the business, which I'll never be forgiven for by some people.

Or am I John Alexander, the respected music business executive in Nashville, with ties to many names in country music? You know, the one who discovered the incredibly talented Patty Loveless in a dive bar in Shelby, North Carolina, and started her on the path to stardom. Or more recently, the one who opened the doors for Kelsea Ballerini, which she proceeded to kick down and rise to the top of the industry. You'll find my LinkedIn profile under that name.

I do know for certain that I am no longer John Anthony, professional wrestler. He called it quits after two ludicrous matches, his sanity winning out over vanity and curiosity. John Arezzi, promising baseball executive, is also long in my past, though my love for all things about the New York Mets continues through thick and (mostly) thin.

What I do know each and every morning is the day will bring something new and unique. Don't believe me? Read on.

2.

GROWING UP CONNECTED

Let's get this out of the way early. I'm Italian and grew up listening to my grandparents speak in Italian, when they didn't want you to know what they were saying. I'm from the Bushwick section of Brooklyn originally and spent my best years on Long Island. So naturally my father had connections to the Mob.

Aside from running a small Brooklyn grocery store for many years, my dad, Salvatore Arezzi, worked overnight at a trucking company. But on the side, he was what you would call a bookmaker. He worked for a pretty high-up organized crime guy, Federico "Fritzy" Giovanelli, a captain or "Capo" for the Genovese crime family in New York.

Dad would take bets on "the Numbers" over the phone. "The Numbers" referred to the last three digits of whatever the race track announced that it took in ("the handle"). So, if they announced that they took in $4,805,125, then "the Number" was 125 that day. For a dollar bet, you would win $500. My dad was part of a team that took the bets. He and the rest of Fritzy's "crew" would work out of various apartments in Brooklyn or Queens. Although it was considered organized crime, Dad's involvement was not with the violent Mob that people immediately picture in their minds.

Dad would go around and collect the money, and at the end of the day on Sunday, he'd head over to turn the dough over to the man I called "Uncle Fritzy."

As a kid, I occasionally helped out my dad in the grocery store on weekends. I wasn't the only one in the neighborhood who helped, either. One kid was Tony Iadanza, whom my dad used to help cross the street when he was a little kid to avoid the busy traffic outside his store. When he got older, Tony delivered groceries, and my father taught him how to pick proper fruit and vegetables. Decades later, Tony Danza of *Who's the Boss?* was on *The Today Show*, talking about those days with my father. My sister Donna got to know Tony well through mutual connections in Little Italy, an area of New York City she frequented often. Tony operated a cheese store there for a while. I got to meet him twice, and both times he gave me a good hug and spoke fondly of "Big Sam," which made me happy.

When I helped my dad, it usually meant putting together the various pieces of the massive Sunday newspapers, then selling them to make a little extra money—but there was bigger money made when I accompanied dad on his gambling drop-offs.

I always loved going with him to drop off the money to Uncle Fritzy. It was absolutely like the characters in *Goodfellas* or *The Sopranos*. There was Frenchy, Louie "The Head," Buddy, and others with street names that were unforgettable. Fritzy always had this big cigar going, and he talked out the side of his mouth.

They called my dad "Big Sam." Uncle Fritzy would see me sitting there waiting for my dad, whom he would call into his office when it was his turn to turn over the receipts, often with a loud voice. After my dad was done, he'd yell, "John Arezzi!" and call me in. He'd pat me on the head, ask how my mom was, and then shake my hand. I loved shaking Uncle Fritzy's hand, as every time I did, there would be some money in it, 20 to 100 dollars. Dad always warned me to say only nice things and to always thank him.

I never gave it much thought, to be honest. You knew that everything wasn't on the up and up, but you kept your mouth shut. You didn't ask questions. It was just part of our life. It was just like all the other Italian families in the neighborhood, at least the ones my father hung out with. They were all in that industry, so to speak, worker bees like my dad.

There was a reason that Dad had three jobs too. My mom, Mary, had mental health issues all of her life, and it was easier for him to be out working than to deal with her.

Though my dad, who did finish high school, worked very hard, there was never a robust income coming into the house. There were always economic problems. We weren't broke, as in living on the street, but nothing was ever simple or easy.

★ ★ ★ ★ ★

My mom and dad came from families from different parts of Italy. Dad's family were from towns close to southern Sicily, and they immigrated to New York from Italy in the early 1900s to pursue the American Dream. My dad was born in the U.S. in 1931. They were a hard-working lot, determined to make a middle-class living.

My mother's side of the family is more of a mess. They were from the south-central part of Italy, Naples, and some made their way to America. Overall, though, they were gypsy-spirited. There could be some Native American ancestry in my blood, through my grandfather on my mother's side, Anthony Guerri. He ran a social club in New York called the Chesterfield Lodge, and died when I was two years old. He was called "Chief" by a lot of people, because he had a darker complexion and a really full mane of white hair. My grandmother, Frances—Fanny—was very rough around the edges. She had a great heart for her grandchildren, but she was a tough cookie. I often tried to get more information on the family from her, but she never cracked. She went to the grave with many secrets. I do know she spent time in jail and was a bootlegger with Grandpa Tony during the Prohibition Era. They ran a speakeasy for a while as well.

★ ★ ★ ★ ★

★ ★ ★ ★ ★ ★ ★ ★ ★ ★ ★ ★ ★

SALVATORE AND MARY AREZZI IN 1955.

When Sam Arezzi met Mary Louise Guerri, two years younger than he was, it was the early 1950s and they were both young teens. Their eventual marriage brought to light the dislike that Sicilians had for Neapolitans back in Italy, and how it continued in America. Knowing that, it should not be a surprise that there was never any harmony between the two families because my dad's side always looked down upon my mom's family.

They had three children. My sister Linda came along in June 1952. I was next, born John Thomas Arezzi on January 25, 1957. A third child, Donna, arrived in June 1962. I know my mom miscarried around 1959 with a boy.

★ ★ ★ ★ ★

Our part of Bushwick had a bit of everything—Blacks, Puerto Ricans, and a heavy concentration of Italians. It was really an ethnic melting pot. We lived on Palmetto Street. Our street, like all the others in the area, had three-story apartment buildings, each housing six families, two on each floor. There was a small candy store on the corner that I used to go to, where you could get a malted milkshake and pretzels as a treat. A small grocery store was nearby as well. Mom used to give me a dollar bill to go to the store to buy cigarettes for her, bread, and milk. Yes, one dollar paid for it all . . .

There was a garment factory across the street from us. One time, it was robbed right before our eyes. Guys came out of it with guns, shooting. Mom just calmly brought us inside. Another time, there was a gang war in the middle of the street we lived on.

Inside the apartment building, I remember a German family living right next door that my mom was really close to. There was also a musician in the apartment building next to ours, because I can remember him playing his guitar, and the window was usually propped open, with the metronome keeping time. He had a mentally disabled kid that was always running away.

It was Brooklyn life. Ours was just more complicated than most.

★ ★ ★ ★ ★

Grandpa Tony gave my mom a nickname that lasted all her life: "Snooky." Any time my mom was introduced to anyone, she'd say (if she liked you), "My friends call me Snooky." If not, it was simply Mary. She was funny, beautiful, and very personable and had a great sense of humor, but she had some hard times growing up. Grandpa Tony was involved with unsavory people, and he was a heavy gambler. He once bet his home on a World Series game, but luckily won. He did owe the wrong people a lot of money and at times there were people after him. My mom told me that they'd have security stay with them as protection.

From all that, she became very paranoid at a very young age, making for a very hard upbringing. That paranoia continued, and, over the course of her life, she had several nervous breakdowns and was institutionalized more than once. Officially, she was bipolar and a paranoid schizophrenic. Her last nervous breakdown was in the mid-'70s, and she stabilized after that. But she was always paranoid and volatile and always afraid on the one side of her personality. On the other side, she was funny, giving, and caring and protected and watched over her kids.

My parents never really got along. There were periods of time when they did, but for the most part, it was not a comfortable childhood. We were always on edge as kids, wondering when our parents would start fighting or when Mom might freak out.

We were Roman Catholic but rarely went to church. Linda and I attended St. Barbara's Catholic school in Brooklyn. That first day of school, I was crying hysterically as I went into the classroom. My mother walked me there. The nuns were so nice. "Oh, don't worry, Mrs. Arezzi. We'll take care of Johnny. He'll be fine." Then as soon as she left, the nun put me in a full nelson, took me to my seat, and slapped me across the head. That was the way they ruled, and corporal punishment was in regular use. It didn't help that I was very introverted and had no confidence; I was petrified of almost everything.

There was a little statue of a saint that each kid got the chance to bring home, and it opened up into a small altar, with a simple message: "The family that prays together stays together." I was excited to get my turn to bring it home, but when I got there, my parents were having a knock-down, drag-out fight. Our group family prayer never worked; instead cops were at the house, called by the neighbors because of the brawl.

WITH GRANDPA JOHN AREZZI AND LINDA IN 1961.

As a family, we would go out weekly to Sunday dinner. Or a special treat would be to go to the local drive-in movies, the Johnny All Weather Drive In. We would all be in the car together, us kids in our pajamas, my dad buying the snacks from the concession stand, and all of us hoping Snooky would be in a good mood. There were family dinners, but compared to other Italian families, both Mom's and Dad's sides were relatively small. We did have one family vacation, in 1960, to the Lake George resort area in upstate New York. It sticks with me because we never went on another trip.

★ ★ ★ ★ ★

In early 1963, we left Palmetto Street in Bushwick and moved into the Ridgewood section in Queens, which was a nicer area. The neighborhood where I was born became crime-infested and was becoming a ghetto. Apartment buildings were beginning to burn down. So we made our escape, and while only five miles away, Woodbine Street in Ridgewood seemed like paradise. One side of the street were all Italians and the other side of the street were all Germans. There was always competition and conflict between the two sides of the street, especially during the winter when we'd have snowball and ice-ball fights with each other. It was wacky. My new Catholic school was nicer than the first, with kinder nuns.

I know that the move was in 1963, since I was there when President John F. Kennedy was killed. He was a hero to me. I remember his presidency, and was glued to every speech he made on television. I was in the second grade on November 22, when an announcement came over the loudspeaker that he had been shot. About five minutes later, there was another announcement on the intercom from the Mother Superior: "Our president is dead." We were dismissed early. Walking home from school with Linda, we thought the world was coming to an end: "They killed the president. Are they going to kill the Pope next?" It was usual to see all the mothers and grandmothers looking out their windows, watching for their kids and talking across the way to each other. We told Mom the news when we got home, as she hadn't heard. She started yelling at us, thinking we were lying to her—until she turned on the TV and saw that we were telling the truth. That night, when my dad came home from work, was the first time that I'd actually ever seen him cry. For the next four days, like everyone else, we were glued to the television. It left an impression on me. Linda and I saw the killing of Lee Harvey Oswald live on TV, which was traumatizing.

★ ★ ★ ★ ★

A year later, in March of 1964, after my parents' four closest friends, Louie and Gracie Esposito and Ann and Michael "Midge" Belvedere, left Brooklyn for the suburbs, Dad decided to follow. We settled in West Babylon, New York, located in Suffolk County on the south shore of the "Island" as it was called. It was a big deal, as Dad bought a house—our first—for $18,000. It was like going out to the country, a fresh start for us all, and we were so happy and excited to make that move. We lived three houses down from the Belvederes on Fifth Street, within walking distance of the Espositos, who lived on Third Street. Midge and Louie, like my dad, were also in organized crime crews. The three families often got together to socialize. There was a real bond between us all.

Our next-door neighbors were the Gallaghers, an Irish family. That was the first time I saw a truly functional family unit—like on *Leave It to Beaver*. The two oldest boys, Michael and Brian, became my best friends, and the family became role models of a sort.

We went to a public school for the first time, Forest Avenue Elementary, and we definitely didn't miss the nuns.

Switching from a black and white TV to a color one was another highlight of Long Island. Getting to watch *Superman* in color every afternoon was amazing. When we got the latest *TV Guide*, I'd circle all the listings for shows that were in color.

Academically, I definitely wasn't a star student; I was just scraping by. Socially, I was still really shy. I can distinctly remember only a few times that I got in trouble as a kid. Once, while still living in Brooklyn, when I was four or five years old, we were at a hardware store, and I stole a mousetrap, of all things. Walking home from the store, my mom noticed that something was amiss with me. I showed her the mousetrap, and she marched me back into the store to hand it back in.

Then during my time on Long Island, I was hanging out with some friends, trying to fit in with the gang. We were in a wooded area overlooking a fairly busy highway. We'd make mudballs and throw them at the cars. We hit one on the windshield and the car skidded, and everyone started running. I was the slowest runner and I got nabbed by the driver.

He didn't call the cops or anything, but yelled, "What's the matter with you kids? You could have killed somebody!"

★ ★ ★ ★ ★

My two sisters each influenced me in their own ways.

Linda, being five years older, was someone whom I looked up to. She would be key to fueling my dual passions for professional wrestling and music. Headstrong and always getting attention for misbehaving, Linda, while cool to me, was a handful. She was a hippie early on. It suited her, free-spirited as she was. She dropped out of school, during one of my Mother's stays at the psychiatric hospital, to get her dresser's license. My sister partied a lot and loved to stir the shit, creating havoc in the house often. She met her soulmate Eddie Behnen in 1971 at a rock nightclub, got pregnant the following year, and at 20 gave birth to my niece Melissa. A small wedding followed, but I didn't get to attend. Snooky got into a fight with Linda the night before the wedding, because my sister chose to wear a red wedding dress. My mom was unhappy, so we were not allowed to go. Linda and Eddie had two more kids: Eddie Jr. was born in 1975 and Michael followed in 1978. Melissa, Eddie, and Michael had

★ ★ ★ ★ ★ ★ ★ ★ ★ ★ ★ ★ ★ ★ ★ ★

LINDA AND ME IN 1958.

a tougher upbringing than we did, as Linda unfortunately also suffered from the sickness of being bipolar. And she and Eddie struggled financially all the time. She developed lung cancer in April 2009 and died in June, just a few months after being diagnosed. Her beloved Eddie died in December 2018.

A RARE PHOTO OF ALL MY FAMILY AT MY NEPHEW DOMINIC'S CHRISTENING IN 1998. LEFT TO RIGHT ARE MY NEPHEW EDDIE BOY BEHNEN, MY NIECE MELISSA BEHNEN-COLUCCO HOLDING HER SON JOHNNY COLUCCO, MY MOM MARY "SNOOKY" AREZZI HOLDING DOMINIC, MY SISTER DONNA AREZZI-DIBIASE WITH MELISSA'S DAUGHTER GABRIELLE, ME AND SISTER LINDA AREZZI-BEHNEN.

Donna is five years younger than me, and she always had this wonderful, bubbly personality. She was also the caretaker of the family. When my mom was going through her bouts with psychosis, Donna cleaned, cooked, and had way too much responsibility for her age. Donna was a model student in school, very social, and involved with many clubs, including being in the school band as a baton twirler and later in the color guard. She always had a huge circle of friends in high school and beyond. I'm pretty sure she keeps in touch with everyone she has met in her life. When asked to describe her, I usually mention Marisa Tomei's character in *My Cousin Vinny*. That's Donna to a tee. She'll come up often in the narrative, as she worked in radio as well, and her son, Dominic, is the light of my life.

★ ★ ★ ★ ★ ★ ★ ★ ★ ★ ★ ★ ★ ★ ★ ★ ★

THAT WAS ME IN GRADE 5.

During my formative years, the three keys to my life developed, my personal Holy Trinity, if you will. First there was pro wrestling, which I'd discovered just prior to moving to Long Island. Then there was baseball, and my love of the New York Mets.

And then there were the Beatles.

Linda turned me on to them. We heard "I Want to Hold Your Hand" on the radio, and then they announced that they were coming to do *The Ed Sullivan Show*. We were all in immediately.

When they came to America on that first trip, they stayed at the Plaza Hotel in New York City, a tidbit we had learned from the news. My sister baited me, "Call the Plaza Hotel and talk to the Beatles!" She wouldn't do it because she was too shy. I deepened my voice as I called, "Hey man, can I speak to the Beatles?" Of course, I didn't get through.

We watched them on *Ed Sullivan* and that changed everything. I just found a love for music, and I owe it all to Linda. It wasn't just the Beatles, either, as she told me about all the great new bands she'd heard. I'd sit with her and her friends as they listened to the latest single or album.

★ ★ ★ ★ ★

Now, West Babylon isn't as full of Italian-Americans as it used to be, but it's still home to Donna and Dominic, and I'm fortunate to rent the basement apartment in the same house when I'm in New York. Our roots are deep in the town.

I'm not sure that either Donna or I could actually count the number of places we have lived around West Babylon—at least a dozen if I were to guess. We had to sell the family home in 1974, because Dad needed the money. He didn't get what it was worth either, since none of us were handy, and when things broke, we just left them.

We moved into a two-family home in West Babylon briefly, and then after my dad left my mom and I went to college, it seemed like she and Donna had to find a new place to live every year or two. Some of the moves were financially driven, but most were because my mom would get thrown out because of her bipolar episodes and fights with landlords, other tenants, or neighbors. From 1974, when we sold our house, to the time Donna got married and moved out, the family lived on Lynn Place, Nims Avenue, Ninth Street, Justice Street, Herzel Boulevard. Get the picture? At one point, we needed a bigger place, since Linda came to live with us, with her baby and her husband.

★ ★ ★ ★ ★

We didn't have the traditional huge Italian family, and small in number though we were, we were fiercely loyal to each other. I found myself jealous of families like the Gallaghers, who seemed so normal. Their mother didn't go off the rails and get carted off to an asylum, only to return months later, like nothing had happened. Since we didn't have a large family, we called my parents' friends, like the Espositos and Belvederes, "aunt" and "uncle" because of how close we were to them. We still get together with the Espositos for most holidays.

In the early 1970s, there was a movement propagating the idea that Italians were being discriminated against. Many people thought that if you were Italian, you had to be connected to the Mob. (We were,

though.) Joe Colombo, founder and leader of the Colombo crime family, started the Italian-American Anti-Defamation League, which became the Italian-American Civil Rights League. A second big rally was held in Columbus Circle, in Manhattan, on June 28, 1971. Colombo lined up this whole day of protests and hired entertainers to perform. My dad took Linda and me with him to the rally. He left us when we got there to find his crew and told us not to get lost.

Colombo got up to start the rally, and he was shot three times. It was a hit by "Crazy Joe" Gallo. The people in organized crime felt that Colombo was bringing too much attention to Italians and the Mafia. Colombo wasn't killed, though, and lingered on for years, mentally incapacitated, before he died. The man who shot Colombo, Jerome Johnson, was immediately killed, on site, by bodyguards. So all these shots were ringing out in the middle of Columbus Circle. We didn't actually see the shooting, just heard it, as we weren't anywhere near the stage, and didn't know what the hell was going on.

It was so hot that day, between the heat and the crowd, that I passed out in the middle of it—but that was after the shootings, and after the rally was canceled. My sister looked after me, and got me through it, and we later found Dad and left. When we got home, we watched all about it on the news. It was horrible. African-Americans were being attacked just for being in the area.

Being Italian has its obvious negative connotations, like that chaotic day. But I accept everything that comes with being an Italian-American and am very proud of my heritage, even more so as I get older.

3.

FRIEND TO "THE KING OF MEN"

The wrestling bug bit me hard in 1964.

My sister Linda called me to the TV: "Johnny, come in the living room, I don't know what this is!" She was sitting on the floor watching midget wrestlers. "There's little men fighting each other." I couldn't believe it and didn't know what it was either. I was drawn in immediately.

As great as that was, up next it was scheduled to be Dr. Jerry Graham teaming with Smasher Sloan against Bruno Sammartino and his cousin Antonio Pugliese. Throughout the match, the announcer kept going, "Bruno hasn't arrived yet." Miguel Perez filled in as a partner to Pugliese. They were getting pummeled and there was a roar from the crowd, and this big, hulking Italian guy wearing a business suit and carrying luggage—suitcases in both hands—ran to the ring. He threw his suitcases over the ropes and proceeded to beat Graham over the head with one. There was blood. Ray Morgan was the announcer, and after the brawl stopped, he went over to Graham for an interview, and commented, "I think you need a doctor." Dr. Jerry replied, "I don't need a doctor. I'm my own doctor!"

That was it; I was hooked. I started watching wrestling every week, because it was fascinating. Wrestling moved around a lot back then, changing timeslots and channels. When my family moved to Long Island, there was a period of time in mid-1965 when I couldn't find it. Then in 1966 it was back, and I was elated. I got to see Spiros Arion for the first time, who was one of my all-time favorites. There was "The Friendly Ox," who later became one of wrestling's greatest heels, as Ox Baker. And of course, Bruno Sammartino was my hero, and I was glued to the set whenever he appeared.

It took awhile, until I was 10 years old, to start pestering my dad about taking me to a WWWF show at Madison Square Garden. I had turned my friend John Belvedere onto wrestling, and his father was game, so we all went together. That show in 1967 was headlined by Gorilla Monsoon against Bruno Sammartino, and we excitedly talked about what could happen on the drive into New York City.

We bought our tickets at the box office and as we were about to go in, we were stopped. We had no clue that you had to be 14 years old to attend the matches at Madison Square Garden; if they announced that on TV, it certainly never registered with me. We returned the tickets to the box office. My dad was pretty pissed and his friend was like, "What a waste of time. We drove all the way from Long Island." It was a sad ride home. I later saw the "Children under 14 not permitted" on the newspaper ads. About three months later, I bought a copy of one of the newsstand magazines, and there was a whole pictorial on that entire card. That was bittersweet, seeing photos of the matches I wasn't allowed to see.

Those wrestling magazines were an entry point to an even deeper world. The first one I ever bought was the January 1967 *Wrestling World*, with a painting of Sammartino on the cover, and the headline was "My three toughest opponents."

That's where I first saw Freddie Blassie.

★ ★ ★ ★ ★

I found it fascinating that there was more than one world champion. Looking at the ratings, I didn't know any of the names. I just absorbed any wrestling magazine I could get. I'd discovered a whole new world. Every single week, I'd go to the local drugstore, Doc's, which was a combination pharmacy and stationery store, and those magazines were on the top shelf next to the adult magazines. I'd pick up everything I could afford. *Wrestling World* and *The Ring Wrestling* were great, and others, like *The Wrestler*, were more salacious, always hyping girl wrestling stories.

Though we didn't have much money, I used what little allowance I was given, and in those days, you could get some things for a quarter here or a dollar there. In 1969, I started working as a paperboy to make extra money.

★ ★ ★ ★ ★

I went to my first actual wrestling show on August 30, 1971.

I had very few close friends on Long Island, but one weekend, John Belvedere and I were invited to go for a camp-out in a tent in Bobby Osmund's backyard. That night, I met a kid I didn't know from my school named Frank Favale. We just started talking and wrestling came up. He was like, "You watch wrestling?" The other guys were talking about baseball, football, girls, whatever, and we just talked about wrestling all night. We became fast friends.

Frank used to go to the Garden shows with his father, and he invited me to go with them. And I was now 14, so I could go without having the worry about being turned away.

The main event was Stan Stasiak against WWWF world champion Pedro Morales. It was actually the only time that Morales ever lost while he was champion at the Garden, though it was stopped due to blood. That night also featured the Funks, Dory Sr. and Terry, against the Kangaroos, in a match that went to a 45-minute curfew draw.

From there, I didn't miss a Madison Square Garden show until 1977, when I opted to stay in Boston for the summer during a college break. I went to every single show, and Frank and I went together regularly for three years or so. Other times, I went with my older sister and some of her friends; there were some shows in the early days where we'd have a group of 10 people sitting together. My dad was not into wrestling. I convinced him to attend a show with me in early 1972, and midway during the action he fell asleep.

For me, wrestling was an addiction. Of course, as my life progressed, I was able to get better seats, and shoot the matches, and eventually be a ringside photographer.

★ ★ ★ ★ ★

In that first newsstand magazine I bought, I learned about Freddie Blassie and a match he had against Bruno Sammartino that caused a riot at Roosevelt Stadium in New Jersey. When I had a little extra money, I would order some back issues, because they were pretty prominent in all the magazines back then, and I focused on back issues that either had a photo of Blassie or his name on the cover, knowing I'd be able to read more about him. Blassie really fascinated me, from his work out in California to Japan but also his reported injuries. He always seemed to be coming back from the dead.

But he wasn't the only wrestler I wanted to learn more about. I'd look for older magazines with Bruno or Spiros. It's a shame, but Arion was a big star that no one ever talks about now. On his debut on *Capitol Wrestling*, taped out of Washington, DC, he won a singles match, and then on the same show won the tag team titles. Antonio Pugliese—also known as Tony Parisi—was teaming with Miguel Perez, who got injured in the first fall of the match. Arion stepped up, and they beat Smasher Sloan and Baron Scicluna for the belts. A star was made, and I became a fan of his right away. I always felt like if there was anybody who could beat Bruno, Spiros Arion would be the guy.

★ ★ ★ ★ ★

As an Italian-American, I can't say enough about what Sammartino meant to me and our culture. He was a hero, at once an upstanding citizen that grandmothers worshipped, and someone who could beat the tar out of any of the dozens of villains that tried in vain to get the best of him. If he would have let us, we would have carried him through the streets, parading him as the ultimate example of Italian masculinity.

Through the years, I got to know him, from being in one of his fan clubs, to meeting him backstage at the Garden, to having him on my radio show, to appearing at my conventions as a guest. Never did he pretend to be anything he wasn't, just a class act through and through.

Bruno left an imprint on me the first time we talked. I was shooting at ringside, and he tumbled out of the ring, and landed on me, but got right back in the action. I was hit pretty hard and tore my pants. After the match was over, I was summoned to the back, and I was worried about what I did wrong . . . It wasn't my fault! Backstage, Bruno apologized. "You guys are at ringside. It's hard for to me judge. Are you okay?" I came away even more impressed about what a quality man he was. Here he was after a brutal match and he's checking in on me.

It was an incredible honor for me to posthumously accept his induction into the George Tragos / Lou Thesz Professional Wrestling Hall of Fame in Waterloo, Iowa, in July 2019.

★ ★ ★ ★ ★

Every good hero needs a good villain, and none was better in my eye than "The King of Men" Freddie Blassie.

I'd read about him in the mags, but the first time I saw him on TV was on Channel 41 in New York, where they played Los Angeles Olympic Auditorium shows. He was a good guy there, but in the WWWF, he always came in as a villain, playing up his sharp teeth like he was a vampire. When he bit someone, the TV would show a big "X" over the attack.

I learned there was a Freddie Blassie Fan Club, run by Jeff Walton, out of Los Angeles. Then the fan club went dormant, but there was a good reason—Walton had parlayed his work into a job with the L.A. wrestling office. That was a very cool career career path . . .

The first time I saw Blassie live was against Pedro Morales in November 1971. I was in awe of the heat that the guy generated and I was head over heels for the heel. I decided to start a fan club for him.

A few of the newsstand magazines had fan club listings and explained how to go about it; protocol was to get a signed permission slip from the wrestler to start the club. Though I was only 14 years old, I wanted to be a part of the wrestling business in some capacity, so I filled out a note to Blassie, and brought it with me to the Garden in December 1971 for his rematch against Morales. He just had to sign and date my note, which read, "I, Fred Blassie, give John Arezzi permission to start a fan club in my honor."

Naïve but ambitious, I told my pal Frank that I was going to get it back to Blassie. He just laughed at me, "How are you going to get that signed? You going to go in the dressing room?" But that's what I did. I went to the entrance to the dressing room and saw the security guards there. I told them my story, that I wanted to start a fan club for Freddie Blassie and needed to get the sheet signed. One guy was ready to throw me out, but the younger security guard took the slip from me and went back to the dressing room. About five minutes later, he came out with a signed sheet.

I went back to my seat and showed Frank. He was skeptical and thought it was fake, which made me question it too. He had signed it "Freddy Blassie," but he was "Freddie" everywhere else. To figure out if it was real or not, I decided to send it to Jeff Walton. I mailed him the permission slip, care of the Olympic Auditorium, to ask him if it was really Blassie's autograph. A couple of weeks later, I got a package in the mail with a letter from Jeff saying that it was indeed Blassie's signature. Not only did Jeff return the permission slip, he put in a bunch of programs and a cardboard Blassie mask that they sold in the arena.

I was in seventh heaven—it was legit!

Now the real work started on the fan club, and I was starting from ground zero. How do I do it? How do I publicize it? What do the members get? How much should I charge? Of course, I had no access to Blassie. I learned what I could from the fan club listings in the magazines.

It took me four or five months after getting the reply from Jeff in early 1972 to put it together. I called it *The King of Men* newsletter. Fortunately, I got some help from a senior in my high school, Bob Colletti, who everyone called "Bruno" because he looked like Sammartino—and Bruno was his idol. And he had a crush on my older sister, Linda, which might have had a little to do with his eagerness to help me. He was on the wrestling team at school. I befriended him and he was more than happy to mentor me a bit. More importantly, he had access to a mimeograph machine.

The first issue of *The King of Men* was about 15 pages, and it covered the matches at the Garden, some info on Fred, ratings—really rudimentary stuff. I charged $3.50 a year and you got the newsletters and a membership card. The key to getting subscribers was to be in the fan club listings in the magazines, so I dutifully sent off copies for consideration to key people in fandom—all of whom who would become my friends—such as Jim Melby, Georgiann Makropoulos, Norm Keitzer, and Tom Burke. Once it was listed, I got my first letters with money in them. I was so excited. And I am still in touch with some of the people that joined, almost 50 years later.

My parents didn't quite understand what I was doing: they didn't see the life skills I was developing with the newsletter, the friendships I was forging. They just saw that I was in my room with the door closed, and they could hear me banging away on my shitty old typewriter, with wonky keys that would break all the time. It wasn't until a couple of newsletters in, where the mail became fairly regular and my name started appearing in the magazines, that they recognized that I was onto something. However, we're not talking big numbers, by any stretch of the imagination, meaning I had dozens of members, not hundreds.

Later, when Bob couldn't print them any longer, my father came through. He was working an overnight shift at a trucking company in Brooklyn, called Eastern Trucking, and he told me that they had these Xerox machines there. I knew the difference between a mimeograph and a Xerox machine, and knew the Xerox machine could copy anything, including photos. That changed the way the newsletter looked, because I started cutting pictures out of wrestling magazines and putting them alongside the articles. It made the newsletter look really good, for its time at least.

Key to it all was Jeff Walton, as he was my conduit to Freddie. I sent him two copies of *The King of Men*, one for him, one for Freddie, and if I had any extra money, I'd ask him for some more Olympic Auditorium programs.

In early 1973, it happened—I got a letter from Fred. It was on letterhead from the Madison Motor Inn, in Boston, and his handwriting was impeccable:

Dear John,

I guess by now you know that I am back here on the east coast. Jeff forwarded your second issue of "King of Men," all I can say is you are doing a great job. Plus, I am happy to have you as President of the Fred Blassie fan club. I know it is a time-consuming job along with not much reward. As you know I was elected and voted as the "Wrestler of the Year 1972." But as yet none of the magazines have carried the story and it was in Oct. 1972 Santa Monica, Calif. Guess that's all for now, hope to see you at M.S.G. Mar. 26th.

Keep up the great work.

Sincerely,
Fred Blassie

★ ★ ★ ★ ★ ★ ★ ★ ★

I STILL HAVE
MUCH OF MY
FREDDIE BLASSIE
COLLECTION:
NEWSLETTERS,
HIS LETTERS,
AND MORE.

I brought Fred's letter with me to the March 26 show, and presented it to security. A few minutes later, the guard came back and told me to follow him . . . and there was Fred. That's where I got to do an interview with him for the first time. He was a babyface in California, but in New York, he was a bad guy, so I didn't know what he would be like at all, whether he'd be friendly or rude. In the end, he was just the nicest guy, very cooperative and very accommodating.

After that, he sent me letters and postcards during his travels, just to keep in touch. It was so cool. I could now say that I knew a wrestler. It was a far cry from standing outside Madison Square Garden at the entrance where the guys came in, with my little Instamatic camera, shooting pictures of the wrestlers arriving.

★ ★ ★ ★ ★

Money was always tight in our household, but around Christmastime, my dad would get bonuses from different people. One year, I got a mini-bike. For Christmas 1972, I pestered my parents for a hand-held 8 mm camera to film wrestling. The one I ended up getting wasn't the most expensive, but it worked. It was cool to do a few home movies over the years too.

But I primarily got it for wrestling. The first time I went into Madison Square Garden with a movie camera was in January 1973, Pedro Morales against Lonnie Mayne, the Vachons were on the card, and the midgets.

I got pretty good at it. Since there was no light with the camera, you had to use existing light, but the wrestling ring was always well lit. Usually, I was anywhere from the seventh to the tenth row. I learned to be ready, when it was the right time to start filming. You watched the match differently, paying attention to when a highspot might be coming, because each reel of film only had three and a half minutes on it. You had to be really aware of when the finish was coming. Over time, I just got better and better at it. It was hard to film, just because of the crowd. It was always frenzied, especially towards a finish. Security were more concerned about fans getting so worked up that they'd riot if Pedro lost. No one told me to stop filming, ever.

Getting the film developed wasn't cheap. At my local Fotomat, it was about five dollars a roll. I'd bring whatever I could afford. Sometimes, I'd only bring three rolls of the five that I had shot. I had to be really conservative because I didn't have unlimited amounts of film—or funds. I wish I could have filmed entire matches, but I could only do highlights.

Main events were my primary target, but I also loved to film people who I didn't get a chance to see on television, like the Vachon brothers. It was like, "Wow, I read about them in the magazines, and here they are in front of me!" Then there was the Funks, Terry and Dory Sr., or Verne Gagne and Mil Mascaras. And Andre the Giant. That's my jewel: out of everything that I've ever shot, Andre the Giant's very first match at Madison Square Garden is the highlight. Nobody else has that.

★ ★ ★ ★ ★

It's really common for people to raise the question, "Don't you know that wrestling is fake?" Wrestling fans are used to it. For me, I sort of knew that it wasn't on the up-and-up, and once I saw the matches live, my suspicion was confirmed.

On September 30, 1972, any thought I had of it being real was out. That was Sammartino against Morales in the match of the century at Shea Stadium. I bought my tickets as a fan, and was just in the beginning stages of the Freddie Blassie Fan Club. But there was a guy named Professor Elliot Maron: he'd take the jackets back from the ring, and he was a guy that all the kids looked up to since he was in the business. We were waiting in line outside the stadium to get in, near the entrance where the wrestlers would be coming in. It was a dreary, rainy, cold day. Professor Elliot came out of Shea, before we're even in, and he said, "It's going to be a draw tonight." I said, "What are you talking about?" I thought Bruno was going to kick Morales's ass. He repeated it. "There's going to be no winner tonight. It'll go to curfew." Sure enough, it went just over 75 minutes and was called on a draw on account of curfew. I was like, "Wow, this stuff is really fake."

And then your education really begins. The wrestlers didn't use blood capsules, but instead used razor blades to nick themselves and start the blood flowing. You find out all these things when you're a teenager, but it made the business more fascinating to me.

★ ★ ★ ★ ★

I decided to join the fan organization called the WFIA, which stood for the Wrestling Fans International Association, and through them, I found other like-minded wrestling addicts. In June of 1974, I attended my first WFIA convention, which was held in Atlanta. To my surprise, I was given two awards: Fan Club of the Year and Best Newsletter. I was shocked. Here I was accepting the awards, and at the head table were Bob Orton Jr., Fabulous Moolah, and "Mr. Wrestling" Tim Woods. Honestly, it felt like I was a part of the in-crowd a little bit. (I was later on its board of directors for a short while.)

Tom Burke, who published the *Global Wrestling News* newsletter, was a big supporter of mine and, it turned out, a teacher too. At the WFIA convention in Atlanta, Tom smartened me up. He had a sit-down with me and told me what kayfabe meant. Kayfabe referred to all this

★ ★ ★ ★ ★ ★ ★ ★ ★

TO MY SURPRISE, *KING OF MEN* WON AWARDS AT THE WFIA CONVENTION HELD IN ATLANTA, GEORGIA, IN 1974.

inside, magic information about the wrestling business and was the key starting point to learning the terminology that was used backstage. The following year, at the convention at the Madison Motor Inn, right beside the Boston Garden, I learned even more, hanging out with the likes of Dave Burzynski and Eric Goldenberg. They mentored me, even if I didn't recognize it at the time.

★ ★ ★ ★ ★

The Capitol Wrestling headquarters were at the Holland Hotel on 42nd Street and Eighth Avenue in Manhattan. There was also a gym next to it where the guys would work out. The Holland Hotel was where the wrestlers used to go and get their tickets if they had any guests.

Determined to get a photo pass to shoot at Madison Square Garden, I staked out a spot outside the hotel. My goal was to corner Willie Gilzenberg, who I thought was the guy who ran everything, not knowing it was the McMahons. He was the figurehead president of the WWWF.

The Capitol Wrestling offices were on the second floor of the hotel, in a little one-room office there. I can remember it distinctly, the Capitol Wrestling sign had a piece of gum that was stuck in the "o." It was there forever, no one ever took it off.

When Mr. Gilzenberg arrived, I followed him into the elevator. I pushed the button for the top floor of the hotel, which had to be 25 stories up. He didn't realize it. "Ah, kid, you made me miss my floor!" I began my elevator pitch: "Listen, Mr. Gilzenberg, my name is John Arezzi. I run the Freddie Blassie Fan Club, and I work for *Ring Magazine*. Here's my press card. I would love to be able to sit at ringside at the Garden." He just listened to me, didn't say a word. When we finally got to the second floor, he told me to follow him.

We entered the office and I saw Arnold Skaaland with Gorilla Monsoon, both of whom I'd seen wrestle. He said the magic words, "Arnie, get this kid a photo pass."

That was the drill prior to every show, though Skaaland never remembered who I was, so I'd have to explain it all again. There was no permanent press pass. Everyone who entered MSG had to have a ticket, whether it said "Wrestler" or "Photo." It was a dingy office in a dingy hotel. There were often other older wrestlers there, a bottle of booze more often than not sitting openly on a desk. They were protective of the business, suspicious of everyone. There were times they'd open the door a crack and peek out. It was like you were going into a speakeasy. One time, I was outside pushing the buzzer, and it took about three or four minutes until the door cracked open, a perturbed Monsoon staring at me. It smelled like someone had just taken a shit. I really don't know how much the Holland Hotel offices were used the rest of the time, but they were always there for the Madison Square Garden shows.

Armed with my photo pass, I could enter through the dressing room entrance. My first time, I sat at ringside next to legendary wrestling photographers George Napolitano and Bill Apter, and they're like, "Who are you?" I knew Bill from sending my fan club newsletter to him. George, I had just heard so much about. Frank Amato was there too. I looked out of place, with my hand-me-down, pawn-shop camera. But I *was* there at ringside, just like them.

★ ★ ★ ★ ★

The Holland Hotel had a restaurant and bar, and it was a good place to hang out and get to know the wrestlers. The underneath guys, like Pete Sanchez and Johnny Rodz, were often there and we all became friends. Everyone had to come in at some point to get a ticket, from Bruno to Killer Kowalski to John Tolos.

After the shows, we'd all congregate at a hidden-away bar called the Savoy, which was across the street from the Edison Hotel on 46th Street, between Seventh and Eighth Avenue. Right after the Garden show was over, that's where everyone would go to drink. Although I was just 18 in 1975, it was legal to drink at that age in New York. I looked forward to hanging at the Savoy after each show, as you felt like a real insider to be there in a tiny bar that held fewer than 100 people. Colorful manager Captain Lou Albano was always the first one there. And he was always willing to shoot the breeze. That Savoy bar was where the girls who wanted to sleep with wrestlers congregated as well; they were called "ring rats" and there were regular faces there every show too.

When Bruno would come into the Savoy, it would usually be with Georgiann Makropoulos, who ran his fan club. When Bruno arrived, we all parted like the Red Sea, allowing him to move to the back of the bar at a table reserved for him. People would come and say hello to him, almost like he was the Godfather. I was too intimidated.

George Napolitano invited me one night to hang out with Andre the Giant, Toru Tanaka, and Mr. Fuji. The place was packed, and George said, "C'mon, we're going to go across the street." There was a little restaurant and bar there, and I had a few drinks, but Andre was drinking like crazy. The stories of his drinking are true. They'd gotten a bunch of cold cuts, sliced roast beef, but no bread, to try to soak up a tiny bit of the booze. Another night, Andre was a little tipsy, and a fan went up to him and asked for his autograph and Andre started chasing this kid. It was an unbelievable sight.

Before the Garden shows, there was another little group of us that would meet upstairs at the bowling alley at Madison Square Garden, which also had a bar and restaurant. Once I got integrated, and got to know Georgiann especially, she would invite me. Hardcore fans from Philadelphia and New Jersey would come in and hang out there too. I developed deep friendships with other "smart" fans like Mike Omansky, who later become a top executive for RCA Records overseeing the Elvis Presley catalog, and was someone I did business with later on.

That's where a lot of people used to buy pictures from me. I'd seen Frank Amato selling his photos to fans, opening up an album for people to choose their favorites, so I did the same. They were maybe a dollar each, and they cost 10 cents or so to duplicate. Fans would come up and say, "What do you got?" I tried to have new photos every month. "Here's Don Leo. Here's Bruno. Here's a posed Bruno with the belt."

★ ★ ★ ★ ★

All these connections paid off as I started to send in photos to the magazines and write stories. It certainly wasn't for the money, but there was a big thrill seeing my name in print. Naturally, the first piece I had published was on Freddie Blassie.

★ ★ ★ ★ ★

One of my subscribers to *The King of Men* was Mike Lano, who lived out in California; he would send me updates on what Blassie was doing out west. He'd even make audio tapes of the wrestling interviews for me to hear. It got to the point where I made Mike the vice president of the Blassie Fan Club.

★ ★ ★ ★ ★ ★ ★ ★ ★ ★

FRED POSES WITH ME AND MIKE LANO, VISITING FROM CALIFORNIA IN 1975.

In January 1974, Mike invited me to come visit him, and go to the Olympic Auditorium to see the annual battle royal. I convinced my grandmother to pay for my trip to Los Angeles, and I can remember that the plane ticket was $179, round trip, on United Airlines. I had never been on an airplane before. My mother was afraid, terrified of me going to the other side of the country, but I went, just shy of my 17th birthday.

The first night, I stayed with Mike and his grandparents. The next night, we stayed at the home of Richard Dawson, the actor from *Hogan's Heroes*, who would become even better known as the host of *Family Feud*. His sons, Mark and Gary, were big wrestling fans, and Mike was their best friend. It was really something to hang out at a celebrity's house and see the way that they lived. I'm from this working-class family on Long

Island, and I'm staying in Beverly Hills. The Dawson kids were different from me, for sure. They weren't snobbish, but they were bratty. They'd gotten everything they'd ever wanted and there was no real discipline in their lives—they were rich kids, and I was not.

We all went to the Olympic together, and it was great to see wrestling there. Andre the Giant won the famed battle royal. I also got to finally meet Jeff Walton at that show. The next day, Jeff got us backstage at the KCOP studios where they taped their TV show. I took pictures of Andre getting a haircut, and John Tolos. Even though Blassie wasn't on the shows, it was a great experience, a real dream weekend.

The last day I was there, I asked Richard to sign a few pictures for my family. He signed one to my mom and one to my sister, and then I asked him to sign one for a cousin of mine. He looked at me and, in his English accent, said, "What are you going to do, sell these fucking things?" That's my lasting memory of Richard Dawson.

★ ★ ★ ★ ★

It's funny how I have so many great memories from that period of my life, but so little of it was about West Babylon High School. As I've said, I was socially inept. I'd sit in the back of the class and wouldn't talk. I was that way really until I discovered pro wrestling and started writing and gained confidence.

★ ★ ★ ★ ★ ★ ★ ★ ★

FREDDIE WITH
A COPY OF THE
NEWSLETTER IN
1974.

The whole turnaround around for me in school was starting the Blassie Fan Club, and then getting more interested in writing. In my senior year, I became the sports editor for a school project called *The Streaker*. I wrote some stories on baseball and wrestling. The teacher, Mr. Nello, complimented me on my writing. He took a liking to me and mentored me. So that was the one class in all four years of high school that I actually excelled in.

I was absent a lot. It was more than the family difficulties with my mom. I just didn't fit in at school. I wasn't athletic, so couldn't play sports. At the time, I weighed about 180 pounds, always 10 to 20 pounds overweight. The only extra-curricular activity I did was working in the school store. I didn't go to my prom. I didn't have a girlfriend. I was just this kid who was in and out of school. When I got my yearbook, so many people had written that they hardly remembered me in school.

In the end, I barely made it out of school. I had to plead to my gym teacher to improve my mark so I could pass and graduate. I did that to a couple of other teachers. I just wanted to get out of school. There was no plan beyond that, as I never took an SAT or any college prep classes. I didn't know what I was going to do. I loved sports, I loved wrestling, I loved baseball. After graduation, I was like, "What am I going to do?"

Eventually, I got a job on a loading dock, at S. Klein's in Farmingdale, New York, unpacking trucks for minimum wage. One day, we were unloading a bunch of garbage pails and some kid who was mentally disabled knocked over a whole row of trash cans that almost fell on me. I just said, "What am I doing?"

Realizing I had to get my life back on track, I called my old guidance counselor from high school, Ms. Sidlow, and scheduled an appointment. She was surprised when I said that I wanted to go to college. She looked at me like I was crazy. "Shouldn't you have thought of that in the four years you were here at West Babylon High School?" She had my records, knew about my family problems, and knew my few strengths. "I don't know what to tell you. I'll do some research, but you really didn't prepare yourself for any sort of college education."

About a week later, I got a phone call from her, and she said, "Well, John, there's one college that might take you, because they'll take anyone."

It was Grahm Junior College. It was a communications school, with a specialty in giving you an education in radio, television, and journalism. I had found my calling.

4.

I AM "MR. WRESTLING"

The admissions brochure for Grahm Junior College in Boston was like looking at the Land of Oz. I knew I had to get in, so I filled in the application and wrote them a several-page letter on why I wanted to go to school. I included some of the wrestling magazine articles that I had written. I submitted everything and checked the mailbox every day. One day, I got home and there was a letter of acceptance, and I was floored.

But I still had to break the news to my parents. While they were both extremely shocked and happy for me, my dad asked, rightly, "How are we going to pay for this?" None of us had a clue about financial aid. After all, no one from our family had gone to college. It was $3,995 for the first year. That included room and board. That was a lot of money then, and even more for us. "Can you wait until next year?" he asked. I knew if I waited a year, I'd never go. "No, Dad, I have to do this! Please!"

My dad didn't have the resources, and began to ask a few friends for money. He asked Uncle Louie Esposito: "No." He asked Midge Belvedere: "No." I remember us driving to his boss Uncle Fritzy's home, parking outside, and him telling me to wait in the car. A few minutes later he came back into the car, dejected. "He said no. Fuck him!" Everyone said it was a family responsibility. I asked him, "What about Grandma Dorothy?" Dorothy Arezzi emigrated from Italy in the early 1900s with my grandfather John and toiled as a seamstress every day of her life, building out her American Dream. Grandpa was the house husband, cooking and cleaning while Grandma worked in the garment district. Together they made a life in Brooklyn. She was always criticizing me and my sisters. She accused my mother of ruining my dad's life once they were married. She was always saying my mom didn't know how to clean house, cook, or take care of us kids. And she was *cheap*. She didn't go for spit, as the saying goes. We knew she saved every penny and had some stocks. We didn't know how much money she had; I'd never even thought about it, actually. All I know is that we felt she hated us all.

My dad was not too confident when the time came to ask her, and we certainly didn't know what she was going to say. We went to her apartment, my dad parked the car and said, "Okay, here we go." We climbed the stairs to her immaculate second floor apartment, in the building she owned, and sat down. I took control. I showed her the letter of acceptance from Grahm and said that I'd be the first ever in our entire family to go to college.

She listened and read the letter from the college. After a few seconds, she just looked up and said, "What's the damage?" We gave her the figure and she shuffled off to her bedroom, and came out a few minutes later with $4,000 in cash. We couldn't believe it. I was elated and hugged her. She said she was proud of me and that I had better do well. I promised I would!

Somehow, I knew getting into college and going away from home was going to save my life. Even though I loved my family, I needed to get away from my mom. I was tired of all the problems, tired of the insanity. And, as it turned out, I wasn't the only one leaving.

When I was packing to go away to college, my dad told me, "I'm leaving too." He had reached his limit and decided that he would move out, and in with Grandma Dorothy. I felt horrible for Donna. She was now going to be the only one left with Mom. Linda, Eddie, and her kids had their own place. So, as happy as I was, my heart was breaking for Donna. While it was an abrupt announcement, given the number of times they had split and reconciled, it wasn't exactly a surprise. He left permanently the same day I left for college.

I just packed a couple of suitcases when it was time to go to school, and I took a train.

★ ★ ★ ★ ★

Grahm Junior College was located in Kenmore Square in Boston and was a non-profit institution as of 1968. I started in September 1975, after the orientation weekend a couple of weeks previous, which only solidified my belief that I'd made the right decision.

The key for me, from that first weekend in Boston, is that no one knew who I was, no one knew about my messed-up family background or about my insecurities. In short, I reinvented myself and came out of my shell.

Though I lived on campus, I requested a single room, which were available for a premium. Grandma came through again and paid the extra for it. To this day, I like serenity, time to myself, and I don't even like sharing a hotel room.

Right from the get-go, I loved everything about college and I made friends immediately, many of whom I am still in touch with. It was the best time of my life, to this day. The experience transformed me into a different person. A big part of that was having a circle of friends, who lived in the same building. You did stuff together all the time, from

★ ★ ★ ★ ★ ★ ★ ★ ★ ★

AH, COLLEGE LIFE.
IT WAS THE CATALYST
THAT ALLOWED
ME TO COME OUT
OF MY SHELL. I
MADE LIFELONG
FRIENDSHIPS THERE,
LIKE JEWELS AND
SPANKY.

classes to partying or concerts. We were all living away from home for the first time.

Mom and Dad, now separated, sent me letters, and Dad would put some cash in the envelope for me. A couple of times, after he'd hit a number, I'd get a little surprise of 100 dollars, but mostly it was 20 dollars, or whatever he could afford. I'd talk to Donna when she and my mom would call from the pay phone near the apartment they lived in. My dorm, Kenmore Hall, had pay phones on every floor. Back home, we only had a phone a few times growing up, as we'd get it hooked up, then not pay the bill, and it would be gone.

Immediately, I loved Boston. Kenmore Square was just a few blocks from Fenway Park, and I was already a baseball fan . . . and in 1975, the Red Sox made the World Series, and that was the dramatic Carlton Fisk home run. There were a lot of local kids at the school, so I was immediately drawn into the Red Sox.

There were concerts everywhere. My oldest sister had turned me on to Billy Joel when "Piano Man" came out. I was walking down Boylston Street with my friend Larry, and there was a little club, Paul's Mall, a little tiny place, and on the marquee it said "Billy Joel Appearing." I convinced my friend to go, and it was four dollars to get in. We were sitting 10 feet from Billy Joel, just before he came out with his new album, *Turnstiles*.

I discovered so much music. I'd always loved music, but the group of friends that I hung around with were into music too, and some played instruments. I learned about the Eagles, Queen, and America, and bands that never made it, like the local Massachusetts band the Pousette Dart Band.

We all had nicknames at school. My crew included Jimmy "Jewels" Clark, Jimmy "The C" Carlson, Michael "Spanky" Santelli, Dave "Flyer" Donlin, "Pancho" Bill Martin, Joe "Golden Rod" Palmieri, Tom "Sundevil" Shaer, Chris "Starsky" Worthen, Sharon "Zing Zing" Taskel, "Harpo" Bruce Chandler, Scott "Man" Menario, Fred "Ferd" Franco, and Scott "No H" Coen. Finally, there was Larry Simmons and his dorm roommate Paul "The Pervert" Rose, from Philadelphia, who inadvertently gave me my nickname. Paul always sexualized every conversation, or changed lyrics in a song to obscene phrases. At one point, we were joking around and he goes, "You're a jit stain." I was like, "What is jit? I've never heard that expression before." "You know, like a jit stain," and he made the motion of masturbating. It became part of my vernacular. I couldn't stop saying it. "You're a jit." And that became my nickname. It's even in our yearbook. The girls didn't know what it was. Some of my closest friends still call me Jit, but in a loving way. It's a pretty messed-up nickname, now that I think about it.

There was a lot of pot and booze. It was a party school. The dorm was co-ed, so there was plenty of interaction. My first year at college, I definitely experienced the Freshman 15. That summer, back in Long Island, I went to the doctor for my physical, and I weighed 266, which was then my all-time high. In my second year, I joined the gym and went on a diet, and I got down to about 210. I then got my first serious girlfriend, Mary Rachele.

★ ★ ★ ★ ★

The opportunities to learn about journalism, writing, and photography, about radio, about television were magical to me, and I dove right in. The lessons would serve me well the rest of my life. I was also heavily involved in the college yearbook, mainly as the photo editor. I took photos of everything: of the kids, the dorms, the teachers.

The college radio station and the closed-circuit television station were known as WCSB AM 660 and WNIR-TV. At one point, they held auditions at the radio station, and I pitched the station directors, Paul Manchester and Vinny Kice (who were both seniors), my idea for a wrestling show, *Pro Wrestling Spotlight*. They thought it was cool, since I had the background writing for the newsstand magazines.

However, the sports director, Lester Singleton, was adamant that he did not want to have a wrestling show on the station, at least not on the sports side of it. He trotted out the usual argument about it not being a sport. This should have been a warning to me of troubles to come.

When the listing came out for who was going to be on the air, I saw Saturday afternoon at five o'clock was *Pro Wrestling Spotlight*. I went crazy, I was so excited. Then I realized I didn't have much of a plan

WRESTLING FOLLOWED ME TO GRAHM JUNIOR COLLEGE, AND HERE I'M SLAMMING VINNY KICE.

besides doing the show, so I did a little preparation and went on the air. I had a script and some soundbites from interviews that I'd done with wrestlers.

The show became a hit in the dorm. People would call in and ask questions, and I became known as "Mr. Wrestling" right away. Of course, prank calls were to be expected given the audience. Really, I was a tiny bit of a celebrity, even if it was just around campus, as the station didn't reach all that much further than Kenmore Square.

I'd mess around with kids at school: "Slam my head against the wall!" "Give me a backdrop!" I'd seen enough on TV that I thought I knew what I was doing, but, of course, I did not.

★ ★ ★ ★ ★

Ernie Roth was a well-known wrestling manager known as The Grand Wizard in the WWWF. Though I didn't know it until I moved to Boston, he was the local promoter for the WWWF, along with Bob

Harmon, who wrestled as Beautiful Bobby. They ran regular shows at the Boston Garden and infrequently in a few other towns near Boston.

Since I already knew Roth from shooting at Madison Square Garden, he was my in, and he let me conduct interviews with wrestlers at the Madison Hotel. They were strictly in-character interviews, never exposing the secretive business of pro wrestling.

Some of my connections from New York didn't translate quite as well.

The New England territory was something of a disputed area. Roth and Harmon had the backing of the McMahon family, who promoted the WWWF throughout the Northeast. Then there was Angelo Savoldi, who promoted smaller shows in various towns in New England and New Jersey.

Through my time shooting at ringside in New York, I developed a decent relationship with Vince McMahon Jr. He'd use some of my photos in the MSG program, and encouraged me to shoot photos of the job boys, like Johnny Rodz, Ricky Sexton, Silvano Sousa, and so many others. Vince told me that the enhancement guys never felt like they got any love from the photographers.

Savoldi would come up and threaten me: "If you do anything for Ernie, you're not going to be able to do anything for me." They put me in the middle of whatever was going on. Then I had to go to Vince, and I explained that I was getting heat from Angelo, and that I didn't know what to do about it. He stepped in and took care of it, and I never learned how. Later, to gain favor with Savoldi, I wrote up a piece for *Ring Magazine* about Mario Savoldi, Angelo's son, who was a young referee.

★ ★ ★ ★ ★

Pro Wrestling Spotlight started out okay, but the Christmas episode in 1975 almost got me thrown off the air. The sports director, Lester Singleton, called into the show once again to debate with me on whether or not pro wrestling was a sport. When he hung up, I muttered "cocksucker" under my breath. It went out over the air. The engineer, Larry Simmons (still one of my dearest friends), who was a really good friend of mine, lost it and started laughing hysterically. I went, "Oh my God, what did I say?"

I tried to change the subject right away, but it went out there and Lester heard it. Later that night, I was attending a Christmas party in the dorm, and he was there, wearing a Santa Claus hat. He went, "You called me a cocksucker!" and he started chasing me, like he was going to beat me up. Though he was drunk and angry, I left out the kicker—he was a little person, maybe three feet tall.

We got called in for a meeting with the adviser for the radio station and the program director. I got suspended for a month or so, but I didn't lose the show. We had to apologize to each other and promise not to antagonize each other—but it was always a one-way street, because I was the one that was being attacked because I was talking about pro wrestling.

There was another time I got in trouble. In the spring of 1976, we decided to put on a wrestling show on the college TV station—with us as the wrestlers. There was no ring, just mats on the floor. We set up a couple of matches in the TV studio, with announcers but no audience. I was one of the wrestlers.

It got a little out of hand. The guys that performed in one of the matches went crazy and started hitting each other over the head, putting ketchup on their foreheads to make it look like blood. But the biggest thing that happened during that taping related to a curtain that wrapped around the studio, providing the backdrop for the entire studio. The guys brawled into it and ripped it. It cost thousands of dollars, and we got into major trouble, and even the dean got involved.

MY FRIENDS AT COLLEGE AND I PRETEND WRESTLE.

The show never aired. I've never even seen a copy of it. We all got our privileges taken away for using the television studio because of that silly wrestling show.

It was a lot of fun doing the first version of *Pro Wrestling Spotlight*, and it ran for two years. For whatever reason, I kept copies of the shows on cassette tape; listening to them now, I am struck by how young I sound. What I wish I had a copy of, but do not, is *Pro Wrestling, A Sport of Controversy*, a documentary that Bill Martin and I worked on together, incorporating my photographs and some of the film I shot at Madison Square Garden; we actually won an award for best documentary at the end of the school year.

★ ★ ★ ★ ★ ★ ★ ★ ★ ★ ★ ★ ★

BILL MARTIN AND I ACCEPT OUR BARRY AWARD IN 1977 FOR THE BEST DOCUMENTARY.

★ ★ ★ ★ ★

Grahm was a two-year school, but I stayed for three, adding a degree in television production in my extra year. I didn't want to leave: I just loved it so much.

Financially, I made it through with a variety of jobs. Fortunately, our family qualified for financial aid, and there were student loans. Plus, there were work/study programs, to make a little money while you were attending classes. One of my jobs that first semester was to exchange the bedsheets from the rooms in the dorm, where they'd bring me the soiled ones and I'd present them with clean sheets. For a time, I worked behind a counter at a liquor store, and I was a bouncer at a disco called Lucifer's. I also still freelanced for the magazines, making a few extra bucks.

In my second year, I decided to stay on campus during the summer. I worked in the admissions department, because they knew how passionate I was about the school. That summer, when kids were visiting, I'd give them a tour and talk about how great it was. I made friends with everyone, from the dean on down, and everyone knew how much I loved the college and how I had excelled. They saw the passion. As a bonus, the dorm was free during the summer since I was working for the college.

One day, comedian Andy Kaufman walked in, because he had gone to Grahm years earlier. He asked to get his college transcript, for whatever reason. I was the person that spoke to him and made that happen. He asked, "Do you mind if I walk around?" I said, "Let me give you a tour!"

So, I took him around. I mentioned that I was doing a pro wrestling talk show at the school, and his eyes lit up. "What? A pro wrestling show?" It was really cool because I knew him from *Saturday Night Live*; he was on that first season. I didn't know how much he loved wrestling, and of course, down the road, look what happened—he started wrestling women on shows and then had a major angle with Jerry "The King" Lawler off an appearance they made on *The Late Show with David Letterman*. A few years later, Andy teamed up with my hero Fred Blassie to produce the hilarious video, "My Breakfast with Blassie."

★ ★ ★ ★ ★

Thinking about my education and what it meant to my family is bittersweet. My dad's brother, Tom Arezzi, was my godfather and my sponsor at baptism. He was a good mentor and very proud of my education as I was the first member of the family ever to go to college, let alone earn three different college degrees. He was a Navy veteran, a straight arrow, totally opposite from my dad. He worked at Pfizer Pharmaceutical his entire career, and was a hunter and fisherman in his free time. He kept himself in great shape. We lost him in December 1998, dying instantly from a brain aneurysm.

**MY SINGLE YEAR AT
EMERSON COLLEGE
HELPED POLISH MY
INTERVIEW SKILLS.**

★ ★ ★ ★ ★

I really wanted to get into broadcasting, whether it was sports, news, or entertainment. My dream was to do play-by-play for the Mets. I worked diligently on completing my education. After my three years at Grahm, I transferred to Emerson College for my senior year to get my bachelor's degree in speech communications. I concentrated on sports announcing for TV. I was on air at Emerson College TV station, doing the sports reports, and I produced one of the daily news broadcasts.

As with Grahm, Emerson's location was at the southern end of Boston Common, on Beacon Street, which meant that we were close to everything cool. I didn't stay at a dorm at Emerson, rather opting to get my first apartment, located in the Back Bay on Bay State Road. The apartment complex was behind the nightclub, Lucifer's, where I worked as a bouncer. It was there that I ran into some unsavory characters, from the Mob boss owner, Henry, to the club manager, Carl. Being a bouncer was not easy, as you had to have eyes on the back of your head. You had to watch out for those who'd had too much to drink—"liquid courage" is how my dad put it. I was in more than one fight there, once getting sucker punched square in the face by a guy who was getting a little too touchy feely with a few of the waitresses. I had enough of Lucifer's when the owner told me to shadow two very tough-looking guys who were known troublemakers. "Just be careful not to get into a beef with them by yourself," Henry warned me, "as they will probably be packing heat." For the minimum wage I was being paid, even though I got to be around lots of hot women, it was not worth getting shot or stabbed. So, I quit and walked away.

At Emerson, the tuition was over $5,000 a year. I covered it with the financial aid grants I received and student loans.

★ ★ ★ ★ ★

Through an introduction from my buddy Jewels, I got an internship at WMEX, which was 1510 on the AM dial in Boston; it changed its name to WITS midway through my time there. It was a talk radio station, and broadcast the Red Sox and Bruins games. I was the one running the commercials ("coming back with more after this break . . ."). I also wrote traffic reports.

My break, if you want to call it that, was producing the weekend overnight show for host Brad LeMack. It was a free-wheeling show, not confined to sports. I wanted to find a way to make it more compelling for the listeners, and to get Brad some cool guests. Each week, I'd place calls to Las Vegas casinos, and try to find out who was performing, and then I would ask to be connected to their dressing room. These were A list names like Rodney Dangerfield, Tony Bennett, Cher, Tina Turner. "I'm calling from the *Brad LeMack Show* in Boston. Would you like to come on the air for a quick interview?" No publicists. And I'd get all these crazy guests. Rodney Dangerfield was like, "How did you get my number, kid? How did you get my number?" And I still have those cassette tapes. The host was often freaking out.

When we had Tony Bennett on, Brad asked him to sing "I Left My Heart in San Francisco." And Tony was like, "Listen, pal, I don't tell you how to broadcast, you don't tell me what to sing." And he hung up.

That brashness helped me on another show I was a fill-in producer for, Dr. Joy Brown's midday show. When I heard Billy Joel was playing in Boston, I went to the hotel where he and his band were staying, and I convinced the members of his band to appear as guests on Dr. Brown's show.

★ ★ ★ ★ ★ ★ ★ ★ ★ ★

THAT TIME I
INTERVIEWED CYBILL
SHEPHERD AT RENO
SWEENEY IN NEW
YORK CITY IN 1979.

Cybill Shepherd was my favorite actress. I found out she was playing at a jazz club called Reno Sweeney in New York City. I reached out to the club and they set me up with a publicist, and I explained I was with WITS in Boston. I got to interview her at the hotel where she was staying. She'd just given birth to her daughter, Clementine, and her husband was David Ford, an auto parts mechanic. I saw her performance and set out to edit the interview. I went to Brad again and asked about playing it. "Well, I really can't do that, John," he said. After he went off the air, and I was supposed to run one of the public-service shows, I played my interviews instead. I was a rebel. I figured I'd done the interviews and I wanted people to hear them, even though at 5 a.m., when he signed off, there weren't many listeners. In fact, if the phone rang, I was freaked out that it would be management upset at what I was doing.

My past in wrestling came back when Vince McMahon Jr. was a guest on the *Glenn Ordway Show* in 1979, which was a huge sports show in New England. Vince came in and really started talking out of character and out of kayfabe about what wrestling is. During the show, I reached out to Ernie Roth and had him call in, and Vince didn't like that. I guess he felt blindsided by it, as the call with Roth was not approved by him, nor did I tell him the idea before executing it. Vince was there to seriously discuss the wrestling business, and his vision of the future of the WWWF. It was a long interview.

★ ★ ★ ★ ★

In May of 1979, I graduated with my bachelor's degree from Emerson College. The entire family made the trek from Brooklyn and Long Island to attend. Both Grandma Dorothy and Grandma Fanny, Uncle Tom, my Aunt Nana, Mom, Dad, and my sisters Linda and Donna all attended. Everyone got along. We celebrated the first college graduate of the Arezzi family. It was a great day, one that I look back at with pride and gratitude, thinking of Grandma Dorothy paying the freight for my first year, the financial support from my dad when he could manage it, and the admiration Donna showed to me. It was a love fest.

After I graduated from Emerson, I was hired full-time at the radio station to do the producing gigs, but it wasn't much more than my internship. I was making minimum wage and still working part-time at Kenmore Wines liquor store. I was working hard to make a living. Once the rent became too much of a burden, I moved in with my two college friends Jewels and Franco, in Revere, right outside of Boston. They had recently graduated as well. Jewels was at WITS. Franco was looking for his place in entertainment. It was my first time rooming with anyone, but we had a great time. On Sundays we'd set up our three TVs to watch all the football games and eat pizza and drink beer. During Christmas 1979, we went to the local Sears and took a "family photo" and mailed out Christmas cards with the three of us decked out in holiday garb.

I was getting lots of pressure from my parents to move back to New York, as a real well-paid job in the broadcast industry eluded me, and after three or four months of really struggling financially, I moved back to Long Island at the beginning of 1980.

My weight had gone back up to 242 pounds when I graduated. I had decided once and for all to get rid of the weight. I went on an Atkins diet and worked out at a gym in New York—that's what I was doing to keep myself busy as I was looking for a job. My weight got down to 190 pounds, making it the best physical condition I'd ever been in.

There were constant interviews, trying to get a better job, and one almost panned out with ABC Sports. That's when I first learned that in certain situations you were guilty by association. Let me explain . . .

Back in the summer of '79, I was visiting New York about once a month. I had leveraged my part-time work with WITS in Boston, or bullshitted if you will, to get press credentials to the New York Mets for the 1979 season. I interviewed players on the field.

Usually, I had my camera with me. One time, I was shooting a photo of Cincinnati Reds catcher Johnny Bench. He started playing catch with a young kid. It turned out to be the son of David Hartman, who was the host of *Good Morning America* on ABC. I sent the photos I took of them to Hartman and got a lovely letter back from him. "I think of myself as being a rather cool and objective father, particularly where baseball is concerned, because I don't want to force my little boy into something that he doesn't want to do," he wrote. "But when I saw the pictures you so thoughtfully sent of little Sean with Johnny Bench, I was absolutely thrilled. They are such fun! Thank you for anticipating my excitement and for making it possible." Then I made my pitch, and I was honest—I was looking for a job. He set me up with ABC Sports for an interview for a production job. I passed the first two interviews with flying colors. I went into the final interview with confidence. Roone Arledge and the other top ABC Sports execs were there. I ended up being deep-sixed by a scandal that I knew nothing about.

At one point, *Ring Magazine* was involved in a boxing scandal, where it had essentially taken money from promoters and managers to elevate their boxers in the ranks. Obviously, my time at *Ring Magazine* was on my resume, so they asked me about my time there. I replied that I had loved it, not knowing that disqualified me from any consideration with ABC. After the call saying I didn't get the job, I was devastated.

I ended up depressed, since I couldn't find a good job. My dad came through for me and asked Uncle Fritzy for help. Fritzy knew a lot of people, from Rupert Murdoch who owned the *New York Post* (and now Fox News) on down the ranks. Naturally, as a prominent Mob boss, Fritzy could make a call or two and get things done. One of his friends was Morris Levy, who ran Roulette Records. If you ever watched HBO's TV series *The Sopranos*, the character Hesh Rabkin was based on Levy. In short, he was deep into music, deep into the Mob. Uncle Fritzy called Levy, and I was told to head over.

I went in for an interview, sat down, and could hear him screaming at his secretary. When he finally saw me, with a cigar in his mouth, he goes, "Who are you?" I replied that Fritzy sent me. "Oh, you're that kid! You start Monday."

The following Monday I showed up, not knowing what my job was or any other details. I worked in customer service. When returns came in from a distributor or warehouse or mail order, I would be responsible for processing those returns. That lasted through the summer. It was my first job in the music business, and certainly not my last.

5.

THE GLORIOUS TWO-MATCH
CAREER OF JOHN ANTHONY

As I was growing up, the newsstand wrestling magazines had been an educational source for me, as I learned about wrestling in other territories. Once I had my first article published by *Official Wrestling Guide* in 1974, on my hero Fred Blassie becoming the manager for Russian villain Nikolai Volkoff, the magazines became a regular source of income for me. (The first one got me a whopping 25 dollars!) I loved seeing my name in print and my photographs published.

It didn't matter which magazine, I pitched photos and stories to them all. But I'm most associated with *The Ring Wrestling*, a sister publication to the better known boxing mag.

In the summer of 1976, my friend Tom Burke, whom I'd gotten to know through our letters and our time together at WFIA conventions, offered me a part-time job at *Ring Magazine*'s office. Tom was an associate editor there, but wasn't often physically in the building, which was on West 31st Street in midtown Manhattan. He still had a day job in Springfield, Massachusetts. When Tom came in, we'd go have lunch.

At *Ring*, I did whatever I was asked to do: file old boxing and wrestling pictures, get coffees, write stories. I was eventually made a contributing editor, but I still freelanced for competing publications.

The floors and writers were creaky and dusty. Nat Loubet was running it, a true legend in boxing journalism, and his daughter Trudy was the bookkeeper. Legendary boxing journalist and radio broadcaster Sam Taub was always there and had great stories to tell. Johnny Ort was another key boxing guy and had seen it all. Nat liked me and arranged for my first press card. Johnny liked me too, which was an accomplishment, since he hated wrestling. I saw so much history, from old boxers coming by to visit to all the photos and stories. It was such a great way to spend a summer, perfect for an 18-year-old.

★ ★ ★ ★ ★

Wrestling magazines can't be compared to any other publications. They walked a strange line between fact and fiction, with the photos usually the fact and the text mostly fiction. But that wasn't tried and true either.

The key was to come up with a good storyline or a good angle, and write it up. In some cases, there's some political motivation in some of the stories that I wrote. Sometimes, I wanted to take care of some of my friends, give them some rub, like Davey O'Hannon and Johnny Rodz. To this day, there's controversy, because Johnny says that Vince McMahon gave him the name "The Unpredictable" and I know I was the first one to give him that name, in an article I wrote about Rodz in *The Ring Wrestling* magazine.

You would talk to the boys, "How far do you want me to go? Do you want to do an interview?"

Jimmy Valiant dismissed me when I asked for an interview. "No, brother, man, just write whatever the hell you want, just quote me, I don't care what you do." Most of them were like that. You'd be liberal in the quotes. You would do interviews, don't get me wrong—I did a ton of them in the back in Philadelphia or Madison Square Garden, Boston Garden, as did my colleagues George Napolitano or Bill Apter. At the beginning, I was shy and didn't do one-on-one interviews, and instead tagged along with Bill or George or Frankie Amato, usually letting them ask the questions.

Around the younger wrestlers, who weren't so well known, I was more confident, and people like Kevin Sullivan would remain friends for years.

Getting the cover story was awesome. *Wrestling Monthly* used a bloody photo of "Superstar" Billy Graham that I had taken on a cover. In another, I had the feature story, Mil Mascaras asking, "Why Can't I Beat Ivan Koloff?" That wasn't my photo on the cover, but they were my photos from an IWA show in the piece.

The money wasn't always there, though. I was stiffed on a few payments, and sometimes you had to stay on them to get paid. I think the most I ever got was 75 dollars, but most were in the 25 to 50 dollar range. Strangely, I never wrote for the "Apter mags," which were published by Stanley Weston, but they did use plenty of my photos.

Weston's office was on Long Island, 20 minutes from where I lived, and I met Stanley a couple of times. I'd often go to the office. I was lobbying for a while to work with Apter in the office, because it was so close. They had a small staff and no one ever left. I developed friendships with Bob Smith and Eddie Ellner, who'd been a member of my Blassie fan club. I loved the atmosphere at the office, and it was a lot like going to the *Ring* offices, just the history. But Apter's office was modern and bright and more into the 20th century, whereas *Ring* was old in every way.

Being a pro wrestling writer wasn't exactly guaranteed fame and fortune, but it did result in a cool friendship. My grandmother lived upstairs from my father's store, and her best friend's daughter was married to Peter Criscuola, better known as Peter Criss from the up-and-coming band KISS. They made it big, of course, but he was still a Brooklyn boy, and I met him at a barbecue. It turned out he was a wrestling fan. He signed a Heineken bottle for me and gave me his address, and I sent him wrestling magazines with my pictures in them, and he used to send me back autographed pictures of KISS.

Later, when I was living in North Carolina and working in baseball, I covered some shows for George Napolitano. Nothing compares to the first Starrcade in 1983, in Greensboro, North Carolina, and the bloody brutality of the dog collar match between Roddy Piper and Greg Valentine.

Through George, I met Jay Youngblood and Ricky Steamboat. They'd just won the Mid-Atlantic tag team titles. They did some local shows in Charlotte that I attended. One night, I hung out with Jay and got to know him pretty well, and we developed a friendship. A few months later, in September 1985, he was dead, while on tour in the South Pacific, from complications from a ruptured spleen. He was only 30 years old.

★ ★ ★ ★ ★

Then there's the most ludicrous idea I ever had, the one where I detail what it was like to be a professional wrestler by actually stepping into the ring. "What a story," I thought. What a mistake is more like it.

In late 1977, while still at Grahm Junior College, I mentioned to Ernie Roth that I wanted to give pro wrestling a shot. "What? Are you crazy? What do you want to do that for?" was his response. "I want to give it a shot. I want to see how I would do." Shaking his head, he agreed to talk to some people on my behalf. It wasn't long before he got back to me: "Alright, they'll use you on the Philly tapes on January 10."

K&H was the place everyone got their wrestling gear, and I bought a pair of tights and a singlet and a pair of boots. My workout jacket would serve as my ring jacket. I was in okay shape for my wrestling debut. I never had definition, muscles, abs, or anything like that, but few of the wrestlers did then either!

When the big day came, I took a bus from Boston to Philadelphia

PHOTO BY GEORGE NAPOLITANO

★★★★★★★★★★★★★★★★

JOHN ANTHONY,
SORTA WRESTLER,
READY TO GO . . .
NOT!

and showed up at the Philadelphia Arena, at 45th and Market. I had my bag with me, ready to work. The only one I'd told about my plan was George Napolitano. He thought I was nuts. I learned later that George had a conversation with Vince McMahon Jr., who had commented, "I didn't know Arezzi was a worker." And George replied, "I didn't either."

Gorilla Monsoon, whom I'd shot many, many times and got wrestling passes from in the office, was my contact. He said, "Ernie said you want to work. Where have you worked?" I lied, "I do a lot of work down south." "You got your gear?" "Yeah." "Heel or baby?" I thought for a second and answered, "Heel." And that was that.

I was even afraid to go into the locker room, and loitered for a time in the staging area, where they did posed shots of the guys. Eventually, I got up enough courage to go into the dressing room. I went up to Ernie, "How does this work? Who am I working with?" He went to find out and came back and told me I was facing Dusty Rhodes.

In the locker room, guys started looking at me because they recognized me as a photographer. Sylvano Sousa, who was a job guy from New England, and somebody that I'd shot not that long ago, was whispering to Monsoon and McMahon and looking in my direction. I don't know what was said. All I know is that my match was changed from a singles match to me and Sousa against Dusty in a handicap match. And in hindsight, I am grateful for that, as the match would have been a bigger debacle than it was.

Monsoon called us together and told us, "Okay, four minutes. Dusty goes over. You guys work it out." We talked about what we were going to do in the ring. Dusty went, "We'll do this, brother. You get me in the corner and start working on me." It was a blur to me, and I was not retaining anything. I kept thinking to myself, "Why am I doing this? What the fuck is wrong with me?"

I had to get a wrestler's license, which was 10 bucks for a temporary one, and it was just a form to fill out. They asked me what my name was going to be, and I went, "John Anthony." Anthony was my confirmation name. I was John Anthony from Boston, Massachusetts, at 220 pounds. There was no physical, no one examined me, no blood pressure test, nothing.

The match started with us both in the ring. We got Dusty in the corner, and I started hitting him on the back and top of the head with my forearm. I found out later that's not really the way you're supposed to do that. Immediately, he got hot, because I had hit him pretty stiff. I gave him a knee and it hit him pretty close to the jaw. He threw Sousa out of the ring, I went to attack him from behind, and he turned around and

PHOTO BY GEORGE NAPOLITANO

★ ★ ★ ★ ★ ★ ★ ★

DUSTY RHODES
HITS ME WITH
A BIONIC
ELBOW.

grabbed me by my hair. He whispered, "I've got to teach you a lesson." Obviously, he realized that I didn't know what I was doing. He started hitting me over the head with the elbows; he had me by the hair and he wouldn't let go, and he hit me on the head with a couple of elbows. I got shockwaves throughout my body, it was so hard, and I was in a daze for the rest of it. I didn't do anything right. He tried to give me a snapmare and I didn't know how to go over properly. He flung me into the ropes, but I ran into Sousa instead of the turnbuckle.

I know Vince McMahon Jr. was cringing, and his line on commentary was "A total lack of coordination from newcomer John Anthony."

For the finish, Dusty dropped a couple of elbows on Sousa, so he's on the mat prone. Then Dusty tried to slam me, and I didn't know to go for a bodyslam, I didn't know how to guide it and share the weight. I was dead weight. He picked me up, but he couldn't lift me. He picked me up halfway and he dumped me stomach-first on Sousa. Then he sat on my head to pin us both.

That was the end of that, and I was totally embarrassed. I was looking out at ringside, and I saw some of my friends with their mouths open; others were just shaking their heads.

Back in the locker room, I found out I was going to be in two more matches, because they were taping three shows. In the next one, I was paired with Joe Turco from Cantana, Sicily—he was a world-famous jobber of that era—against Peter Maivia and Chief Jay Strongbow. The third taping was supposed to be me working against Bob Backlund.

While Monsoon was telling us about the tag match, where Maivia and Strongbow would go over in seven minutes, I just wanted to get out there. When we went to talk about it, obviously they'd all been tipped off that I didn't know what I was doing. Strongbow called the match and said, "You don't get in the ring at all. You stay outside the ring until the very end. The whole match, you're going to try to tag in, and we're going to pull Turco away. At the very end, when you finally get tagged it, we'll throw you, you'll get a headbutt, and we'll cover you 1-2-3." That's how the match played out. I was outside the ring, and every time I was close to being tagged in, Strongbow would laugh and pull Turco away. People were just laughing, so it was more of a comedy match than anything else.

★ ★ ★ ★ ★ ★ ★ ★ ★ ★ ★

**TAKING ADVICE
FROM MY PARTNER
JOE TURCO.**

Finally, I was tagged in, and Strongbow threw me over the top of the rope—I vaulted pretty well, actually—and I got picked up and he threw me into Maivia, who was outside the ring. He gave me a headbutt, and then Strongbow pinned me 1-2-3 and it was over.

When I got back to the locker room, Monsoon came up to me and said, "Okay, you're done for the night. Thank you." In a way I was relieved that I didn't have to face a legitimate shooter in Bob Backlund in that third match! I got paid 90 dollars, in cash. Everyone got paid in cash.

One of the memories that stuck with me was that, in the locker room, Tony Garea got his money just after he'd gotten out of the shower. He took the money and slapped it on his wet ass, and he started walking around the locker room with dollar bills falling off his ass. It got a lot of laughs.

It was fascinating to me even being there in the locker room, especially because I sat beside Spiros Arion. Here's a guy I was such of a fan of. I don't remember a lot of specifics, beyond the atmosphere, since it was so surreal to me.

My head was killing me. I suspect I had a concussion. I was very disoriented. I took a bus back to Boston and I was just out of it. But I continued to question why I did it. The payment for the eventual story I wrote, "*Ring Wrestling* Magazine Writer Tries His Luck in the Ring," was not worth it.

The only good thing to come of it was the reaction of my pals. The matches aired a couple of weeks later, and the engineer at the college TV station taped them for me, and we had viewing parties. It was on Channel 56 up in the Boston area. The whole dorm was hanging out in one of the common areas, waiting to watch me work against Dusty Rhodes, and then the following week in the tag team match.

Donna got our mother to watch wrestling that week. She didn't want to, so my sister pleaded, "It's really going to be good tonight. Please watch it with me. Johnny's going to be there." "Oh, Johnny's going to be there? Okay." She didn't tell her I was going to be in the ring, getting my ass kicked. That was a surprise to my mom, and my sister got a laugh out of watching our mother get freaked out. My dad was like, "What are you doing that shit for?"

Years later, when I started *Pro Wrestling Spotlight* on mainstream radio, I called myself "former pro wrestler John Anthony," and I didn't use my real name until after the first year of the show.

I'd travel from Boston to Madison Square Garden to shoot the matches, and the next one was February 20, 1978. It was a big night, with Superstar Billy Graham defending his WWWF world title against Bob Backlund.

I set up at ringside and flipped through the program . . . and there's me wrestling Strongbow. It was a George Napolitano photo. My immediate thought was "Oh, shit, I'm in the program." A few minutes later, Mel Phillips, who brought the ring outfits back to the dressing room, approached me and ordered, "You've got to leave." I didn't understand. He said, "Come to the back." I collected my stuff and went to the back, and was told by Mel that I couldn't shoot pictures any longer as I was a wrestler. I was still allowed backstage and watched Backlund win the title from outside the curtain leading to the dressing room.

I had wrestled my way out of a photographer's gig, which I found ironic and kind of funny. (Also funny, John Anthony actually made the Japanese newspapers covering the matches.)

From that moment on, my days in professional wrestling were numbered.

Or so I thought.

6.

I SHOULDA STAYED IN BASEBALL

Did you ever love a baseball team so much that you stole a piece of turf from their home stadium and planted it in your backyard? I did. Yep, back in October 1973, right after the Mets clinched the National League pennant in Game 5 of the Championship Series against the Cincinnati Reds, I snagged a chunk of Shea Stadium sod and tried to get it to grow in our backyard in West Babylon. (I had sold my coin collection to buy seats for the series.) I'm not exactly sure what I was thinking would happen; maybe old Mets coming out of the Iowa corn field like Shoeless Joe Jackson in *Field of Dreams*.

It's certainly a good metaphor for my fandom, my obsession, for all things New York Mets. Living mostly in Nashville, I splurge on the full baseball TV package so I can watch every game, from spring training through the end of the season. If I can't see it on TV, I'm following the game on my phone during a concert or secretly under the table at dinner.

I owe the curse of my love for the Mets to my Uncle Sonny, who was my mother's brother. He took me, along with my cousin Anthony, to my first Mets game on July 3, 1966, at Shea Stadium. It was magical and hot—over 100 degrees. I fell in love with the magnificent green playing field, the crack of the bat, the players scurrying to make a play, the loud boisterous crowd, the smell of the fresh peanuts. Ed Kranepool got several hits and became my hero and to this day my all-time fave Met. Steady Eddie wore number seven, which was also worn by his cross-town rival on the Yankees, who happened to be Mickey Mantle. Uncle Sonny was a great guy, with a terrific sense of humor. I was very close to him. Everyone loved Sonny. In January 1995, he died a few months after being diagnosed with congestive heart failure, as a complication to his long-time diabetes. He entered the hospital with some breathing difficulty, and within days he just deteriorated and was gone. The ironic part was that he was a diehard Yankees fan. The Yankees were not home that week in 1966, and if they had been, I would have become a Yankees fan, and would have enjoyed many more winning seasons during my life.

In 1969, when the Miracle Mets won the World Series, I was 12 years old. During the team's run in September, my mom was going through one of her nervous breakdowns. As much as I was filled with joy watching my Mets battle their way to first place that September, I was also being overwhelmed as I watched my mom sink into another abyss. She ended up being committed in a very violent way, and it traumatized my family. But the World Series was on, the Mets' *first* fall classic. On the morning of October 15, my aunt, who stayed with us during that time, woke me up and said, "Your dad wants to see you." I went into his bedroom, and he said, "You're not going to school today." He paused, and I wondered why. Then he answered, "Because we're going to the World Series." It was Game 4, the game Tom Seaver pitched, the game Ron Swoboda made that miracle catch, and the Mets won in the 10th inning on a bunt play. It was a dream come true. I have no idea how he got the tickets, but he did; it was a lot like when he got Linda and me tickets to the Beatles at Shea. Being connected had its benefits.

The next day was Game 5, and the Mets could win it all. The Gallaghers next door were allowed to stay home for it, but my dad made me go to school. Armed with a transistor radio, we listened to the game in my eighth-grade class. The teachers let us listen until the moment the Mets won, and then we were told to shut it off.

Baseball and pro wrestling were my twin passions, and I started putting together my own Mets magazine, which covered the team and

Eddie Kranepool. It was mainly for my own amusement, but a few friends saw it, and it helped me polish my writing skills.

Though I didn't get to go to many games, finances being what they were, I followed the team religiously. When I was in Boston for college, the Red Sox were really good, and the Mets weren't, so I enjoyed going to Fenway for games; they were in different leagues anyway, so it's not like I gave up on the Mets.

The mention of college is important though, since one of my classmates, Larry Simmons, a dear friend to this day, went to the baseball winter meetings in 1979 and got a job with the San Diego Padres in the minor leagues, with their affiliate in Walla Walla, Washington. He knew that I didn't have a career path in front of me and encouraged me to consider it. "You should go to the baseball winter meetings. They have a job fair," he said.

The 1980 MLB winter meetings were in Dallas, at the Lowes Anatole Hotel. Larry had been in the game for a year, he'd gone through the process, so we went down together. He wanted out of Walla Walla and quickly got a new job with the Class A Anderson Braves, in the South Atlantic League. Traditionally in baseball, you move around a lot, not only as a player but as an executive.

Since most of the jobs available were entry level, it was a pretty informal deal. You signed up for the job fair and hoped that you found a match. Your resume had been submitted as a part of the registration, but from there, it was up to you to be aggressive and find the people that were hiring.

That first day, I scoured the list of job postings, and I saw one for the Mets. "That's the job I want!" But I didn't know to navigate it much from there.

It was getting frustrating to me, because it was a three-day convention, and I had gotten interviews, but not for the job in the Mets organization. One interview was with the Clinton (Iowa) Cubs, and the offer was something like 75 or 100 dollars a week. My initial thought was, "There's no way I'm going to Iowa for a hundred bucks a week."

The Mets job was with Jack Farnsworth, who was a long-time owner of minor league franchises. He was an independent owner but had secured what were called PDCs, or player development contracts, with the two major-league clubs. The Mets affiliate he owned was in Shelby, North Carolina, and the Cardinals team was in nearby Gastonia. The latter had, until recently, been a Pittsburgh Pirates town. Both were also in the South Atlantic League.

Mr. Farnsworth was impossible to pin down, and I was getting very concerned that I would not connect with him before the winter meetings ended. So I thought about how to make it happen, and I ended up calling his room at the Lowes. His wife, Nina, picked up the phone, and I explained who I was. I laid out about being a Mets fan forever and wanting to break into baseball, a pitch not unlike the one I gave to Willie Gilzenberg back in the day, for my wrestling press credentials.

Her response was "I think my husband needs to talk to you. He's downstairs at a meeting, but I will make sure he gets your message, so stay put." Of course, there were no cell phones, so I had to wait by the phone in my room. She set off to find him. Within 10 minutes, she returned the call and said that Jack wanted to talk to me, and that I was to find him in the bar. So that's what I did.

He was a very old-school Southern man, with a deep accent and a cigar in his mouth. "Why do you want to work for me?"

"I love the Mets."

"You know you won't make any money."

"Yeah, I understand that. I'm willing to do the work."

At the end of the meeting, he wrote down on a napkin, "January 11, 1981," and his address, and said, "You're hired. You want to be a Mets man, you can be a Mets man." He gave me the job and then asked me what I wanted to do. I answered public relations and marketing. "I'll make you public relations director, how's that?" Of course, I agreed. It was all happening so quickly. Up next, he told me my salary would be $125 a week, so $500 a month. I said okay.

The rest of the time in Dallas was really celebratory for me. And if you were a baseball fan, the winter meetings were a great place to be. You'd run into George Steinbrenner in an elevator. Larry knew a couple of girls who worked for the Atlanta Braves, and we were all hanging out in our hotel room partying. Who comes into the room but Hank Aaron with some of his friends. We ordered another case of beer from downstairs to share with Hammerin' Hank.

Later, we went down to the bar, and sitting there was Billy Martin and Mickey Mantle. I went up and introduced myself. All of a sudden, Billy puts his arm around me, like I was a pal. It was so surreal.

Since I had my job, I called up a girl I knew from the WFIA convention in Dallas a few years back and asked if she'd like to get a drink. She agreed and made plans to meet me at the bar at the Lowes. It was a night that I will never forget. When she saw me, she was blown away, because the last time she'd seen me, I was 250 pounds, and I was around 190 now and looking pretty good. We hit it off. As we were settling down in my room, the phone rang. It was my sister calling from New York, telling me that John Lennon had been shot. I was stunned and devastated, and immediately turned on the TV, and during *Monday Night Football*, Howard Cosell made the announcement that Lennon was dead.

While my friend consoled me, the mood was gone. That was the only bad memory of the trip.

I had my job in baseball.

★ ★ ★ ★ ★

Upon my return to New York, I shared the news. My dad couldn't believe how little I was going to make. "How are you going to live on that?"

"I don't know, I'll figure it out." He and the rest of my family were sad, as I had just come back home to live in New York after spending five years in Boston. Of course, having lived in big cities, I didn't have a clue about small-town life, with its overall lower cost of living. I gave my notice at Roulette Records, and they didn't really care.

"Okay, see you later."

I packed up my car and drove to North Carolina. Our first meeting, in early January, was at Jack Farnsworth's house. It was in an upscale neighborhood in Gastonia, which was just outside Charlotte. In the room were six or seven other people that he'd hired for the two ball clubs, the Mets in Shelby and the Cardinals in Gastonia. One of them was Mike Koperda, the general manager of the Shelby Mets of the South Atlantic League (South Division). He had four or five years of baseball experience, but was two years younger than me. Mike was the youngest general manager in all of baseball at that time. He was very animated and a real character. He was hyper, with no off switch. However, we hit it off immediately, and though he was my boss, we were pals.

It was like a boot camp, and we soon found out what Mr. Farnsworth was about—money. He needed to meet his expenses, which included the deal with the teams and the costs of putting on the games too. Generally, the major-league teams took care of the player salaries for their signees, as well as things like the uniforms.

The key for minor-league owners to make money was always the stadium, since you got revenue from ticket sales, concessions, parking, and all that. Unfortunately, that was a huge problem in Shelby, where we played at American Legion Stadium at Shelby High School.

My assignment was basically to do everything. While my primary job was to sell advertising, including the fence-sign ads and program ads, and to arrange promotional nights with corporations, you never knew what you'd be called upon to do that day. On top of sales, I did announcing and even booked the talent to sing the national anthem.

We got our marching orders every morning at 7 a.m. at a sales meeting. You'd cold-call companies and people all day. There was an hour for dinner, from 6 p.m. to 7 p.m., and then from 7 p.m. to 10 p.m., you were expected to do more calls, telemarketing, from your home. At night, it was mainly about calling individuals about season tickets. It was non-stop. You'd go to sleep, wake up, and do it all over again.

It was not something that I really minded, because it was baseball and I was affiliated with the Mets.

The first day of selling was one I'll never forget. I'd met an operator of a large furniture store there, and she was another northerner, who had migrated down there. She bought two fence signs from me, on the outfield wall, for $1,500 each and two program ads for $500 each, as she had two separate furniture businesses. At the conclusion of the day, we'd go to Mr. Farnsworth's house and have a meeting. "What'd you do today, big man?" he asked me. I announced the two fence signs and two program ads, $4,000. "Holy smokes! Hot dog!"—he said that all the time, "Hot dog!"—"This man can sell. I knew there was something about you." It made me feel good, but the other salespeople looked on enviously.

I quickly learned that not every day was like that, or even close to it.

★ ★ ★ ★ ★

Another aspect of the job was housing the ballplayers. The Mets had a booster club, so you found some places with them, where a family would take in a player, providing room and board for a fee, and usually tickets too.

On my decidedly minor-league salary, I found myself needing to sublet part of the house that I was renting for $240. My roommate was another rookie salesperson with the team, named Don. He was a nervous wreck and couldn't handle Mr. Farnsworth's terrifying tactics. I'd find him weeping in his room, and the day before he left for good, he shit his pants in the car on the way home from the sales meeting simply out of fear.

My next roommates were players from the team, and while the experience gifted me with a couple of great friends, I did learn that ballplayers are slobs. No one took care of the place, except for me. They wouldn't clean up in the kitchen. Then they'd go on these road trips, and things would fester. To this day, I'm manic when it comes to cleaning and having my stuff in its proper place, and it stems from Gibby and J.P.

Gibby was a top prospect in the Mets organization and a first-round draft pick. He was a catcher named John Gibbons, who was born in Montana but grew up in San Antonio, Texas. Upon learning that he was staying with me, he immediately gave me a pitch to house another player, J.P. Ricciardi, an infielder from Worcester, Massachusetts. Initially, it was the three of us, and then we were assigned another player, a switch-hitting outfielder named Mike Hennessy, who was from the Bronx originally but grew up in New Jersey. We paid 60 dollars a month each. We were all kids. I was 24, and they were a couple of years younger than me.

It was fascinating because baseball players are so different from regular people. For one, they are so superstitious. When Gibby got on a hot streak, you'd find him asleep cradling his favorite bat. Note that I didn't say he was in his bed. There was not enough room for all of us in the house. I had a bedroom that I didn't share. In the second bedroom, there was a queen-sized bed, and we had a couch. There would be shifts, where one night, a guy got the bed, and the next the couch, and the other guy on the floor, and they'd rotate the next day. So they'd look forward to a road trip as they'd be guaranteed a bed.

I'm from New York and would curse every once in a while, and J.P. would say, "You're not going to go to Heaven if you keep saying stuff like that. God doesn't like that."

One night, at 3 a.m. or so, I heard someone trying to break in through my bedroom window. I grabbed a bat and went to see, and it was Hennessy, as he'd misplaced or forgotten his keys. I didn't get along with Mike as well as John and J.P. Mike was a crazy Irish guy, arrogant, full of himself, and very New York. I've recently gotten back in touch with him through Gibby. Mike was a handful, and Shelby was his last stop in professional baseball—he was out at age 19.

J.P. and John were so unique, from such radically different backgrounds, yet the best of friends. Gibby made the majors as the Mets starting catcher in 1984, but was injured in a collision at the plate during spring training of that year, fracturing his cheekbone. When he returned, he hit only .220 in limited action. Once the Mets traded for Gary Carter of the Montreal Expos in the winter of 1984, Gibby's fate was determined. He was called up during the Mets' championship run in 1986 and batted .474 in eight games, and earned a World Series ring as the non-roster bullpen catcher during the playoffs and World Series. J.P.'s future lay in management. After his minor-league days fizzled out, Ricciardi spent time as a coach in the Yankees organization, before catching on with the Oakland A's, during general manager Billy Beane's Moneyball days (Beane had played with Gibby and J.P. too). The Toronto Blue Jays hired J.P., in November 2001, as their general manager, and he then hired Gibby as his manager in 2004, before firing him in 2008; Gibby had a second go-round with the Jays, under new management, from 2013 to 2018, including two runs to the American League Championship Series.

John and I remain close. Over the past few years, I've been helping open doors up for his daughter, Jordan, who is a fledgling Americana/ alt country artist. I'm perfectly willing to admit that I have hit both John and J.P. up for tickets on numerous occasions over the years. After all, I did clean up after them for an entire season . . .

★ ★ ★ ★ ★

The season itself was tumultuous; it was exciting, but it was grueling because of how many hours you'd have to put in every day. When the season started, I was also the announcer on the public address system in the stadium.

Both Mike Koperda and I were from New York, and brash and aggressive compared to the aw-shucks folks around Shelby. We set a goal right from the start: to have a record crowd at Shelby for an opening day. Mike and I hired models as ball girls, and they all wore jerseys with the number 10 on them—Bo Derek's movie *10* was still on people's minds. The ballpark held maybe 5,000, and we shoehorned in 7,000 fans.

My sales were really good, and not just to the businesses but also the season ticket sales, the corporate sales, the group sales. It was such a small town, we were almost kings, walking around in our suits. People knew we were with the Mets.

But that celebrity didn't always translate to sales. You'd go into the office or the business and try to sell them something, and the real Southern ones would take a look and go, "Where you from, boy?"

"I'm from New York, sir."

"Well, you're just a Yankee."

You heard that all the time. After a few experiences like that, I got used to it, even if it was like nothing I'd ever seen before. I did come up with the proper response, though: "No, sir, I'm with the Mets."

We did promotions that worked, tried and true draws, like the San Diego Chicken and "The Clown Prince of Baseball" Max Patkin. Then there were the promotions that didn't go so well. My love of wrestling, in all its forms, resulted in a Mississippi mud wrestling night on a Friday. The ring was on wheels so we could take it out and fill it with mud. However, we didn't know what we were doing, and it was filled with dirt that was wet, like you'd find in an infield. Before the game started, we had the girls wrestle in the mud, not realizing there's a special kind of mud for mud wrestling. Ours had pebbles and was not smooth. During the fight, one of the girls got something in her eye and she jumped out of the mud pit. She ended up in the hospital, and that was our last mud wrestling night.

★ ★ ★ ★ ★

The slogan for the New York Mets in 1980 was "The Magic Is Back." It related to the new owners of the team, Fred Wilpon and Nelson

Doubleday Jr. For the 1981 Shelby Mets, we used the same slogan, "The Magic Is Back in Shelby." It was on the promotional ads, in the program, and even on the business cards.

I worked with the local radio station, coming up with different music bits to use during the game. For example, when the Mets hit a home run or we won a game, I'd play "Magic" by Pilot, which was a big hit in the '70s, or The Lovin' Spoonful's "Do You Believe in Magic." It wasn't like today, where the players choose their theme music as they head to the plate.

Any time one of the Shelby pitchers would strike out an opponent, I'd play "Another One Bites the Dust" by Queen. I do remember one situation, with Don Mattingly, who was with the Greensboro Hornets. He struck out. After hearing the song clip, he turned around and gave me a "if looks could kill" stare. I was reprimanded after the game: "These guys are trying their best, so maybe that song isn't right." I continued to do it—just not when Mattingly was at bat.

★ ★ ★ ★ ★

Everything with the Shelby Mets went through the Farnsworths. Jack owned the team, of course, and his wife, Nina, was always around, helping with concessions. Their son, Dan, who was an attorney, was in the picture too. They'd host dinners, including the local mayor and other notables from around town. The sales meetings were at their house, the bonus being that Nina was the voice of reason. "Jack, don't be so hard on them," she'd scold.

It was always an adventure with Farnsworth. He was never happy about the money we were bringing in, thinking he'd go out of business, or lose his shirt, or lose $50,000 that year. If I wasn't doing well, he'd threaten me with "I'm going to put you over to the Cardinals, and see how you'll do there." He used intimidation to get his way, not a very conducive atmosphere to success.

His main business was selling Bibles, and he'd bring in his hot-shot Bible salesmen to sell baseball. Normally, they'd last a week or so and then they'd be out, because they couldn't sell baseball.

★ ★ ★ ★ ★ ★ ★ ★ ★

SHELBY METS ON THE FIELD IN 1981.

Racial discrimination was still prominent in small Southern towns. Farnsworth was a racist, there's no doubt about it. He'd sit with me and say, "We had this Black boy that worked for me and eventually made it to New York to work for the Mets, and he was one of the finest Black boys I ever met." It was uncomfortable hearing things like that, given where I grew up. He would hire these poor Black kids to be at the games, and it was their job to get the foul balls back from the fans in the stands that caught them. "Those baseballs are expensive. We'll lose our shirt if we keep giving them fans the foul balls!" They would be paid in food, like hot dogs and sodas.

The more I got to know Mr. Farnsworth, the more I disliked him because of the way he operated, because of the prejudices that he had. He was constantly worried about money; it was never about the joy of the game.

★ ★ ★ ★ ★

In June, there was a draft, and we got some new players. One of them was a very loud, cocky guy named Lenny Dykstra, who became one of the most beloved Mets ever, a catalyst of the 1986 World Championship club. When I ran into Lenny years later in 2017, at the induction weekend of Mike Piazza in Cooperstown, New York, he was promoting his book,

House of Nails: A Memoir of Life on the Edge. I introduced myself, and he was still Lenny.

"John, how the fuck are you, man?" He asked what I was doing now, and I told him about the music business. "You must be fucking loaded, bro."

Then he recounted a story I'd forgotten, about me picking him up when he got to town. "I'm all excited and I get off the plane and you pick me up from the airport. I'll never fucking forget it. You took me to the field, and it was a fucking high school field, and it was the shits, and I couldn't fucking believe that I had to play at a fucking high school field." He didn't show that disappointment or that anger that day, in 1981, but he remembered it years later.

Lenny was a player that you knew was going to make it. He was just so aggressive and so fast on the basepaths, and had a quick bat. He was this dynamic player that sparked the team when he was on it. His nickname was "Nails" during his exciting baseball career. However, after baseball he was called "Lucifer." Given his up-and-down life both during and after his baseball career, that should not come as a surprise.

★ ★ ★ ★ ★

At mid-season, we were not doing very well in the standings, but the pressure was on to keep selling. If you have a winning ball club, people attend; if you don't have a winning team, even in the major leagues, crowds are sparse.

We were promised outfielder Darryl Strawberry, and that never happened. Farnsworth was pissed off about that, because Darryl was the big Mets signing, anointed to be the big star from day one.

The season ended in August, and the Shelby Mets limped to a 59–83 record. Six of our players eventually made the majors: Gibby, Lenny, Randy Milligan, and La Schelle Tarver as players, and Jay Tibbs and DeWayne Vaughn as pitchers, which was a pretty good ratio for a Class A team.

★ ★ ★ ★ ★

The players used to call Shelby "Hellby," since there was nothing to do, no bars, no nightlife. As a tiny Southern town, it was hit or miss whether they appreciated you being there or treated you as an outsider.

Yet, it was where I had my greatest social life. When we had any time off at all, Mike Koperda and I would party. He had a girlfriend who would come down pretty frequently, but I was a serial dater. It helped that I was nice and thin for the first time in my life. I'd go out and always have a girl accompanying me. My confidence was at an all-time high. Even though I was only making $125 a week, I felt I was really part of a special thing that was going on in town.

Going out was complicated by the fact that Shelby was in a dry county, so liquor was restricted. There was no place that would sell you a drink unless it was a private club.

One night, there was an ad in the paper for a band playing at the Stardust Lounge. For alcohol there, you could bring it in, then check it in, and buy it back from them, for a couple of bucks each. I called Mike up and we went out to blow off a little steam.

Straight Up was the band. It featured a beautiful lead singer wearing red spandex, with reddish, short hair. She just started singing covers of Journey, Linda Ronstadt, Bonnie Raitt. Her voice was amazing. So good in fact, that I wound up going to see them at that club all the time. They were the house band, often playing five hours a night. After a few shows, I got up the nerve to talk to the lead singer, Patty Lovelace. Country music fans would know her later as Patty Loveless.

To me, she was a talent, and I convinced myself—and her—that I was the man to be her manager and take her to stardom.

So much for baseball.

★ ★ ★ ★ ★

At the end of the season, I told Farnsworth that I didn't want to work there anymore, and that I was going into the music business. He thought I was crazy. "You could have been an executive with the Mets. You're good, you have talent."

Somehow, he convinced me that I could make a ton of money selling Bibles for him. "I'll start you off at $300 a week." I was making $125 a week with the Mets. I gave it a shot for a week.

He was on the road, so his top sales guy trained me on selling Bibles. In the evening, we had adjacent rooms, and you could hear Farnsworth on the phone through the wall screaming at this guy for not making enough sales that day—and that was his top guy. I decided, "I don't need this."

Baseball was very rewarding, but it was frustrating, because you were working for a guy that was never satisfied, no matter what you did. It was a great learning experience, and it was a great education for me on the art of selling and the art of taking rejection from sales calls. And also knowing that if you have a passion for what you're doing, and if you're selling something that you're very passionate about, it doesn't matter if people say no to you, because there are enough people saying yes to make it worthwhile and fulfilling.

★ ★ ★ ★ ★

Jumping ahead into 1982, I was back in New York, selling radio ads at WNYG, but I wanted to get back into baseball. Many people in the Mets' New York office knew me from my time in Shelby. Al Harazin was the assistant to the general manager, and Jay Horowitz was the head of public relations. The Mets were putting up a new "Diamond Vision" scoreboard, and they were interviewing for someone to run it. I'd also had some exploratory interviews with MLB in its head office.

For the Mets job, I went through a couple of rounds of interviews, and I was one of the finalists. I was so psyched, thinking I could be the guy running the video screen on the scoreboard. Then I got a call from Harazin saying I came in second, and the only reason I was second was that I didn't have enough video production knowledge, so they hired someone who was a better fit.

But Al went to bat for me and directed me to MLB's in-house show, *This Week in Baseball*. I interviewed with legendary baseball TV producer Larry Parker there and was hired for an entry-level position as a production assistant/viewer for *This Week in Baseball*. Essentially, I watched several games at a time on their TV monitors and time coded the major moments—home runs, big catches, managers arguing with umpires. They'd choose the best segments for Mel Allen's show (though I never met Mel). I made about $250 a week to start, and I was still working WNYG in sales; it was ironic that I was making more money part-time than I was with my full-time job at MLB.

MLB had a very meticulous hiring process, and they were looking for people who could go all the way in the company, one of them being Sean Mooney. Mooney went on to produce and host segments for MLB. He became an anchorman for New York TV station WWOR as well. But he is best known as the host of several WWF shows, including *Prime Time Wrestling*. He and I have recently reconnected, which was a bit surreal.

When I was hired at MLB, there were suggestions that I could move up into marketing or sales but that this was where everyone started. I stayed a few months, getting up early, taking the train to the city as a part of my commute, and then watching games all day. It just wasn't challenging enough, and I didn't have the patience to wait it out until I could move into another position.

In the end, I quit the baseball job to go full-time at WNYG—and I quit that job within a few months, because another radio station found out about my sales record and hired me away; that was WLIR, a historic, New Wave station back in the early '80s, which broke new acts like Duran Duran, Billy Idol, and the Romantics.

As my uncle did for me by taking me to my first Mets game in 1966, I have done the same for my nephew Dominic. I took him to his first game and shared my passion for the game and the Mets with him. We are bonded for life through the team. We've gone to Mets games all across the United States, and our annual spring training vacation to Port St. Lucie is our favorite part of each year. Dominic is not far away from getting his Master's degree in Sports Management, and has a desire to work for the Mets upon graduation. That would be the ultimate for me to see!

7.

PATTY

It's not correct to say that I discovered Patty Loveless. She was close to becoming a star as a teenager but left Nashville before that happened. She would ascend to the top of the country music industry after I left the picture. Instead, I was there during her darkest times, the partying and drug use, the troubled marriage.

I was this nutty Italian New Yorker who saw the best in her, encouraged her, stood by her, reminded her constantly that her dreams of being a success could come true.

I did it out of love.

★ ★ ★ ★ ★

Like Loretta Lynn, Patty Ramey was the daughter of a Kentucky coal-miner. Raised in a large Southern Baptist family, music flowed through the Ramey life. The Swinging Singing Rameys were her brother Roger and sister Dotti. By age 12, Patty was earning money as a singer, and she soon replaced Dotti in the duo. In 1971, country music superstar Porter Wagoner caught their act, took an immediate liking to Patty's style, and encouraged her to write and perform on her own.

Famed country singers Teddy and Doyle Wilburn, who'd discovered Lynn, brought Patty to Nashville in 1975. She was signed to a writing deal with the Wilburn's Sure Fire Music, and had an early hit when Ronnie Smith performed her "Country I'm Comin' Home." She was mentored by Dolly Parton—who taught her how to put on makeup for the stage—and fame seemed around the corner for Patty Ramey.

While touring with the Wilburn Brothers on the Americountry Express Show, Patty met a much older drummer, Terry Lovelace. To the dismay of everyone around her, she married Terry and he moved her out of Nashville and took her to his hometown, Kings Mountain, North Carolina.

In the new environment, Patty left country music behind and transformed into a rock 'n' roll singer in her husband's band, belting out cover tunes in seedy bars for drunk patrons. They were not playing in venues where talent agents would be scouting for the next stars.

But then I wasn't a talent agent.

★ ★ ★ ★ ★

My first conversations with her, while I was working for the Mets, were about learning her story. She was so talented yet stuck in the shit-ass club.

I challenged her, "Don't you still have a dream to be something in the business?"

It floored me when she said, "That dream is over. I'm married now."

She was three weeks older than me, born January 4, 1957.

"How can you say that? You're 24. You have your whole life ahead of you."

When I wasn't working, I'd hang out at the club, and I started to develop a friendship with some of the other Straight Up band members. During shows, I'd sit with their girlfriends or wives. It was really interesting to me, since I was a New York guy, very metropolitan, and I felt worldly compared to the folks in Shelby. They were all from other small towns around North Carolina, from working-class families. Their lives centered on partying on the weekend. I integrated myself into their world.

★ ★ ★ ★ ★ ★ ★ ★ ★

HANGING OUT IN
THE TRAILER THAT
PATTY AND HER
HUSBAND, TERRY,
OWNED IN KINGS
MOUNTAIN, NORTH
CAROLINA. A
KEROSENE HEATER
KEPT THE TRAILER
WARM.

One night, I was invited to party with them and some of the band members after one of their shows, and I went to the trailer where Patty lived with Terry. Everyone was doing drugs. It was more than pot. There were pills. One drug they used to call "Mad Dog." The scene was not something that I was comfortable with. I'd smoked pot since my college days, so that never really bothered me; I drank some but not a lot. Yet I got drawn into this lifestyle, and it was a conflict for me with the Mets and this rock 'n' roll stuff. Something had to give. The Mets lost.

★ ★ ★ ★ ★

Patty was so enchanting. She was beautiful, talented, with an incredible voice, and she had an aura about her, that indelible "it" factor. She looked like a star, she sang like a star. But she had this other side of her too during that time, and I think it stemmed from unhappiness—that's my personal opinion. It was the loss of her father and the struggles she and her husband were encountering, living in a trailer with just a kerosene heater.

As for Terry, I hate to use the term "backwoods redneck," but that's what he was. He was a good drummer, but he was not the nicest guy in the world. He did not like me, because I was talking to his wife about pursuing her dreams and how talented she was. It was disruptive to his simple, comfortable life.

I saw something in her that I'd never seen in anybody before. For me, it was not just a professional relationship; I was smitten by her, right from day one, and that was a turning point in my life. I knew this girl was a star and I knew I wanted to do something to help her. Wanting to be around her was the main driving factor of my decision to work with Straight Up.

★ ★ ★ ★ ★

Looking back, I sure had a lot of nerve to pitch myself as a manager. I must have learned something at that crummy job at Roulette Records, right? No, but I did make some good contacts. Bob Lapoff still worked there, and I taped Straight Up off a soundboard and sent a cassette to him. He immediately agreed that she was really good and agreed to help me try to do something with her. I also had the support of my Mets pal, Mike Koperda, and Marilyn Hoyle, a close friend I had met in Shelby, who we hired to work with us at the ballpark, and who fell in love with the band as well. Marilyn and Patty hit it off, and to this day, they remain the best of friends. They both helped my confidence, assuring me that I wasn't insane, even though many people, including my family, thought that I was.

With Bob as my mentor, and Marilyn as my cheerleader, I quit the Mets and made a plan: get her out of the club; hit other venues; get her a record deal; make her famous. As a start, I blindly began calling booking agents, pitching her talents. My sales experience helped as I called up clubs to convince them to give Straight Up a try. (I wanted to rename the band Patty Lovelace and Straight Up, but no one went for that.) I used my photography skills to shoot some publicity photos of the group, wrote up a little bio, got an article in the local newspaper about how this guy from New York was managing this band. There was a list of all the cover songs they did but oddly no originals, even though Patty had been a songwriter. She was a belter, singing loud, whether it was mainstream hits by Journey, Pat Benatar, .38 Special, Molly Hatchet, or lesser known groups like Spyder and Toronto.

The first gig that I booked was a week-long stay in Myrtle Beach, South Carolina. It might have been $1,500 for the week, and my commission was 5 percent. It went up to 10 percent and 15 percent as time went by. The crowds were small, the accommodations were shitty—they put you in band houses, which are exactly what you'd think, barely more than a flophouse. But it was the start of a couple month period that was really tumultuous, as we ventured out onto a circuit in the southeast—Atlanta, Columbia, Greenville, Greensboro.

PATTY IN STUDIO, LAYING DOWN A TRACK IN CHARLOTTE, NORTH CAROLINA, IN 1981.

Everyone was fired up, thinking this New York guy was going to get a record deal, but I didn't know what the hell I was doing. I was just flying by the seat of my pants, and then reporting up to Bob in New York what was going on.

There were constant struggles, there was always turmoil. And more importantly, it was still an atmosphere with a lot of drugs. After every performance, there was booze and drugs. And Patty drank to get drunk.

Me too. I was drinking more, taking some drugs. I was introduced to Quaaludes through the band. It's a drug that isn't around much anymore, but it gave you a euphoric feeling. One night, Patty said, "Let's go take a walk." We walked on the beach in South Carolina. It was a beautiful night, and I had taken a Quaalude for the first time with her. The high made me even more in love with her, but I did not act on it.

When she wasn't on stage, Patty was the most down-to-earth, simple person. She got joy out of any little thing. She loved to cook, she loved to clean house. She was domestic at home, and on stage, she was a different person.

Despite my best efforts at hyping Straight Up, we never seemed to get repeat bookings. For the few that were in the crowd, they made an impression. The crowds were better in tourist spots, as people were out for the night to see a band, and it didn't matter what band.

At gigs, I was more than just the manager. I also served as the sound man, the light man, the road manager, booking agent—all of it. It was all-encompassing for someone who had no experience whatsoever in this world. There was a lot of pressure and stress.

One night was particularly bad. We were at D-Fords in Atlanta. I had a '73 Chevy Caprice, and I had Patty in my car, while the band was in a truck with the gear, usually driving behind us. We stopped at a liquor store and Patty bought a fifth of Seagram's. By the time the first set went on, she had drank enough to be feeling good. At one point, she asked me to dance with her, but she continued to drink.

We got through the first set okay, but then at the beginning of the second, she wasn't able to do much. The song was Styx's "Too Much Time on My Hands," and she slurred her words when she introduced it. "We've got a problem here" was my reaction from the soundboard in the back. She couldn't continue, almost doing a Bette Midler from *The Rose* . . . She fell.

Normally, they did four or five sets, so I got her off there, while the band continued on with some covers without her. She was just so drunk and depressed. Her vocal cords were also giving her problems, eventually requiring surgery in the 1990s. Terry was never understanding; it was always about the money, pushing her to work.

Patty later told me that she thought about attempting suicide that night. Thank God she didn't. But it was that bad.

★ ★ ★ ★ ★

Since I wasn't making any money, I started borrowing some. An uncle in New York lent me $1,000—and that was a lot of money in 1981. He helped me even though he couldn't believe I'd quit my job with the Mets. When I asked my father to help me, he said, "I'm not helping you with no rock 'n' roll band and no singer. You went down there to work for the Mets, a good job with a future. You just threw it all away. She sounds like a coyote singing in the woods!" It caused a real rift between my father and me.

My percentage on Straight Up's shows—when they had gigs—was too low, probably lower than minimum wage at the time. I had band meetings and tried to tell them what to do, what songs would work better, but no one ever listened to me. It turned into an ugly scene, and I was struggling big-time financially. While I hadn't made big bucks with the Mets, it had been a solid job.

To make ends meet, I applied to a bunch of places for a paying job. I ended up at a portrait photography company. After taking someone's photo, you'd sell them the various packages of prints. It was a traveling job, so I'd be in Winston-Salem for three days, set up in a hotel. One gig might be shooting photos of a bank's employees, their families, and their pets. There were salespeople selling them the packages, and I made commission as well as a salary.

Even my housing was in flux. Initially, I was staying with one of Straight Up's guitar players and his girlfriend in a trailer. I'd be on the road taking photos for this new job, and then I'd come back to the bedroom in the trailer, and there'd be dog shit or cat shit on the bed. It was just a horrible existence—my life had spiraled downward.

And so had the band.

After one of my trips, I got back to the trailer, and the guitar player told me the band had broken up. This mattered, because I had still been getting commission from them, since they were under contract to me.

Those six or seven months were among the most tumultuous of my life. I just decided to drop it all and go back to New York, which I did in March 1982.

There was tension between Patty and me, since I'd never come through with all that I promised, but we had a good bond and worked it out.

★ ★ ★ ★ ★

Back in New York, I was hired as an account executive for this little daytime radio station, an oldies station, WNYG 1440 AM, located on Route 109 in West Babylon, New York. I started selling and making some money in radio ad sales. It was not my endgame, because I knew I had bigger and better things to do.

Patty and I kept in touch. It was mostly by letter, as neither of us had access to a phone on a regular basis. She wrote that she'd founded another band and that Terry was more open to her pursuing a music career. "Sounds like you really like your job. I'm really glad for you. I hope good fortune comes your way soon. So you can back a good R&R band. Hint hint," she wrote on April 20, 1982. "We've had a good tape made of us playing live. It is great, John! You'd be surprised how *tight* everyone plays together. It feels so good. I'll send you a tape of it as soon as we make copies. I think you'll like it a whole lot better than Straight Up."

It led to me going to visit, and I was once again drawn in by her talent, and I knew that I still had feelings for her. With that mixed-up thinking, I signed her to another management company, in the fall of 1982, but as an individual. Terry agreed reluctantly.

I started managing her again, and through Bob at Roulette, I met a producer named Red Neinkerchen. Red was mostly a jingles producer. We talked about Patty; I played him some tapes, showed him pictures. "I'll produce her, maybe we'll write a song."

★ ★ ★ ★ ★

The plan was to record her in New York, and after a few deferrals on her part, she finally made it up in September 1982. Since it was her first trip to New York, I made sure that she had the time of her life. She stayed with me and my family. It was a whirlwind week. We went to Manhattan, and I showed her around, and we had dinner at some nice restaurants. We went to see a John Lennon tribute play together, and even the Playboy Club with my dad and his girlfriend. Patty was a big

fan of a band called The Babys. Their lead singer was John Waite, and he had just put out a solo album called *Ignition*. It so happened that Waite was playing at a famous New York City club called The Ritz. Patty and I went and rocked out together. After the set, I told her to come with me, and I took her backstage. She couldn't believe we just walked in there, and she got to say hello to John. Directly after the concert, we went to Tower Records and bought the album. Then we went back to WNYG, where I had the keys to the building, and we played the album there, smoking a joint.

For me, I was falling even more in love, the deepest love I ever felt for anybody. That week just solidified it for me. I was going down a path that was going to be destructive to me. She was married and I didn't cross those boundaries; I never would. But there were some signals . . . whether they were misinterpreted or not, I'll never know. During that trip, there was one time in Manhattan when she grabbed my hand and held it for a while. I was nervous, excited, scared. I really don't know if she ever had feelings for me. In my heart, if she did have the same type of feelings I had for her, it would have been a different story. It was one-way love.

But the trip was about music, and I got her into the studio with Red. He gave her a rock song he co-wrote, "Lost Days, Lost Nights." They knocked it out in a couple of days. It was good, a stepping stone, we hoped, to something bigger. But then what do you do with just one song? I certainly didn't know what I was doing. I was trying to navigate through this whole mess.

"I just can't seem to tell you in words of how much I enjoyed my trip to New York. I had a wonderful time; one I'll never forget. I was really in great company," she wrote me after the visit. "Thank you so much for the great places & times we spent together. I'm glad everything went as well as it did with the recording. Like I said, 'I please myself by pleasing others.' Your family are good people. Send everyone my love."

★ ★ ★ ★ ★

I started taking weekend trips to North Carolina to see the new band, Caliber, with Patty still as the singer and Terry as the drummer, but no one else from Straight Up. I would leave work on Friday, drive all night to get to North Carolina, and get there in the morning. She'd play Saturday night, and then I'd leave for New York on Sunday. That's how crazy it was for me. Often, I'd bring a friend just to keep me awake.

On one trip, when Bob Lapoff came with me, we convinced Patty to come back to New York to shoot a music video for "Lost Days, Lost Nights." One of my friends from college, Bill Martin, worked for a television station in New Hampshire, so we had a place to shoot it—all my friends knew about my "thing" with Patty, as I'd always bring it up when I talked to them.

This was the point where I changed her name, because of the how actress Linda Lovelace was associated with the 1972 porn move, *Deep Throat*. Terry protested, but I explained why, and going from Patty Lovelace to Patty Loveless was not a big change in the end.

★ ★ ★ ★ ★ ★ ★ ★ ★

CALIBER POSES
FOR A BAND PHOTO
IN SEPTEMBER OF
1982.

In November 1982, Patty came up for the video. I bought her a few outfits, and Joan Jett was just breaking at the time, so I put her in a black spandex outfit. I also took her to get some new promo pictures taken by my wrestling buddy, George Napolitano. When we arrived in New Hampshire, Bill, Patty, and I went out the night before the video shoot. We had a few and stayed out way too late. When she woke up, Patty had puffy eyes. It was just a mess. The video had shots of her walking in the foggy early morning woods, or close-ups of her looking out over the lake. MTV was only just starting, so we didn't have a template to work from, and Bill had never shot a music video before.

Patty went back to North Carolina, and I was all over the place job-wise, trying to make more money, trying to cover my expenses going back and forth to North Carolina, trying to promote her career, trying to make a living. I left WNYG to go to WLIR, which was the hottest New Wave station at the time, a very innovative, historic station. I kept Patty in the loop: "I'm going to a bigger station now. Maybe this can help us." Four months later, I was gone, since I was never focused on the task at hand, because I was obsessed with Patty and North Carolina, going there to be close to her.

She seemed to confide in me, whether it was in person, on the phone, or in letters, and I wanted to be there for her. "Again I'm sorry for giving you a scare. You know me, when I lose my voice, it's like a death to me, and it depresses me so," she wrote in February 1983. "But, Saturday night

I went to pieces. I just had to have a *good cry*. But, John nothing entered my mind, like the thing I *almost* did in Georgia. I was just close to a state of depression. I *hate* being sick or anything wrong with my singing. I'll let you know what the doctor says."

I did try to move on. Through one of my advertisers on Long Island, I met Dawn, a pretty Italian girl. She ran a modeling agency and was trying to grow that business. I integrated her into WNYG and she got a job there so she could make some money. Even though I worked at WLIR, I was still close to many of my friends at WNYG. One night, one of my radio friends called my apartment to say they were at a bar and that Dawn kept asking about me, and that she missed me. "Come on and meet us, Johnny A," said my friend, "Dawn wants you to come out." So I went. I liked her and thought a relationship might get my mind off Patty. We danced and by the end of the night, we were kissing. I was walking on air.

As I headed back in the family apartment (which was now just my mom and my sister), I had all these feelings racing through me, about Dawn, thinking ahead. But as I entered, my mom was on the phone with Patty. "Patty, calm down. Johnny's here." So she puts me on the phone and Patty's crying. "John, I can't take it anymore. Things are bad. I want to come back to New York with you." She was going through whatever she was going through down there, and I just told her I'd come get her and bring her back with me. I was the guy she called.

Her next trip to New York in the spring was meant to shop her around, to meet key music people, but really it was so she could be close to me. Since I knew their history, I bought us tickets to Dolly Parton in Atlantic City and encouraged Patty to reach out, since Dolly had told her in the past that she was always welcome. Patty did but didn't hear back until after the show. Patty and I shared a hotel room: separate beds. It was tough since I was so in love with her.

★ ★ ★ ★ ★

Out of the blue in mid-1983, Patty's brother Roger came back into the picture. She'd been estranged from her family for a while, because they didn't like Terry. Roger lived in Nashville and was working at the Country Music Wax Museum, owned by a wealthy Korean businessman, Daniel Hsu.

Patty told me that Roger wanted to meet with me and to talk about Nashville. "Patty needs to get back to country music. Patty is a country music artist. Patty loves country music, even though she's in the rock 'n' roll world, she's not cut out for that," is what he told me. I didn't argue and thought it was a great idea.

My first trip to Nashville was to see Roger, and he was a good host, showing me around town. We talked a lot about Patty, and about how she was not happy. When I met with Daniel, I brought along my whole Patty Loveless press kit, the demo, and music video. "How much do you think it would cost for Patty to come here and try and get a record cut?" he asked.

While I didn't know a lot about those specifics, I guessed $10,000. He said okay, that he would invest. Roger was like, "Holy cow, it happened that quick? I've known this guy for years and never asked him for anything!" We drew up some paperwork where he would get paid back his investment with a few points if anything happened.

I went back to North Carolina for a sit-down with Patty and Terry, confident my showing them the $5,000 check would spark excitement and hope. That was not the case. Terry was not happy about it at all, and Patty was trying to contain her enthusiasm and happiness that we'd secured some money for her to go to Nashville. Terry really didn't want her to go. I think he saw her as property. He never really respected her. There was something about him that was not right, and I don't know what happened behind closed doors with them, but I know she wasn't happy. At the time, she didn't make the commitment to go, and Terry certainly didn't give her permission to go. I went back to New York dejected and with knots in my stomach.

Back on Long Island, I was going through some personal issues. My older sister, Linda, was becoming more and more paranoid, beginning a total nervous breakdown. It brought back memories from my childhood, seeing my mom go through the same illness. It got so bad that I spent three days trying to keep her from going off the deep end. She was afraid her husband was out to get her, then the government, then my dad's boss Fritzy. I was driving her around and finally took her to the local police station, where they committed her to a psychiatric hospital.

I decided that I had to get away from New York because of the turmoil. I had gone through enough trauma as a kid because of my mom's frequent nervous breakdowns. As an adult, I had a choice to stay or leave. I decided to leave. But I also I wanted to be near Patty. I began applying for some jobs in North Carolina. I set up some interviews and got hired by a big Charlotte station, WEZC-FM "Easy 104."

Next came the biggest mistake that I ever made in my life.

Since the $5,000 was in my account, I used about $1,000 of it to cover my move. Having scratched and clawed for money for so many years, I was too tempted by a chunk of change I had access to, especially when I decided I needed to escape from my family problems in New York.

In North Carolina, I kept meeting with Patty and was frustrated with her, for not fighting harder now that the opportunity had presented itself, and with Terry for holding her back. It broke my heart to see her waitressing. She was wasting away, and I didn't understand it. On my side were Roger and Daniel, who was patient about the investment.

Like we were breaking up as a couple, Patty encouraged me to seek out other acts to manage, and I did, primarily a band called Panic. That got me out on the road and away from her. "John I do appreciate all you've tried to help with. But, you see now, I believe, working with another group, things are similar in bands," she wrote me. "Well, I better end this before it turns into a book. But, in closing I want to leave you with this. Even though I'm not performing, *I haven't given up on the dream*. Take care of yourself, cause you are special to me."

Managing Panic, I did okay, but kept dipping into the money that was for Patty's deal, until finally it was gone. I reached out to Daniel and told him that Patty was stagnant, but that Panic was one to watch. "Would you transfer the $5,000 for Patty to Panic?" I wrote him a letter about that possibility, and he replied but did not approve the transfer of the money into Panic. That was the last I heard from him.

Patty, meanwhile, finally came to the realization that she wanted to do something with her life. She took a cover-band job doing country music in Charlotte, and then talked to her husband and brother, and decided, finally, to return to Nashville.

Our contract was pretty well just a handshake over the last year and a half. "I need to get that $5,000, so I can go to Nashville and do this demo," she said, and I had to tell her that I didn't have it, which was the hardest thing I've ever had to do. I didn't want to disappoint her, and I didn't want to mess up her chances to go to Nashville. I was sick to my stomach when I told her.

She was disappointed, shocked, angry, and hurt.

She was also destined for something I could not give her—stardom.

★ ★ ★ ★ ★

The rest of the Patty Loveless story goes on without me.

In Nashville, she recorded a demo with Roger helping her, then landed a record deal at MCA, and became country royalty. At the end of the day, what I did for Patty Loveless was put a fire back into her belly to convince her that she really needed to go for it, back in 1981.

When it looked like Patty would finally succeed, Terry started wigging out, threatening her, and was abusive. She eventually got enough courage to leave him. Later, in 1989, she married her producer, Emory Gordy Jr., and they moved to an estate in rural Georgia.

Five of her songs hit number one on the country charts: "Timber, I'm Falling in Love," "Chains," "Blame It on Your Heart," "You Can Feel Bad," and "Lonely Too Long." The Academy of Country Music named her Top Female Vocalist in 1996 and 1997, and she joined the Grand Ole Opry in 1988. Oddly, she has not been inducted into the Country Music Hall of Fame, but she will be.

★ ★ ★ ★ ★

We have seen each other over the years. Our friendship maintained itself in a very low-key way. It took me years to get over those personal feelings I had for her. She always knew that I believed in her. She knew that I loved her. She always knew that I had the best of intentions for her, but the timing was bad, and my experience was non-existent. She had to be ready.

I wasn't the bad guy, I was trying to help her. But the misstep on the professional level was that $5,000. Once I started making money, I never forgot about it, and I offered to pay it back, but never heard back about that specifically.

Patty was really close to my family. She called my mom "Snooks," and Donna and her were two gal pals, putting on their makeup together and gossiping. Her letters and Christmas cards always mentioned them.

I'd go watch her perform, whether it was in the greater New York area or at the Opry. It became a professional relationship, albeit one with a deep history.

In 2007, a few years after moving my mom to Nashville, she took ill and didn't have much time left. I had run into Patty at a recording studio and told her about my mom. Patty asked where she was, and later that day went to the hospital to see her. My mom loved Patty, and her eyes lit up when she walked into the hospital room. I'll always remember that.

★ ★ ★ ★ ★

You won't find John Alexander (or John Arezzi, for that matter) in any biographical information on Patty Loveless.

Those years I was associated with her were the darkest years of her life, that's when there was the drugs, the alcohol, the rock clubs, all of the stuff that Patty was not proud of. She's not that person today, and I'm not the same person that I was back in those days. That was a dark period for me too. So I get it.

But in the end, she changed my life, and I think I changed hers. In my heart, I know that if I hadn't walked into that club that night, and if I

PATTY AND ME, REUNITED IN 2014.

hadn't met Patty when I met Patty, I don't think she would be alive today, because of the road she was traveling and the crowd she was traveling with, and the husband that she was married to at the time. Patty was in a really bad place.

For me, if I hadn't walked into that club that night, there's no telling where I would have been professionally. I might still be working in baseball.

8.

STRAIGHT UP,
STRAIGHT DOWN

The music industry is littered with bands that had great talent, with managers that believed in them, that just never broke big.

Like Panic.

They were a New Wave band in North Carolina, and the bass player, Gary Lyon, had played with Patty Loveless. She wrote me about him in February 1983: "A friend we used to play with [Gary Lyons] of Wheels came by tonight & stayed for a long time. . . . He is the bass player I brag about all the time. He's one great guy. They changed their name to [Panic]. . . . I hope someday you will meet him. Excuse this hand writing. I've been drinking a little wine with Gary & Terry—to celebrate seeing him again."

I wondered why Patty wanted me to work with another band, since I really wanted to be by her side. In my mind, I convinced myself that if I helped Panic become a success, then it would get Patty to believe in me more. Had Patty been more active with her own career, and in a better headspace personally, I don't think I would have represented Panic.

The first time I saw Panic perform was at a nightclub in Charlotte, North Carolina. They were very tight, had charisma, and blew me away. They were really good, really seasoned. They had been a rock band previously, playing that Lynyrd Skynyrd–sounding Southern rock, and a lot of people hated them for the change; in the Deep South, New Wave music had not hit, and never really would.

The lead singer was David Duke Simmons. His father was a preacher in North Carolina, and David was this wild, scraggly-looking blond dude who was also a fabulous percussion player. The other lead singer and lead guitarist was Todd Washburn, who was an incredible, charismatic performer. He was really good-looking and the girls loved him. Neither Duke nor Todd was the best singer in the world. Gary was on bass, David Harper was the keyboard player, and Scottie Thomas was the drummer in the initial stages, before he left.

While the majority of their set was covers of Duran Duran and all the artists that were on the radio at that time, they were also writing music and had an independent album out, so there was something there for me to market.

I agreed to help them. Their booking agency, Showtime, was run by Mike Uzzell. Mike had been in a very prominent regional band, Nantucket, which made a lot of headway down in the South, and then he started his own booking agency. He also had another band, Sidewinder, which came in second in the very first *Star Search* TV show, losing to Sawyer Brown.

Panic was an outcast at Showtime, since they had changed their musical style. But I felt they were on the cutting edge of what was going on in music at the time. What I started doing for them was reaching out to college radio stations and setting up interviews. It seemed to get some traction. Their biggest markets were definitely the college towns, since the progressive minds were living there, and not every bar was aiming at hard-rock rednecks.

I started meeting with agents and promoters of other bands. Panic got some airplay on independently owned stations. Things were starting to catch fire regionally, although my job at radio station EZ-104 WECZ as a sales rep started going into the toilet because of my lack of interest in selling radio ads and my desire to sell Panic. I got fired from my job at the station because I wasn't concentrating—and for another reason.

Personally, I hit a low point. One night I was out with a friend from the station, Ralph Rhodes, who was the program director. It was the same month that the drinking laws changed in the Carolinas, with stiffer penalties. I got so drunk that I threw up outside of the club. Since I was wearing my business clothes, like an idiot, I took my tie off, and I tied it on my car antenna—is that a red flag or what? Sure enough, I get pulled over and get a DWI. You can't be an on-the-road salesperson if you have a DWI, and my license was suspended for a year.

After I lost my job in late January 1984, Panic invited me on the road as their manager.

★ ★ ★ ★ ★ ★ ★ ★ ★

PANIC MAKES A RECORD STORE APPEARANCE IN CHARLOTTE IN 1984.

Panic opened up for the Romantics and for Sheila E, but the big one was getting to open for Billy Idol, who was really hot with "Rebel Yell" just out. There was trouble from the start, as the road crew for Billy Idol threatened us at the first show: "Unless you guys can provide us with cocaine, we're not going to give you any good sound or lights." I didn't participate in that, but we got good sound and lights.

In short, there was a lot of partying going on. There were girls and drugs every night. We partied our asses off.

The money was okay. I was getting a percentage but not a full manager's commission. I think it was 10 percent. The band was grossing maybe $5,000 a week.

Without the job in Charlotte, I had moved to Garner, North Carolina, just outside Raleigh, where I rented a house with Todd and one of his girlfriends.

There were two agencies in town, Showtime and its rival, CMC. CMC had a major label act, Dave Adams, who was the lead singer for Glass Moon, and they had another band that was starting to blow up, Old Boy, three women doing new music. I tried to get Panic to go over, but that never happened, as they were loyal to Showtime.

I went into CMC and started booking acts for them, one of which was a Beatles tribute act. I saw CMC as a place that I could learn and network and get to meet some of the label people. Bill Kane ran it, and he'd been one of the original managers of Alabama. He had a bright, young guy named Tom Lipsky who was the head of the management division. I learned things there but never made much money, and certainly didn't have much in the way of quality acts to sell.

With Panic, I tried and tried to move the needle, but it just never happened. The vocals were not there. The charisma, the stage presence, the fan base and groupies were there, but the songs were not. We didn't have any hit songs, though the guys were constantly writing. When you're on the road, though, songwriting never gets the attention it needs. But they were a terrific cover band, maybe the best in the Southeast at the time. And they were a great group of guys, including their roadies Jimmy "Jim Bob" Mock, Bruce Agnew, and our great soundman, Roy "Skinny" Moore.

At the end of our one-year deal, they thanked me and we parted ways. The progress I had made for them wasn't enough, so I understood.

★ ★ ★ ★ ★

Panic wasn't the only band I worked with while I lived in North Carolina.

Back when I was in New York, and still representing Patty, whenever I made a sales call, I'd have a cassette tape of her and a portable radio to let people hear her. On a call to Spirit Insurance, my rep pointed me to a salesperson, Tony Guma. He was a drummer in a band called New World, which played alternative New Wave. Tony gave me a demo tape. It was really good—their vocals were great, the songs were good, lyrically not the best but I saw potential.

Phil Vassil was on guitar and lead vocals, Tony Clemente was on bass and also sung lead, and Kevin Keegan was on keyboards. When I was working in North Carolina, I brought them down to appear on a couple of local TV music shows.

But after Patty told me she had signed with MCA Records, and after Panic and I parted ways, I decided to head home to New York in the fall of 1985.

Before heading back, I placed a call to an acquaintance I had met in New York while managing Patty. Let's just call him Johnny O. Johnny O had been interested in helping Patty, when I met with him back in 1983, and had introduced me to his father, who offered to loan me money to get her off the ground. Then I told my dad what I was up to. He knew of Johnny O's dad and would not permit it. He said he did not want me involved with them because if I could not pay the money back, it could be dangerous. I listened to him then, but I reached out to Johnny O anyway.

That big dream was still out there for me: to discover and manage a breakthrough act.

I met with Johnny O, and he was interested in helping me and introduced me to some acquaintances of his. I always liked Johnny O; he was a genuinely nice guy, soft-spoken, and impeccably dressed—classy. And he liked me and my passion for music.

Johnny O arranged for a meeting at a fancy New York City Italian restaurant. I pulled up in my rusty old Mercury Monarch, and I felt confident, but nervous about the people I was about to meet, and what I might be getting myself into.

I made my pitch to Johnny O and the other gentlemen there. I told them that I needed investment capital to begin a management company, and I stressed that I knew how to identify talent. There were stories about my time with Patty and Panic. I claimed to know the music business, but I was really an apprentice, and not a full-fledged music professional. I'd only really been on the fringes and didn't really have any relationships to take anyone to the next level.

Johnny O and his closest associate there listened and remained quiet, but their accountant, Ken, was over-the-top excited. He loved the idea. Ken ran an investment and accounting firm out of Jericho, New York. Ken was there at the restaurant with his cousin, another potential investor, who ran a taxi company on Long Island. It was agreed that night that we were opening a business! Ken provided the start-up money and an office in his building, and my salary was $300 a week, along with a leased car—the first new car I ever owned—a 1986 Mercury Cougar.

That's how Straight Up Management Company began.

★ ★ ★ ★ ★

The first thing I did was place ads in the local entertainment newspapers. It worked, and I got plenty of responses, but most of the acts I sat down with were shit.

There were gems that came out of it, though, and a few that later succeeded in the music business, although not necessarily the way we envisioned at the time, and not under Straight Up.

★ ★ ★ ★ ★

The one that really could have been something was Carl and the Passion. The lead singer, Carl Allocco, was a rock 'n' roller, a cross between John Lennon and U2's Bono, with influences ranging from Tom Petty to David Bowie, just a real talented guy. His keyboard player, Paul Doherty, had answered the ad and convinced him to have a meeting.

Carl scoffed that someone would put an ad in the paper to find acts. He was so defensive when he came into the meeting, but he said I won him over because I had "sincerity and puppy-dog eyes."

Carl and the Passion already had a development deal with MCA Records on the table when we met. They were being produced by Richie Cannata, who was the sax player for Billy Joel, and had connections in the music business. Earlier, Carl had been managed by Tommy Mottola and had a deal at RCA with his band Dreamer.

After Carl signed up with Straight Up, he told Richie he didn't want the development deal and made me the middle man. I'd never spoken to Richie before, and he called me up: "John, this is Richie Cannata."

"Hey Richie, how you doing?"

"What do you mean, how the fuck I'm doing? Who the fuck are you anyway and how the fuck did you convince Carl not to do this MCA deal?"

I said, "He just doesn't want to do it; he wants to get a full-blown record deal."

He threatened me. "I should go over there and fuckin' break your fuckin' neck." It was not a pleasant scene.

When I told Johnny O, all he said was "Nobody's breaking anybody's fucking neck. If you have any problems, give us a call." Ritchie never came over to break my neck—and it was probably good that he didn't try.

★ ★ ★ ★ ★

Radar was a five-person rock band with two women up front. They were doing commercial '80s rock 'n' roll, really good stuff, really good songs, with good hooks. The two principals were Mary Tamburo, the lead singer with a fabulous bluesy sound, and Debbie Michaels; also involved were brothers Steve and Russell Salerno, and Jose Ferro. Debbie played lead guitar and was the leader of the band. They were all in their late 20s, so they were seasoned and ready for the next level, but it never happened. Radar left Straight Up within six months, and internal problems caused them to break up.

★ ★ ★ ★ ★ ★ ★ ★ ★ ★ ★

RADAR HAD THE HAIR, BUT NOT THE MANAGER, TO BE STARS.

Todd Washburn, the lead singer of Panic, reached out when I started Straight Up. He asked if I would manage him. I said yes, moved him up to New York, put him in the studio, and let him write solo for the first time. He was a real brilliant, out-of-the-box New Wave–centric writer and composer, and had been since the age of 16, when he composed and conducted his first symphonic piece. At Appalachian State University in North Carolina, he learned all kinds of instruments, and that's where Panic began. Later, he set up his own production studio in Virginia and became an award-winning writer and composer for countless television shows. He also ran an indie label, Lure Records, celebrating roots music. Unfortunately for Todd, he blew out his vocal cords and lost his voice. He just tried so hard through the years. He talks in a whisper today.

★ ★ ★ ★ ★ ★ ★

TODD WASHBURN COMES BY THE STRAIGHT UP OFFICE IN 1987.

★ ★ ★ ★ ★

New World didn't last much longer as a band, but the lead singer, Phil Vassil, changed his name to Nick Phillips and went solo under Straight Up. I did get him a deal with Profile Records, and he had a song titled "Is That Love?" which made it to number 14 on the dance charts. I tried to help him after Straight Up closed down but didn't have the resources to get much done. Not long after, he got a record deal with a band called

Vibrolush, and they had a few hits and were hot for a while. Later, Phil became a painter, showcasing his work in galleries, which he still does today. Tony Clemente became a big-time real estate executive.

★ ★ ★ ★ ★

With my experience in marketing, I immediately set out to create a showcase for the major acts signed to Straight Up. I had New World, Radar, and Carl and the Passion perform at a charity event for multiple sclerosis and arranged a deal with Malibu, the hottest club on Long Island.

Through George Napolitano, I got Captain Lou Albano to serve as the host, and he'd already done work to raise money for multiple sclerosis. The other two celebs, both hot at the time, were Long Island's Jackie "The Joke Man" Martling from *The Howard Stern Show*—which also got us some plugs on the show—and Larry "Bud" Melman from David Letterman's show.

The result was a packed house at Malibu, and we raised a lot of money for charity.

★ ★ ★ ★ ★

Managing artists, your main job is to create opportunities for them. All the acts were essentially in the same place, and I didn't know enough about the music business. In short, I overloaded myself with talented people, but I didn't know how to get them to the next stage with a record deal.

The biggest mistake was having too many acts, all in the discovery or emerging phase of their careers, and they were all jealous of each other. Any time someone made progress, the other acts were like, "Why did you do that for them?" and "How did they get this?" It was a juggling act for me.

I put them all in the studio, recording songs. Carl and the Passion were a little more elevated since they were on the New York circuit and had a bit of a buzz.

★ ★ ★ ★ ★ ★ ★ ★ ★ ★ ★

**ME AND CARL ALLOCCO
IN LOS ANGELES IN
1987.**

It took some time, but we did secure a singles deal—"Everybody Walks Too Fast"—for Carl and the Passion, and that was for overseas distribution in the U.K. We made that connection at a music seminar. Carl got close many, many times. Really big labels, like Epic Records and Warner Brothers, really liked Carl, but Carl was an alcoholic. He would go out drinking at noon and spend all day in a bar just getting toasted and pontificating—that's what he called it. He'd smoke cigarettes and get drunk and meet girls. He sabotaged himself more than anyone I have ever met.

With all the buzz Carl and the Passion had, I set up a showcase at Studio Instrument Rentals in Manhattan. Several labels came out to this private showcase. Carl showed up a little inebriated, but not sloshy drunk or slurring. He performed his set and did well. The last song in the set was a cover of the Motown song "Money" the Beatles had popularized—he always did one Beatles song in a set, and the rest were originals. During that finale, he had a water bottle with him and he proceeded to spray water on all the talent scouts that were in attendance (A&R for artists and repertoire in music lingo). Needless to say, that didn't work out well.

Michael Caplan was a big-time wrestling fan and the vice president of A&R for Epic Records, where he was very prominent for many years, signing many big acts. He really liked Carl. For *WrestleMania III*, we invited Michael over to Carl's house to watch the show, and Carl hated wrestling—he still does. It was really about developing and nurturing a relationship. Carl liked to tease people and never respected anybody, and was busting Michael's chops for liking wrestling, so that was an awkward night. But Michael knew talent and came back, this time to see Carl and the Passion play at Nirvana in Times Square. After the set, in the dressing room, Carl paid no mind to Michael, changing his clothes in front of him, all drunk and aloof. Michael was turned off and walked away.

Carl also holds the distinction of being the only performer I ever got physical with. I was sleeping at the Straight Up house, and one night, very late in the evening, he called me up and said, "I'm coming over. We're going to go out." I said no and told him not to come over. "Come on, were going to go out drinking!"

"I am not going to do that. Don't show up here tonight. If you do, we're going to have a problem." Sure enough, 10 to 15 minutes later, there's banging on the door. I opened the door and grabbed him by the throat. I pushed him down on the couch, and I was ready to start punching him. He just started laughing at me. "Get off of me, you fat fuck." He didn't take it seriously.

Aside from the deal for the U.K. release of "Everybody Walks Too Fast," Carl and the Passion were also nominated as Best Male Artist by the New York Music Awards, as well as Best Independent Single. He didn't win either of them.

For all their issues, Carl and the Passion was our best shot.

After Straight Up Management, Carl went on to find other representation, including Camille Barbone, who was Madonna's former manager and had helped break her big. He moved to Nashville and did a couple of independent things. Basically, he was done in New York; he had pissed off so many people in Manhattan that he was actually banned from Bleecker Street, in the Greenwich Village area, and therefore from clubs like the Bitter End and Kenny's Castaways. To skirt the ban, he grew his hair out, changed his name, and called himself Charlie Dog.

To this day, I know that Carl is upset that he never had the big hit record. It gnaws at him. How do I know? I went into business with him

30 years later, mentoring and teaching young artists not to make the mistakes that he did.

The most successful people from Carl and the Passion were Paul Doherty, who became a world-renowned architect, and Doug Genuard, the lead guitarist, who made a fortune, believe it or not, as a wedding band singer.

★ ★ ★ ★ ★

We hired a pretty high-powered entertainment lawyer named Stu Silfen to shop deals for our acts and didn't get a bite. The music business is so incestuous, and it's all about previous relationships, and there I was just being aggressive with some good acts.

At the New Music Seminar in New York City, I booked a table, printed up a shitload of cassettes, and handed them out in the gift bags. There were also a few trips to Los Angeles in an attempt to get the bands to break.

We rented a house for the company in Hicksville, Long Island, and turned it into an 8-track recording studio instead of paying for space at a proper recording studio. There was a bedroom there too for the bands, and an office for me. Eventually I brought in Dave Adams, who I'd known in North Carolina, as a producer. He was producing Carl and Todd, and created his own new material, but I just couldn't get him a record deal either. Dave was such a brilliant talent and he should have broken big, but that wasn't my fault. He had opportunities with his record deal. Glass Moon was his first band and they had a hit with "On a Carousel," a cover of a Hollies song. Then his independent project came out on Elektra Records. He's still in the Carolinas and involved in music. I still listen to his music.

We were spending a lot, and making slow progress, but no money was coming in. My help would come and go. I'd hire an assistant, and they'd be gone weeks later.

My Italian partners were never around. If I needed money for a session or even to get my paycheck, Ken was available. The rest would show up once in a while at a gig, say hello, and leave.

I had great relationships with all the partners. They all liked me, and they knew I was a hard worker and that I was honest. I never did anything but try to succeed, and doing it in a way that was really maybe sometimes too honest. I never signed artists to restrictive contracts.

My philosophies were not those of my partners. They would act on their own, making promises. "Hey, my friend has a really good act. We're going to manage them." All these acts were coming and I had to say yes to them.

It's impossible to remember everyone that was on Straight Up at various times. A few stand out, like Rita Coolidge's niece, Laura Satterfield, and a band that was signed to Warner Brothers called Teen Dream. They were three young, Black girls from Columbus, Ohio. Benny Medina, the A&R star at Warner, had signed them, and I was decidedly an outsider, this white guy in a very tight-knit African-American music community. At my first meeting with Warner Brothers, they were like, "Who the fuck is this guy?" There were internal problems with Teen Dream that I didn't know about when I was told that I was managing them. The lead singer, who was 17, got pregnant, and Warner Brothers dropped them.

★ ★ ★ ★ ★ ★ ★ ★ ★ ★ ★

LAURA SATTERFIELD PUTS HER HEAD ON MY SHOULDER, AFTER PUTTING HER CAREER IN MY HANDS IN 1987. SHE IS THE NIECE OF RECORDING STAR RITA COOLIDGE.

★ ★ ★ ★ ★

One act did become the biggest band in the world for a time, but unfortunately, that wasn't under my management.

You might have heard of them—New Kids on the Block.

In 1988, we had been spinning our wheels and there was frustration from Ken, who felt he was the only one investing. It was a financial drain. Along came someone who promised us record deals with Columbia just because of his connections. For that to happen, we were told we needed new demos, produced in Boston via a connection, Maurice Starr, who had discovered New Edition.

Starr's brother was a guy named Michael Johnston, from a band called the Johnston Crew, two hip, very cool, Black guys, and he had had a studio up in Roxbury, right outside of Boston. We went up there with three of our acts. The fee was $100,000 to record.

The idea was that Starr and Johnston were going to take the tapes to Columbia Records and get a deal for everybody.

And at the same time, Starr was producing a new act in the studio. They needed management. It was New Kids on the Block. I went into the studio and listened to them. "Holy shit, they're fucking good. They're *really* good," I said.

"Oh yeah, we just got them signed to Columbia. If you want management on them, they need about $70,000 to pay off a little debt," said Starr.

I went back to my partners. "Maurice introduced me to this new band, New Kids on the Block, and they just got signed to Columbia. Let's do something with them. It'll cost us $70,000."

Johnny O was stonefaced and replied, "We've got enough fucking bands. We're not making any fucking money with the bands that we've got. We don't need another band. And we're going to be getting deals with Columbia Records anyway!"

The deals never happened for us, and those New Kids on the Block did okay. The connection I had paid off with tickets for me to take my niece to one of their sold-out concerts though.

★ ★ ★ ★ ★

Then Ken started acting strange and stopped writing checks. When some bills were due and I came looking for money, he said he was done. "Go to Johnny O and get money from those guys, I am tapped out!" I set up a meeting with Johnny O and told him about what Ken had said. All he said was "I guess that's it. We're closing up." "What?" "We're closing up. It's over."

Just like that, in early 1989, Straight Up Management was over, though I was the one that had to tell the bands.

It wasn't as tough as you might think to break the news to them, as musicians are really good at rolling with the punches. I think everyone just thought, "Okay, this is over. On to the next thing!" As far as loyalty goes, it's not like anyone was hurt.

Everybody knew that I was sincere in my efforts, that I gave it my best shot, that I never lied to them. But I was very inexperienced. I learned by going into the trenches to try to make things happen, figuring out things as I went along. I was networking and developing relationships, but it takes years to do that.

When it was over, it was over, and everyone moved on with their lives. But they like to reminisce about those days, because those were some exciting times, especially when you have a management company that's investing money in you.

I was overwhelmed most of the time, overworked, underpaid, stressed out, always worried about money. And if you add them all up, I was probably responsible for the day-to-day personal management of 30 people. As a personal manager, you are a business adviser, a psychiatrist, a consultant, a trained ear, and you got calls in the middle of the night.

★ ★ ★ ★ ★

Naturally, we had to get out of the house in Hicksville. I had an office and a bedroom, and even kept some of my memorabilia there. I walked in to start packing and a water pipe had broken and flooded the place out. I lost a lot of my baseball memorabilia, pictures, tapes.

It was a fitting end as Straight Up Management took its final breath.

★ ★ ★ ★ ★

Ken ended up in the witness protection program after it was revealed that he was embezzling money from his clients. There is no doubt in my mind that a lot was going on with my partners that I did not have a clue about. Johnny O was always a true gentleman, and I really liked him as a person and partner. Ken was always fun to be around, and I really liked him as well. However, the other businesses they were involved with together caused havoc in all their lives. I was lucky to escape without a scar.

It was fun while it lasted.

9.

IN THE *SPOTLIGHT*

You need a scorecard to keep track of *Pro Wrestling Spotlight*, its various incarnations, and the myriad of radio stations and various timeslots that aired it. It started in college, where it barely reached listeners off-campus, and by its third incarnation reached a huge audience on WEVD, which could be heard throughout the Northeast.

It got to the point where listeners would tape the show off the radio and mail cassettes to other fans across the country. There were other wrestling radio shows in other cities, but once I established my footing, there wasn't anyone else covering pro wrestling the way that I was, as a legitimate journalist, getting the best guests and asking the tough questions.

Some of my big-name guests included stars from the past, like Bruno Sammartino, Freddie Blassie, Killer Kowalski, Buddy Rogers, Fabulous Moolah, and John Tolos, and hot current stars like The Ultimate Warrior, Eddie Gilbert, Ric Flair, Konnan, Rey Misterio, Sgt. Slaughter, Eddie Guerrero, Chris Benoit, Sid Vicious, Wendi Richter, Madusa, Brian Pillman, Nikolai Volkoff, and many more. I got to trade quips with managers Paul E. Dangerously and Teddy Long and learn from announcers such as Jim Ross, Chris Cruise, and Mike Tenay. Others were virtual unknowns, like this kid from Long Island, Mick Foley, who called himself Cactus Jack Manson.

I'm proud of all I did with *Pro Wrestling Spotlight*, but it didn't come without oodles of angst, stress, and financial headaches.

★ ★ ★ ★ ★

In 1985, I moved back to New York and went to the first place I always went when I needed a job, WNYG. I was hired to sell ads again. But I had a bigger plan in mind this time.

I pitched the idea of *Pro Wrestling Spotlight* to the station's co-owner, Mrs. Horenstein, and she agreed to give me an hour. I asked my friend from the magazine business, George Napolitano, to host it with me, and he was all in.

George was a good co-host as he was so well connected. Everyone loved George. He wasn't as gregarious as, say, a Bill Apter, who had a joke or an impression for everyone, but George was solid and trustworthy and kept things close to his chest. If someone tells him something in confidence, he keeps it in confidence. He doesn't like to tell you the whole story; you have to dance around to try to get a story from him.

We'd traveled up and down the roads together to shows, and George and I both had an undying love of the New York Mets. He's always been there for me, opening doors, introducing me to the right people. He was a mentor in the truest sense of the word. So he was the right choice to be on *Pro Wrestling Spotlight* with me.

We went on the air in late '85, when wrestling was crazy hot. The first *WrestleMania* had taken place at the end of March, and Hulk Hogan and his WWF buddies were everywhere, media darlings.

In the first week, we had Tully Blanchard as a guest. He was a buddy of George's and called in to talk about what was going on in Jim Crockett Promotions, which was ramping up its efforts to compete with WWF. There wasn't a lot more to the show than that, since it was the first episode, and there weren't many callers.

Come the next week, and George and I could see this having potential. We booked someone we both knew, Captain Lou Albano, to call in, and we played one of his songs, "Captain Lou's History of Music," to boot. He was always a great interview, so quick and witty.

However, the other owner of the station, Mr. Horenstein, was present while we were broadcasting. Whatever was on the air was broadcast throughout the building, and he heard the Captain Lou song and declared, "I don't want this on my station." And that was it: he took us off the air. We had a two-week run and then were given the boot. But I still stayed on at WNYG to sell ads.

★ ★ ★ ★ ★

WKRP in Cincinnati had nothing on WNYG.

Sol Horenstein and Muriel Horenstein were the married couple that owned the station, under its official title, Babylon Bay Shore Broadcasting Corporation (it was based in Babylon, Long Island). They were two of the most memorable characters I ever encountered in any business or personal setting. The Horensteins were certainly well known on Long Island.

★ ★ ★ ★ ★ ★ ★ ★ ★ ★ ★ ★

THE HORENSTEINS WERE THE OWNERS OF WNYG AM. WHAT CHARACTERS THEY WERE!

I had quite a long history with them, not so much with Mr. Horenstein (besides him kicking the second version of *Pro Wrestling Spotlight* off the air), but with Mrs. Horenstein. As Muriel Matthews, she had been a publicist in her early career, and she met the much older Sol when he was working as an attorney on Long Island. Ambitious, in

1961 they purchased the biggest heritage rock 'n' roll station on Long Island, WBAB-FM, and its AM partner, WNYG.

They ended up selling the big station, no doubt for a decent profit, and ran the AM station as a little mom-and-pop place. Mr. H really didn't know what was going on for the most part, as he was older and still established in his law practice.

But Mrs. H? She ruled the roost.

And she was something, a unique character who would love you, detest you, fire you, and hire you back. As long as you were generating money for her, you were her best friend; if you got into a little bit of a sales slump, or got into disfavor with her, then she'd become your enemy. Both Mr. and Mrs. H were small in stature, little more than five foot four, I'd say. Mrs. H dressed impeccably, with coiffed hair and lots of jewelry. Mr. H was a suit-and-tie guy, with the occasional sighting of him in a golf shirt.

She was a piece of work. She called everybody she liked "Cookie."

"What did you bring me today, Cookie? . . . Go out and get a trade deal with this restaurant, Cookie."

A lot of clients would pay cash, and she'd just grab the cash. Her bookkeeper, the foul-mouthed, cantankerous Pearl Greenburg, was in cahoots with her. Mrs. H got into all kinds of trouble. There's a story where the IRS was coming in for an audit; she jumped out the window of her office to avoid talking to them.

The station was run haphazardly, and each payday, everyone was worried that their checks weren't going to clear. On Friday when people got paid, it was a race to the bank to cash the check, and you'd hope that you got there before the money ran out.

There were a lot of trade certificates handed out as bonuses for good performances. I do remember a Christmas bonus, which probably goes down in history as the weirdest Christmas bonus from any employer: bottles of ketchup with past-due expiration dates. We all thought it was a joke, but it *wasn't*—that was our Christmas bonus.

I got my sister Donna a job there not too long after being hired myself for the first time in March 1982. She stayed many years, leaving and coming back a few times (just like her big brother). She was there for the very end, after the Horensteins sold the station, and it was overtaken by Colombians. They turned the downstairs offices into bedrooms. My sister's office was down there, and there were people walking around in their pajamas. It turned into a hellacious place at the very end.

I don't know if she was ever serious or not, but Mrs. H would always tell us to kill her husband, and that we'd share the insurance money. She'd go, "Push him down the stairs, Cookie." She said that to everybody.

One day, Donna almost accomplished that. She was a very energetic person, but was always late for meetings, running here and there. She had to run out of the radio station for something, and downstairs there was an entrance going into the station where there was a screen door and a heavy wooden door. She was running to leave and pushed open the heavy door, and Mr. Horenstein was coming in at the same time, and she slammed the door into him. He was a slight old man, probably in his late 70s or early 80s at the time, and dripping wet might have weighed 110 pounds, and he tumbled to the ground. She started screaming, "I killed Mr. Horenstein!" He was bruised but okay. She didn't get fired; in fact, she might have gotten a bonus from Mrs. H.

★ ★ ★ ★ ★

For all the Horenstein stories, the fact is that an enormous amount of talent came (carefully) through those WNYG doors. For many, like me, it was a first job in the industry because they had very liberal hiring practices. It was also a place to go if you really needed a job, because there were seemingly always openings, whether in sales, programming, or production. She'd bring you back if you left too.

The office was a collection of first-time executives with lots of potential (and many top radio people got their start there) for the misfits who would come, go, or stay for years. Everyone who was part of WNYG shares the bond of having survived life with the Horensteins.

This was my sixth time working at WNYG. When I'd been there previously, I'd done sales too, but I was also the sports director and I had a baseball show, *The New York Baseball Report*, which gave me press access to the New York ball clubs. We did a trade deal for season tickets with the Mets, meaning we could give away tickets on the air. It was a weekend show. As the sports director, I did all the sports reports during the morning and evening rush-hour drives. I enjoyed that. But unless I was performing as a sales rep, bringing money in, those on-air perks were taken away. You never received compensation for the on-air appearances.

And everything had to be sponsored. So for my sports reports to air, I'd have to go out and get an advertiser. For a time, a local topless bar called the Gaslight Lounge was my sponsor; Mrs. H. didn't care as long as there was money coming in.

The selling part was very challenging because the station didn't get results. It was a small signal and the success of radio advertising lies in reaching a big audience, but also in having frequency, which means that your commercial is running three, four times a day in different parts to get the maximum exposure for your audience. At WNYG, they would sell these packages where it would be 100 dollars a week and you get two spots a day and a promo announcement, and that was it. Plus, when you first signed up, you got a free clock to put in your office.

Tom Rosenbluth—Tom Ross was his soliciting name—was one of those unforgettable key personalities at WNYG. He was a very eccentric guy and a little hygiene-challenged, let's say, so naturally they kept him in a little room in the basement. His job was to get leads for the sales-people. He called the businesses on behalf of the station, and if there was any interest, a sales rep would head over.

Many of the clients were hit and run. You'd go in, sign a client, and then you'd never see them again. The station would send collectors to get the money for the spots, and that was their only job. Those collectors were kept busy collecting accounts mainly for longtime sales manager Larry Walsh. Among them was my brother-in law Thomas DiBiase, who was also a part of WNYG for years.

So many clients would cancel and not pay after three or four weeks that Mr. Horenstein, shrewd lawyer that he was, added a clause to the advertising agreement in the fine print which noted that if they defaulted, the bank note gave WNYG permission to go into their bank account and take their money. Most clients signed it.

This leads to one of my most memorable sales efforts. I signed the West Babylon–based Pines Motel Lodge to a deal. It was one of those places where the daytime business, in and out so to speak, was key. The owner was James Sammartino—who was no relation to Bruno—and he'd never done radio before, so we came up with the idea that anyone who came in and mentioned WNYG would get a free bottle of champagne. That was the main point of the spot.

In general, I went back to the client to collect the money, since I saw my role as being helpful and not confrontational. After the first week, I got the check, and James said no one had come in. I mentioned that radio advertising takes time to work. Second week, same story, and he's getting frustrated, so I promised to get him a few bonus spots. And so it continued until the fifth week, when James was livid. "I don't want to do this anymore! I bought a whole fucking case of champagne and not one person has asked for it!" It wasn't smart, but I replied, "Well, you have a case of champagne, let's have a party!" He just went nuts and threw me out, and I went back to the station and told Mrs. Horenstein, who arranged to call in the bank note.

A couple of months later, I was out on a Friday night with WNYG's sales manager at the time, Mel Adler, heading to the liquor store before going to a party. We ran into Sammartino at the liquor store. He saw me and began yelling "It's *you*, it's *you*! You took money out of my fucking bank account." "That was the station, not me. I didn't have anything to do with that." But that ended my dealings with the Pines Motor Lodge.

The show most associated with WNYG was *The Original Italian Hours*. Goombadi Joe was the originator of the show, and it grew into the station's most popular program. It was bilingual and played Italian music. My dad would listen to it in the 1970s, and I'd call to make requests. After Joe, the host most people remember is Lilla Savona, who was a very buxom, animated, over-the-top, self-indulgent personality who used to flaunt her assets to get advertisers to advertise. Lilla was a full-blooded Italian, but her sales ability got her the gig. When Lilla was away, I guest-hosted. I wasn't bilingual and just played songs that I liked that were Italian-themed, like Frank Sinatra.

WNYG had various formats over the years. After the sale of WBAB-FM in 1976, the station changed its call letters from WBAB-AM to WNYG, and its format to gospel programming (New York Gospel). That lasted until 1979, when the format changed to CHR (contemporary hit radio). It was changed again in the early 1980s to oldies/gold (New York Gold). It then flipped to Spanish when the Horensteins got out. Going full circle, the station went back to gospel when the station changed hands again in the early 2000s, under former WNYG DJ Phyllis Rose. It no longer operates.

★ ★ ★ ★ ★

After my failed foray into music management in the spring of 1989, I was back at WNYG and, soon enough, back into professional wrestling.

Once again, I pitched Mrs. H. on a wrestling radio show. She said okay, as long as there was advertising to support it, so at first it was a revenue share deal, meaning that the ad money kept the show on the air, not me buying the time—that came soon enough.

The third go-round of *Pro Wrestling Spotlight* debuted on April 9, 1989. Just before that aired, there was a National Wrestling Alliance (NWA) show in New Haven, Connecticut, and George Napolitano got me clearance and backstage to conduct a couple of interviews. I quickly got caught up on the storylines so I could do the interviews, as I'd only been following wrestling on a very peripheral level.

Honestly, it was a little bit of a whim. I didn't see it as a full-time gig for sure, and I hadn't looked down the road. I started reaching out to old friends, like George, Georgiann Makropoulos, Don Laible, Tom Burke, and Bill Apter, and reintroduced myself to people I hadn't really been in touch with since 1978. Dave Meltzer gave me a plug in *The Wrestling Observer Newsletter* before the show went on the air, meaning that I had callers on the first show, and then more callers on the second show. It proved to me right off the bat that I was onto something, that there was an audience, even with the limited range of the station. I had hope.

Those first shows are embarrassing to listen back to now—and for the most part, I have all of my shows recorded on cassette tapes—and not just because they were mostly kayfabe, meaning that I was keeping with wrestling storylines rather than being a journalist. I cringe hearing them, as I'm not in control in the studio, and guests like the Power Twins (Dave and Larry Sontag) run roughshod over me in a circus-like atmosphere. There was a rotating cast of characters coming into the studio, including the usually quiet Broadway Sonny Blaze (Al Schaefer) and the miscast ring announcer Marty Pereira. The people at the controls, whether engineering the board or taking calls on the whopping two phone lines, changed constantly too.

And for some reason, I called myself ex–pro wrestler John Anthony, never mentioning that "John Anthony" only ever had two squash matches in which I had embarrassed myself on WWWF TV.

Right from the start, I got top-name guests. To my surprise, when I reached out to WWF, I was put in touch with the head of public relations, Steve Planamenta, whom I knew when he was a kid and I was writing for the newsstand magazines in the 1970s. We caught up a bit, and we were both excited for each other's successes. Steve stressed that to get WWF guests and tickets to give away, I'd have to stick to storylines and offer up softball questions. With *WrestleMania V* on April 2, 1989, Jimmy "The Mouth of the South" Hart was on my first show in a taped segment. I thought there would be plenty of WWF guests going forward. How naïve I was.

On the second show, I called in a favor from Georgiann Makropoulos and lined up my hero, Bruno Sammartino. It ended up costing me big time. In the pre-taped interview, we started off with easy talk about Bruno's career, but then he just went off about WWF, saying a lot of things that alarmed me, including that all the guys were taking steroids and using recreational drugs. He also slammed Vince McMahon.

I was so concerned about it that I reached out to Planamenta and told him I'd talked to Bruno for my second show. Automatically, his guard went up. He asked for details of Bruno had said, and I told him the subject matter, and that Bruno was not kind to WWF at all. Steve said that if I ran the interview, WWF wouldn't work with me any further. Before I made any decision, I played it for our station director, Warren Green, and he brought in the station's attorney, John Lander, who worked at Mr. Horenstein's firm. He warned that we were opening ourselves up for slander charges if we ran it.

When I came to the inevitable decision that I couldn't run the interview in its entirety, I reached out to Bruno to record a second interview, and we toned it down quite a bit. But even the toned-down version ended my association with WWF.

That was the moment that I knew that *Pro Wrestling Spotlight* couldn't stay kayfabe and needed to be more insider. My own knowledge of the inner workings had grown so much through my subscription to *The Wrestling Observer Newsletter*, which I began in 1988, as well as other so-called dirtsheets. To suit my changing tastes, a good, compelling radio show would have to include some insider news, but those early shows walked a fine line, where I played along with what was on TV but mixed in some real news. I didn't want to insult anyone's intelligence.

★ ★ ★ ★ ★

The first key newsworthy interview that I did was in August, when I had Ricky Steamboat on the show, talking about his ongoing contract dispute with WCW, which resulted in his departure from the organization. I'd gotten him at the gym he owned in Charlotte, North Carolina. To that point, wrestlers never talked about contracts or money, so the news rippled out from there, with various newsletters covering my interview with him. Then the following week, Jim Herd, who was running WCW, came on to address Steamboat's claims. I look at the Steamboat interview as a key moment, where I had turned a corner and knew what I wanted, and now how to deliver it. A couple of months later, "The Dragon" was proof that I had listeners, when I brought him up to a personal appearance at a plumbing company, and fans lined up around the corner. The owners were shocked, the station was shocked, and even I was amazed by the turnout. No one had ever seen WNYG's limited signal ever bring that many people out. That really gave me an indication that there was a market for the fans to meet with wrestlers and laid the groundwork for my future conventions.

The personal appearances continued through the years, with names like Davey Boy Smith, Jim "The Anvil" Neidhart, Road Warrior Hawk, "Leaping" Lanny Poffo, Missy Hyatt, Woman, and many more. The signings always made money, at least for the store, and raised awareness for the show. I made money from their advertising dollars, and the client paid for the live remote feeds and for the talent to come in for the appearance. It was really a little cottage industry for me, a sideline hustle.

★ ★ ★ ★ ★

The show started to really grow, but Mrs. H. was never satisfied by the amount of money the station made from it. It was such a challenge to sell ads on a show about pro wrestling with limited coverage. After five months, my sweet deal for the show—a revenue share—came to an end, and Mrs. H. made me buy the time from the station, meaning that she always got her money. At the same time, my ad sales for the rest of the station probably suffered as I focused on my show more than I probably should have.

Buying air time would be the model going forward at all the homes for *Pro Wrestling Spotlight*. It was always a struggle and there was never time to take a breath and go, "Okay, I have enough money for the next month." Because it wasn't just the show, I still had my own rent, my own bills, and my family. I survived, I did okay, but I never got rich off it by any stretch of the imagination.

Donna hated that I struggled all the time. She used to say, "Just get a job somewhere." She had a personal interest, since I was the one paying Mom's bills. But there were plenty of times during the struggles when Donna helped financially, buying groceries when I didn't have money. She chipped in as much as she could.

★ ★ ★ ★ ★

My advertisers through the years ran the gamut, to say the least, and they came and went, with a lot of turnover. The few that succeeded with me knew the market I was catering to and had businesses that benefited from pro wrestling fans. An ad buyer wanted to see results, and a few did, like L&S Comix, a store on Long Island that sold wrestling merchandise and videos.

★ ★ ★ ★ ★

Some of my regular guests later became among the most important figures in pro wrestling. Mick Foley was Cactus Jack Manson when he made his first appearance with me on September 17, 1989. He was a Long Islander too, and I met him through Broadway Sonny Blaze. Foley was a little more on the kayfabe side than the shoot side, but he sat in with me for the whole two hours on one show, just before he had his first run with WCW. We became friends, and he'd come over to my house to watch wrestling video tapes or pay-per-views.

The other was Paul Heyman, who was a manager and announcer as Paul E. Dangerously. Like Foley, he lived not too far away, so he was always willing to do an interview. He was sent home by booker Ric Flair from the NWA in '89, and he came on and took calls from listeners. His wit was fantastic and those old interviews with him stand the test of time simply because he was so great.

★ ★ ★ ★ ★

PAUL E. DANGEROUSLY (AND HIS
CELL PHONE) AND SONNY BLAZE
AT THE 1989 WNYG CHRISTMAS
PARTY, IN HICKSVILLE, NEW
YORK.

There were so many great moments, but if I had to narrow it down to just a few highlights, here they are:

- On August 27, 1994, Shane Douglas won a tournament to crown a new NWA world champion over Too Cold Scorpio, on a show promoted by Tod Gordon. Douglas then tossed down the title and went on a rant that would lead to the formation of what would later be called Extreme Championship Wrestling, run by Heyman and Gordon. It was a turning point in wrestling history. Not only was I at that show in Philadelphia at the bingo hall that would become known as the ECW Arena, but·on the day after the screwjob, NWA promoter Dennis Coralluzzo was on the show, and Paul E. was on with Douglas, and then Gordon. They were arguing and fighting—separately—about what had just taken place.

- On September 17, 1989, Cactus Jack Manson (Mick Foley, Mankind, Dude Love, and just Cactus Jack—come to think of it, he had more names than me!) made his first appearance on *Pro Wrestling Spotlight*. Cactus appeared more than any other guest in the show's history. I met him for the first time when he entered the dingy WNYG studios, and he stood up for the entire two hours, in a very entertaining, free-wheeling style. I opened the mic and let him go. I knew that minute that this guy was destined for greatness.

- On March 15, 1992, on the night before the historic Phil Donahue show, with my partner Vince Russo watching from the control room and *CBS Evening News* filming in the studio, several personalities appeared to discuss the WWF sex scandals. In the studio were Dave Meltzer, "Superstar" Billy Graham, Barry Orton, and me. On the phone, Bruno Sammartino, Billy Jack Hayes, and midget Lord Littlebrook all weighed in. It was an explosive show, one of many newsworthy events that took place during that period.

★ ★ ★ ★ ★

It was confidence boosting to know that I had regular callers, even if the phone lines at WNYG were the drizzling shits, meaning that we'd lose guests and callers, or just have so much interference that we had to abandon the call. I can rhyme many of them off: Vinny from West Babylon (who later helped me produce the show); Steve from West Hempstead; TJ from Deer Park; Nick from Massapequa; and Joey from North Babylon. Another listener, Ski Wiskowski from Hicksville, was a big, goofy, lovable guy who happened to be mentally disabled; he was so loyal and came out to everything I did, and he got to know Cactus Jack and other wrestlers through his association with the show. Ski was a legend to *Pro Wrestling Spotlight*. He sadly passed away in the early 2000s.

Then there were the listeners who were young and later went on to other things in the wrestling business. The ECW "Stud Muffin" Joel Gertner was one of my weekly callers. Mike of College Point went on to better things as respected wrestling journalist Mike Johnson of PWInsider.com. Brian Last enjoyed the broadcasts so much that, decades later, he sought me out for a podcast. The end result was my own podcast, *Pro Wrestling Spotlight Then and Now*. The podcast has created its own stars from those early listeners.

The most beloved caller to the show in its early days was a young kid who went by George from Lindenhurst. His weekly calls are now legendary on my podcast; he would ask off-topic questions or about wrestlers like the Ultimate Warrior and Zeus that I never enjoyed discussing. And the podcast's listeners love him and love the way he annoyed me back then.

These people thank me to this day because they got into the business after listening to, and learning from, *Pro Wrestling Spotlight*. It gave them a love for the business along with an education.

In fact, one of the listeners put together a design for a T-shirt, "*Pro Wrestling Spotlight*, Listen and Learn." I liked it and used it on T-shirts. Later, I got hooked up with the Long Island Bowlers Association and we started a *Pro Wrestling Spotlight* bowling league on weekends.

Interacting with my listeners became key, both on the air and in person. Sports bars were a good fit and I'd arrange to be at one to watch a pay-per-view or a Clash of the Champions special on TBS. On air, I'd invite fans to come out and join me. The bars were always happy with the results. Those fan gatherings were so important, as they built further fan loyalty and friendships. There was a couple that met at one of my promotions, and they fell in love and got married. Recently, they reached out to me to let me know that they're still together. I couldn't have run the bus trips or the conventions without the dedicated fan base. I frequently put small ads in the Long Island newspaper *Newsday,* and in the *New York Daily News*, adjacent to "The Slammer" wrestling column, to promote the radio show and the conventions. Mostly, I'd take out advertising because the show moved from station to station, and the ads would promote the new time slot or new station.

I couldn't have succeeded without the support of the wrestling newsletters. I got so much love from the big three newsletters: Meltzer's *Observer*, Wade Keller's *Pro Wrestling Torch*, and Steve Beverly's *Matwatch*, which focused a lot more on the TV side of wrestling. All of them were regular guests, as well as Bob Smith from *Pro Wrestling Illustrated* and veteran journalists Bill Apter and George Napolitano. They helped build my audience in the Northeast. When the newsletters got plugs from me, they noticed an uptick in their local subscribers because of it. That meant that together we were actually smartening up the local audience to the wrestling business. The callers became progressively more intelligent, more insider, every week.

★ ★ ★ ★ ★ ★ ★ ★ ★ ★ ★

BRUCE JACOBS, SONNY BLAZE, AND ME IN THE WNYG STUDIO IN 1989.

In the studio at my side was Bruce Jacobs, a local West Babylon guy, whom my sister Donna introduced me to. Bruce was a salesperson at the local P.C. Richards electronics store. Bruce wanted to get into radio, and Donna set up a meeting for me to meet with Bruce. I had no idea what to do with him, but he was hungry, willing to learn, and worked for free. He was a die-hard Mets fan like me! He came in as the "producer" of the show. As the weeks progressed, Bruce became a vital part of the show, screening calls, and getting guests live on the air that I had arranged. Bruce became a close friend and ally, and wound up staying for the duration of my WNYG tenure and later came back to work with me in 1992 at WEVD. He also accompanied me as my ring announcer and assistant during my Southeast Asia tour for International Wrestling All Stars.

Bruce went on to get his own sports show at WNYG, and did the morning and afternoon sports reports. For that, he was paid a whopping $25 per week by Mrs. Horenstein. That experience turned into a successful career in talk radio, including working for FOX Sports Radio. He is currently a broadcaster in the Phoenix area.

My right hand during the *Pro Wrestling Spotlight* years was Don Laible. Don was the person who had my back throughout all my years in the wrestling business. He was a wrestling photographer, journalist, and occasional wrestling bad-guy manager called "The Bug," wearing a hood and carrying a fly swatter. Don is also a fellow lifelong Mets baseball fanatic. I met Donny very early on, in 1975 at the Wrestling Fans International Convention in Boston. He gets easily excited and animated in a way few people I've ever met do. Our friendship grew over the years. He lived close to Grandma Dorothy in Brooklyn, and he'd come over when I was visiting her. Don was a wrestling encyclopedia, and when I launched the *Pro Wrestling Spotlight* on WNYG, he shared his vast Rolodex with me. That got me Stu Hart, Lou Thesz, and Killer Kowalski, to name a few. As the show grew, Don's involvement did too. I gave him a weekly news segment at the top of each show; Don covered all the latest news and rumors from WWF, WCW, the independent leagues, and Japan.

Later, when I began promoting my conventions, Don was all in, assisting in whatever way I needed and serving as my official photographer. I later took Donny on tour to Venezuela where, as The Bug, he managed Nikolai Volkoff. Don got burned out on the business a few years later than I did and then concentrated on covering sports for the local paper in Utica, New York. He is also the beat reporter for the Mets Triple-A team, the Syracuse Mets. He is a trusted ally and friend.

★ ★ ★ ★ ★

Not all my listeners succeeded in pro wrestling, of course. Some were smarter than that.

A dedicated teenage listener, Andrew Goldberger, called in regularly and came to my conventions. Maybe I saw a little of myself in Andrew, nerdy but smart, and obsessed with wrestling. On a couple of occasions, I invited him to the studio to sit in as we did the show, one time with Foley there.

In late 2019, he found me on Instagram and said that he'd been hunting me for more than 20 years. Andrew wanted to say thank you, as

the experiences he had through *Pro Wrestling Spotlight* helped him gain self-confidence. He developed a tech platform that facilitated donations for churches, and he eventually sold it for millions of dollars. He retired at the age of 38. He lives in Spain and has a place in New York. This kid, who was a listener of mine and later followed the Grateful Dead around, is now this brilliant success and has an interesting way at looking at life. I am pleased that he is back in my life.

But there's a controversial aspect to what Andrew contributed to pro wrestling: Vince Russo. Though to better understand the issues that Vince and I had, you have to understand the times and how the WWF was rocked by scandals.

10.

THE SCANDALS

There were many newsworthy interviews on *Pro Wrestling Spotlight*, but none compared to one with former WWWF champion "Superstar" Billy Graham on March 25, 1990. It was explosive and controversial: he named names and addressed how the steroid culture had overtaken professional wrestling.

Less than a year later, the renamed WWF found itself in court, talking openly about performance-enhancing drug use by its roster, and I found myself in demand, reporting on the trial.

We'll never know just how much of a role my interview with Graham played in the federal case against a Pennsylvania doctor for distributing steroids, but there's no doubt in my mind that it was an important part in the proceedings.

★ ★ ★ ★ ★

"Superstar" Billy Graham was not the famed evangelist, of course, but rather the renamed Wayne Coleman, who was a football player and a competitive bodybuilder before learning the ropes of pro wrestling from Stu Hart. With his chiseled physique and a spell-binding gift of the gab on the microphone, he was a drawing card from his early days in the sport, even if no one would ever call him a polished technical wrestler.

At six foot four, and weighing 275 pounds, Graham rose to the top of his profession on April 30, 1977, when he beat Bruno Sammartino for the WWWF world title. He held it until February 28, 1978, when he lost to Bob Backlund.

Graham had already started speaking out about steroid abuse and how his own usage had damaged his body. One of his interviews had been on a Los Angeles TV station. I heard about it and wanted "Superstar" on my show to elaborate on that appearance, and to see if he would go deeper into the subject. He had never been on my radio show before. I'd known him from my days photographing WWWF shows. We socialized some back then as well, having dinner on a few occasions.

It ended up being one of the longest phone interviews I'd ever done. We talked for about an hour, and he was incredibly forthcoming. He believed there was a huge problem which had not been noticed by the public, and that meant that no one was doing anything about it. Thanks to all that I'd learned about steroids from Dave Meltzer in his newsletter, I was plenty prepared to ask the proper questions of Graham. In his wrestling column in *The National* sports newspaper, Meltzer was the first to mention on a major platform that there was a major issue brewing.

It got such a big response from my listeners that I replayed portions of it in subsequent weeks, and the various newsletters shared the info as well. Graham's honesty and transparency was so refreshing in the secretive world of pro wrestling. People were both fascinated by it and saddened.

★ ★ ★ ★ ★

Though we didn't know it at the time, the U.S. government had been building a case for two years against George Zahorian, a 43-year-old urologist who moonlighted as a Pennsylvania Athletic Commission doctor. It makes sense that if Graham was talking to me in March of '90, that investigation was ongoing, and he was maybe trying to position himself in a better light for the feds, or maybe providing information to them at that point. Who knows?

I certainly didn't know how my life would be upended by it all.

★ ★ ★ ★ ★

When the investigations became public, I dove into the story in a very substantial way, from coverage on the radio show to being present when the trial started. Meltzer and I covered it more than anyone else, and we both ended up with a higher profile because of our hard work.

The trial started in Harrisburg, Pennsylvania, in June 1991, and I got a hotel room in town and set up shop, staying for the entire time. One of my listeners was Fred Hornby, who was one of pro wrestling's greatest historians, but more importantly in this case, he worked at 1010 WINS, the largest news station in America, and he arranged for me to cover the trial as a stringer.

Each day, I went to the courtroom and made my notes, and then got soundbites outside from witnesses or the attorneys during breaks or at the end of the day. I'd call the New York radio stations with my reports. I was also on a couple of major radio talk shows, including with sports talk legend Bill Mazer, who was very prominent in the New York market at that time.

Since I knew so many of the principals involved in the Zahorian trial—I actually picked up Graham at the airport when he arrived—I found myself really involved, perhaps too much so. Witnesses were testifying about this stuff Zahorian was doing. There were stories about FedEx packages that were going to Hulk Hogan. Aside from Graham, the wrestlers who testified at the trial—Roddy Piper, Dan Spivey, Brian Blair, and Rick Martel—all admitted to buying and using steroids at least during the investigation period, which was from '88 to '90. A few huge names one would have expected to be there testifying were not, for reasons unknown. Those names included key figures Vince McMahon, whose name was brought up many times by Zahorian, and Hulk Hogan (Hulk was subpoenaed to testify but was excused from appearing, as a judge ruled that his privacy took priority).

The world knows a lot more about steroids, the apparent benefits and the side effects, now than it did in 1991. Steroid use was a secret in the wrestling business, yet everybody knew because of the size of the guys—you could just look at them and see there was a massive problem. When the movie *No Holds Barred* came out, I railed on my show against Tiny Lister, the juiced-up actor named Zeus, as case in point for steroids hurting wrestling performances. He could could barely move in the ring. In the business that I grew up with and loved, the wrestlers were normal people, just bigger than the rest of us, with colorful personalities. It had all changed into this circus of blown-up guys. On top of it all, remember that on a federal basis, steroids were declared illegal with the Anti-Drug Abuse Act of October 1988. And in pro wrestling at the time, you didn't get a push unless you were big.

But when you have a ringside doctor like Zahorian, who technically worked for the state athletic commission, but was compliant and kowtowing to WWF, distributing steroids, painkillers, and whatnot, it's obvious to everyone that it was a corrupt situation. Zahorian had developed this cottage industry, and as the stories went, the guys used to line up for their "candy" as it was called.

There wasn't a lot of media coverage, certainly on a national scale. It wasn't like ABC or NBC or CBS had a presence there.

I never felt overwhelmed by all the "real" reporters, and they never looked down on me for hosting a wrestling radio show. Really, I had more skin in the game because I was in the business. I was a journalist trying to get to the bottom of what was going on.

My allies were Meltzer, Keller, and Beverly, guys on the inside who knew the fight. Certainly, the other radio shows that were around at the time, like Larry Katz's show in Baltimore, Joel Goodheart in Philadelphia, and Rich Mancuso who had a huge platform on WFAN in New York on Saturday nights, didn't cover it in anything like the depth I did.

Then, at the end of the week, I had to piece it all together for my *Pro Wrestling Spotlight* show. It was stressful.

In the end, Zahorian was convicted, sentenced to three years in prison and fined $12,700 along with two years of probation after his jail term.

ABOVE: The Arezzi family in 1968 at our home in West Babylon on Long Island. Left to right: Linda, Sal "Big Sam," me, Mary "Snooky," and Donna.

LEFT: This Christmas photo of the Arezzis from 1991 is the last one we have all together.

With Grandma Dorothy Arezzi and Grandma Fanny Guerri at my graduation from Boston's Emerson College in 1979.

Backstage at Madison Square Garden in New York City on March 26, 1973, when I got to meet Fred Blassie for the first time.

My best friend in wrestling was Don Laible, and here we are fighting over Pedro Morales's WWWF title in Tom Burke's house/museum in 1975; Tom bought the belt in a pawn shop!

Making my pro wrestling debut; note Vince McMahon on commentary!

My wrestling license.

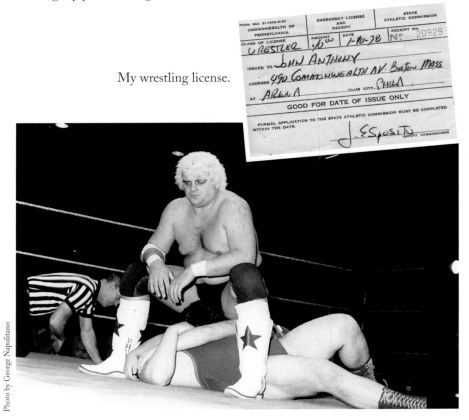

Dusty Rhodes pinned me by sitting on me!

I'm interviewing Mets manager Bud Harrelson in 1990 when I worked at WNYG.

Working for the minor league Shelby Mets, we even had "Mets Models"! The girl on the right, Jackie Pecora, is from my hometown in West Babylon, and went to high school with my sister Donna.

The Magic is Back in Shelby!

JOHN AREZZI
PUBLIC RELATIONS DIRECTOR

P.O. BOX 2197
SHELBY, NC 28150
484-0172

SHELBY METS
CLASS A AFFILIATE
NEW YORK METS

Patty Loveless and me in June 1981 at the first show I booked for her in Myrtle Beach, South Carolina. I also fell in love with her that weekend.

Patty and me in 1996, backstage at the Paramount Theater adjacent to Madison Square Garden.

Straight Up poses for a photo. Left to right: Larry Huffstickler, Terry Lovelace (Patty's husband), Patty, "Boo" Canipe, and Steve Mobley.

ABOVE: At the WNYG studio with Rockin' Robin Smith, sister of Jake "The Snake" Roberts, in 1989.

RIGHT: Rey Mysterio Jr. and me at an ECW show in 1994.

The legends and me at 1992's Weekend of Champions. Back row, left to right, are Jushin "Thunder" Liger, Jimmy Valiant, Bruno Sammartino, Nikolai Volkoff, and Killer Kowalski looming over me; front row is Ivan Koloff, Wendi Richter, and Captain Lou Albano.

Sarah Darling and I met at this Halloween party in October of 2009 at stylist Michael McCall's home.

Backstage at the Grand Ole Opry in 2014 with Brad Paisley and Sarah Darling following their duet that evening.

While at GAC, I was chosen to judge a talent contest in Tennessee in 2004, along with country artists Tammy Cochran, Anita Cochran (no relation), and Deborah Allen.

RIGHT: I was a regular at the Palm restaurant in Nashville—and even had a caricature of me on the wall with the other VIPs!

BOTTOM LEFT: My nephew Dominic hanging out with Miley Cyrus.

BOTTOM RIGHT: It was great working with Dolly Parton on a few projects while at GAC. Here we are reacquainted at a concert in Forest Hills, New York, in 2017.

The steroid issue didn't go away. On July 16, 12 days after Zahorian's conviction, Hogan went on Arsenio Hall's show and lied about his steroid use, claiming that he had only used steroids on three occasions for injuries.

★ ★ ★ ★ ★

WWF's knee-jerk reaction to Zahorian's conviction was to call a July press conference to talk about its intention to put together a steroid-testing program. Meltzer told me about the press conference, which was scheduled for the Plaza Hotel, but I didn't get an invitation. Naturally, I called up the WWF PR department, but I was told that I didn't know what I was talking about and that there was no press conference. I fought them on it, since I knew the date and time, and I wanted credentials. A little while later, I called in under an assumed name from a different radio station and I got the information I was looking for. (In hindsight, I could have walked in anyway, but it was about the principle of it.)

At the press conference, I stood out, as I asked Vince McMahon several hard-hitting questions only an insider would be able to, like why he pushed wrestlers with larger physiques. With a group of reporters hovering around him after he left the dias, I asked, "Why didn't you invite the wrestling media to this?" He said, "I didn't know we didn't invite the wrestling media." Steve Planamenta, who was next to him, said, "None of them called." I flat out called him a liar to his face. Another WWF rep pulled me aside and asked what station I was with. Once I said WGBB, she said that they do a lot of advertising with the station and maybe they would not any longer. They were not used to someone holding their feet to the fire.

My Italian temper rising, I called Phil Mushnick at the *New York Post*, who had done a little coverage of the Zahorian trial. I told him what had happened and he was fascinated by it, and I got to talk extensively to him. Mushnick was outraged at WWF's behavior and saw right through its bogus new steroid policy. In Mushnick, I had an ally, someone to vent to.

I had unleashed a beast. No mainstream journalist has called WWF/ WWE to task more through the years than Mushnick, and it was me that set him loose. We talked many times after that. Phil often warned me about what a terrible industry pro wrestling was, and he said that if WWF went down, the whole industry probably would too. I saw it as an opportunity to correct a lot of the things that were wrong in the wrestling business. The steroid stuff was just a precursor to the explosiveness to come.

★ ★ ★ ★ ★

Six months later, on January 9, 1992, Mushnick wrote another explosive column, stemming from accusations that "Superstar" Billy Graham and another wrestler, "Dr. D" David Shultz, had made on *Pro Wrestling Spotlight*—the former on the bigger station, which aired a couple of days earlier. It was probably the most explosive article ever written on WWF, about the lies, the corruption, the Hogan mantra of "eating your vitamins and saying your prayers" that was constantly pushed. The article was huge and I was in the middle of it again, and it was just a whirlwind of shit.

Then on February 26, 1992, Mushnick started the ball rolling on sexual misconduct accusations. He would later name Mel Phillips, who had worked for WWF in various capacities, including as a ring announcer, and Terry Garvin, who had helped with storylines and was in charge of the ring crews.

From there it all blew up, the mainstream media had a field day, and wrestler after wrestler had their tales to tell. Because it was salacious, it was so much easier to report on than steroids. Not only did you have the underage-sex scandal, but you also had the harassment allegations, and it was pro wrestling—it was already a circus industry. It was easy fodder for mainstream media to jump on, without any real desire to get to the bottom of what was going on.

Jeff Savage's *San Diego Union-Tribune* article on March 11 further rocked the boat, and Mushnick expanded on it the following day, when more wrestlers revealed how they had been harassed. It became a zoo.

★ ★ ★ ★ ★

My own personal experience with Mel Phillips definitely skewed my coverage.

AT THE 1975 WFIA
CONVENTION IN BOSTON.
FROM LEFT, MEL
PHILLIPS, DONNY LAIBLE,
ME, TOM BURKE, AND
ERIC GOLDENBERG.

I first Mel Phillips in 1974 at the WFIA convention in Atlanta, where he won the Wrestling Fan of the Year award. He was smart and charming, and the big draw was that he was in the business. We became friends. I'd plan to go to the Philadelphia taping, and the next day would be Hamburg, and Mel would suggest, "Come with me, I'm driving Stan Hansen or Bruiser Brody." He was giving me access. At the time, I was 17 or 18 years old.

When he was coming to New York, he'd ask about staying at my house. I'd ask my mom, but it was always okay. He had these two young boys—and I won't mention their names, because I'm still friends with them—on Long Island, and he'd go seek them out and start wrestling with them in the backyard. I wondered why he was doing that.

Then when I started college in Boston in '75, Mel would come visit me, and he would get upset because I didn't really want to hang out, since I had a girlfriend. Mel did meet one of my friends in the dorm and he'd seek him out when he was visiting and again would wrestle him. I never put two and two together, which I should have. The thing about Mel was that he was always hanging around young boys.

In 1977, I'd had enough of the creepiness, and I distanced myself from him. There were always rumors about him, like he was a foot fetish guy. It was commonly known in the back that Mel was a guy to keep your eye on, and he was always around. Eventually that resulted in a job as a ring announcer.

When the allegations did come out, it all added up, finally; somehow I'd never figured out that the guy was a pedophile. I think I was a little bit old for him to be attracted to me. The thing that made it worse, for me, is that I knew so many of the people involved in the cover-up, people who worked for WWF through the years. That's part of the reason I was so committed to the coverage of the trial.

But by the same token, my closeness to the situation meant I was biased. I leaped when I should have waited and given proper consideration to my words and how it would affect the people involved. Since I was brokering my time, I wasn't getting paid by the station, so their lawyers didn't pay attention to what I was saying. Later, when I was at the much bigger, 50,000-watt WEVD, the station started getting letters from the WWF lawyer, Jerry McDevitt, alleging my lies and threatening a lawsuit. My account rep at the station would call me and go, "I got another letter from the WWF lawyer. We're just going to ignore it." I was like, "Okay." There was never any formal legal action.

There were allegations made by the likes of Barry Orton (brother of Cowboy Bob, uncle of Randy Orton) against Phillips, Garvin, and Pat Patterson. I reported on the allegations as if they had happened. Patterson, who was a high-ranking WWF executive and was involved in writing the storylines, should not have been mentioned in the same sentences as the other two, and I have apologized repeatedly—and do so again here—that I should never had reported that Patterson was involved in the incidents. I'd known Patterson for years, and he was always flirtatious, and him being gay certainly was not a secret in the industry, even if he did not come out publicly for decades. But he was not a pedophile and I was wrong to include him in the allegations. I am sorry, Pat. He was done wrong in the sex scandal frenzy in 1992. I had promised that if I ever encountered Pat again at a wrestling event I'd apologize, but sadly will never have the chance, as he passed away in the fall of 2020.

Terry Garvin I didn't know very well, but I had met him through Sonny Blaze, who had booked him for several WWF TV tapings as a jobber. Sonny and I would be backstage at a few WWF events, and I always hoped that it would lead to better access to wrestlers for my radio show, but that never happened. When the sex scandals broke, Sonny defended Terry to me, and when I offered him a spot on the show to explain, he declined and distanced himself from me.

It was a challenge to get information on the three: Phillips, Garvin, and Patterson. WWF covered it all up and we never got straight answers on anything. Was Phillips fired? Suspended? Did he quit? Who knew what and when? I truly believe he was caught a couple of times and that no one did anything about it. I'll never understand why he wasn't removed from his position and fired earlier, in the 1970s. Who knows how many kids were abused, but could have been spared had someone acted properly. Mel had his favorites, of course, but there were always new kids around him. Phillips never made a move on me, so I couldn't have been one to point the finger, but for anyone experiencing similar creepy vibes today, they would have acted and told someone; it's one small way the world has improved when it comes to reporting child molesters.

In the end, we don't really know exactly what happened. People left their jobs, but no one went to jail. No one knew what deals were going on, what deals were being cut as a result of the allegations, with any of the kids who had been abused. McMahon was doing everything in his power to keep all of this quiet. It was hard to cover it week after week because there were no arrests, there was no trial.

My phone began to ring more than ever before—people in the industry, journalists, media professionals. It didn't stop for weeks.

I made a lot of appearances in my so-called downtime. I was on everything from *CBS Evening News* to a spot on Comedy Central. With the respected *Eye on America*, they came into the studio and filmed me. Dave Meltzer was filmed in my studio too. There were plenty of other shows. I was a guy in the middle of it all, because I was in a major media market and easy to get a hold of. When one show booked me, the next one wanted me too.

★ ★ ★ ★ ★ ★ ★ ★ ★ ★ ★ ★ ★

"SHOWTIME!" DESCRIBED
MY TIME ON THE *PHIL
DONAHUE SHOW* AND MY
NEWSLETTER.

The big one, though, was an episode of *The Phil Donahue Show* which aired on March 16, 1992. Phil Donahue was a nationally broadcast talk show host who never avoided controversial topics. It was fascinating to be a part of such a big production. A number of the guests were there the day before to go over the plan, including myself, Barry Orton, "Superstar" Billy Graham, Dave Meltzer, and Bruno Sammartino, who was a guest on the phone. At the same time, CBS News people were getting soundbites of their own.

The day of the show, they sent limos to pick us up. Earlier in the day, I was out running some errands, and when I got home to the apartment that I shared with my mom, she goes, "There was a knock on the door. There were two guys looking for you."

"What did they want?"

"They asked if John Arezzi lived here. I said, 'Yeah, my son lives here.'" They said, "Tell your son he lives in a dangerous neighborhood," and they left. She was pretty concerned. I perceived that as a threat.

As for the show itself? Wow.

I was a part of one panel, with Meltzer and Vince McMahon. The looks I was getting from Vince that day were not nice; if looks could kill, I'd have been dead. The conversation went to Hulk Hogan on *The Arsenio Hall Show*. Meltzer and I had talked several times a week, and during one conversation Dave mentioned that Vince had said he was devastated when Hulk Hogan made those statements on Arsenio. I asked Vince about this. He said, "I wasn't devastated."

Dave jumped in. "That was the word you used to me. You used the word devastated." He caught him in a lie in front of a national audience. People were laughing and hooting it up. Vince gave me another look, almost like he was accusing us of setting him up for a fall.

Plenty of other things happened too, like Tom Cole, one of the ring boys who made the allegations, switching sides—he was supposed to be on the show itself, but when it was taped, he was sitting in the crowd with Linda McMahon and Miss Elizabeth. They had settled with him right before the show, gave him a job, and gave him a check. We were all shocked as we expected him on the show with us. Looking at *Donahue* now, I cringe; weighing in at almost 400 pounds and wearing my dark glasses, I looked more like a freakin' con artist than an impartial journalist.

As a funny side story, my mother went to the *Donahue* taping, with my sister and my brother-in-law. There are a few good, close-up shots of my mom during the show, looking puzzled. At the very end, with the cameras off and people packing up, my mother went up to Vince McMahon. "Mr. McMahon, I just want to shake your hand. I admire you so much."

"Oh, thank you, ma'am."

"I'm John Arezzi's mother." His look was priceless, like someone had shit in his cereal and he wanted her away from him as quickly as possible. On the way home, I couldn't stop laughing about it, because it was so crazy. But that was my mom.

Out of my Donahue appearance, *Pro Wrestling Spotlight* exploded with listener growth. We started to get tons of calls and countless letters.

I was this crazy crusader who was covering pro wrestling in a mainstream way as it had never been covered before. That two-year period of 1991 and 1992, with the steroid trial and then the sex scandal, was a wild time. The terrible death of Owen Hart and the double murder-suicide of Chris Benoit may have gotten more press years later, but for sheer impact on the industry, nothing has ever compared to the double whammy of the steroid trial and the WWF sex scandal.

★ ★ ★ ★ ★

It's an aside in retrospect, but when the steroid issues with Zahorian had concluded, McMahon decided that he had to present an olive branch of sorts to the wrestling media, to those of us that were seriously covering the business.

Out of the blue, I got a call from Planamenta, inviting me to meet with McMahon, along with Meltzer and Keller, as well as photographer Mike Lano. It was convenient because they were all coming in for a wrestling convention that I was running. They sent a car for us to get to Titan Towers, which was in Stamford, Connecticut. That was on August 23, 1991. Notable people were not invited, like George Napolitano and Bill Apter, meaning they were targeting the insider writers and not the newsstand magazines.

McMahon himself gave us a tour of Titan Towers. They were friendly and embracing. Sitting down, it was like a classroom with McMahon at the lectern and we were the students. He urged us to work with WWF, to reach out if we had questions, and not to assume and report on rumors. Aside from making peace, I felt it was a sales job of sorts, trying to get us to lay off, that WWF was taking care of things. He was trying to smooth everything over.

I saw through the ruse, but was pleased when WWF started cooperating with my radio show, however briefly. After asking for two years, I finally got Freddie Blassie on my show, live for two hours. Not long after, the cooperation ground to a halt.

Less than a year later, in January 1992, WCW hired a new boss, Kip Frey, and he invited the wrestling media to Kansas City to sit down with him. That was cool to do, even if it was on my own dime. The best part was that I got talk to Dusty Rhodes about our time in the ring together—which he didn't remember—and got him to sign *The Ring*

Wrestling magazine that had a story about me, their reporter who got into the ring to wrestle.

★ ★ ★ ★ ★

There was a second steroid trial, in July 1994, when Vince McMahon was charged with conspiracy and possession with intent to distribute anabolic steroids. The trial was held on Long Island, near the Nassau County Coliseum, so only about 20 minutes from where I lived.

By then, I was a certified enemy. With the first steroid trial, WWE tried to have détentes and cooperate, but when the sex scandal coverage began, my goodness, I was an enemy of the state—and I assume that I still am. Part of the reason was my prominence, and that's partly because I was in New York, the media center of the world, and available to appear on any show that wanted me.

Unlike the Zahorian trial in 1991, the New York media was out in droves, along with even more of the wrestling media. I spent a lot of time with Wade Keller, but Georgiann Makropoulos of *Wrestling Chatterbox* was there, and even a young kid who had a newsletter, Jeffrey Mengles. Plus, there were wrestling fans in the courtroom, and they'd hoot and holler until silenced.

Vince's children, Shane and Stephanie, weren't very old, and I can remember feeling sorry for them, that they had to see all of this. Speaking of sympathy, Vince wore a neck brace for the entire trial, as he was having some neck issues, but a lot of people thought that was a work.

The trial only lasted a couple of weeks, and it was odd, since none of "The Boys"—his wrestlers—testified against him. Those that spoke were Tom Zenk, Tully Blanchard, Warlord, Hulk Hogan, and Nailz (Kevin Wacholz). The most tense time in the courtroom was when Nailz was on the stand. He and McMahon hated each other and he had alleged that McMahon had attacked him. You could tell that McMahon had more disgust and disdain for Nailz than for anyone else, just from watching his face when Nailz came into the courtroom.

In the end, they couldn't prove that he suggested that anyone get on steroids. It was a fair trial. He got off, and the fans in attendance popped.

When he was acquitted and left the courtroom to all the smiles and jubilation, McMahon announced that it was time for him to get back to work. (WWF had set up a contingency plan, with veteran Memphis promoter Jerry Jarrett brought in, if Vince had faced prison time.)

This go-round I didn't do much more than report on the trial for my radio show.

★ ★ ★ ★ ★

In this retelling of the Zahorian steroid trial and the WWF sex scandal, I have left out one name. It's time now to tell my side of the Vince Russo story.

11.

IT'S ALL MY FAULT

I am to blame for Vince Russo being in the wrestling business and, depending on who you ask, I'm either the Antichrist or the man who opened the door for professional wrestling's most successful run ever. If you listen to Russo's arch-enemy Jim Cornette, I am "patient zero" in the plague that was and is Vince Russo.

For those of you unfamiliar with his name, here's the long and short of it. He used me as a springboard into professional wrestling and got himself a job with WWF, first as a writer on its magazine and then talked his way into becoming a scriptwriter. He was one of the key people behind Dwayne "The Rock" Johnson and "Stone Cold" Steve Austin becoming household names in the Attitude Era of WWF. Later, Russo worked at competing companies, to varying degrees of success. At one point, he even made himself, a 39-year-old former video store owner from Long Island, WCW world heavyweight champion. He's a polarizing figure in pro wrestling.

It's time to set the story straight on my role in Russo's saga—as what he wrote in his autobiography, *Forgiven*, was not entirely the way I remember it.

★ ★ ★ ★ ★

In mid-1991, a regular listener to *Pro Wrestling Spotlight*, Andrew Goldberger stumbled upon this video store, Will the Thrill Video, in Coram, Long Island, and immediately reported back to me that the owner was a wrestling fan with a huge collection of wrestling videos. He'd even had a few wrestlers into the store for promotional events. Looking out for the show, Andrew suggested that Will the Thrill Video would make for a good advertiser and had told the owner, Vince Russo, about me. I called Vince up and was invited down to chat.

I pitched him on advertising and he was intrigued, and later came on board as an advertiser. The relationship started as a client-advertiser deal, and that's it. He paid for his ads, and I'd promote whatever deals or sales he was having. I booked the Honky Tonk Man for him, as part as a promotion for a neighborhood street fair.

As I got to know him, Vince told me about his journalism degree and his desire to write, and how the video business was suffering from Blockbuster and other big stores coming in and muscling out the mom-and-pop stores. He really wanted to get into the wrestling business. He was a big fan of old-school wrestling.

Vince was very Long Island, aggressive, animated, and in-your-face; he moved at 100 miles an hour, with a short attention span. His biggest asset was working hard, putting in long hours to make his video stores go, though it put pressure on his marriage. When he was enthusiastic about something, wow, could he get excited; likewise, if he didn't like it, boy did he let you know.

There was something in my gut that didn't quite feel right about him, an instinctual thing. I wanted his ad dollars, but part of me wondered how long I'd be able to put up with him.

It turned out to be short lived—a few months as an advertiser and only three months as my business partner.

★ ★ ★ ★ ★

Russo wanted to start a newsletter, to put his journalism degree to use, and to capitalize on the built-in fan base with the radio show. Publishing a newsletter was never something that interested me. I felt that the industry was well covered by the likes of *The Wrestling Observer Newsletter* and *Pro Wrestling Torch*. What would the spin be for a *Pro Wrestling Spotlight Weekly* newsletter? But he convinced me.

Vince wanted the newsletter to be entertainment, not analysis, but I saw myself as a respected journalist in the not-so-respected world of pro wrestling.

We divided up the responsibilities. Vince reviewed the TV shows and the new video tapes and did some special features. In the first issue, he had an interview with Sunny Beach. I wrote a front-page editorial that looked at Hulk Hogan and the lie about steroids he had told on Arsenio Hall's show, and mused how things would play out in 1992. The tales of "Superstar" Graham and David Shultz shooting up Hogan with steroids had only just come to light at that time. Also in that first issue, I started a Mat Memories column to look back at my own experiences.

The thing I didn't anticipate was Russo's editorializing on everything he wrote. He wasn't the polished writer that he claimed to be, and everything had a juvenile tone to it. His writing style certainly didn't mesh with the true insider voice that I had on the radio show. He was doing entertainment writing and not insider wrestling stuff.

In print, our voices conflicted.

★ ★ ★ ★ ★

Credit where credit is due—it was Vince that pushed me to get *Pro Wrestling Spotlight* onto a bigger station. He was always badgering me about lost opportunities. One day, I just told him that if he thought the show should be on a bigger station, then he should find me one. He landed us on WEVD, 1050 AM, which was a 50,000-watt station that brokered time. It was a legacy station and used to be WHN, which was a huge country music station for a lot of years. It had one of the biggest, most powerful signals in radio, and in the evening, it could reach from the southern edges of Quebec down to Virginia.

He brought the deal to me, but the key was how much it would cost us. It was a whopping $1,053 a week for a single hour. That was a huge jump from $400 a week—and I was having a hard time paying the current fee.

Russo was a salesman and worked on me, buttering me up over my sales skills, and tying in the launch of the newsletter with the move to the new station. I eventually agreed. I was comfortable at WGBB, and I had a very loyal following on Sunday mornings from 10 a.m. to noon. It was a good slot and I got a lot of calls. The station managers at WGBB extended credit to me if there were weeks when I couldn't pay the $400. I was hesitant to move, but I did want to grow the business.

The pluses outweighed the negatives. I could sell ads to a wider clientele with the new station, reach more listeners, and ideally attract more fans to come on the bus trips, which usually were a moneymaker for me.

ONE OF THE NEWSLETTERS I DID WITH VINCE RUSSO.

I made the deal with WEVD towards the end of 1991, and we were set to debut in January 1992. We went ahead with the *Pro Wrestling Spotlight Weekly*, with the first issue dated January 13, 1992.

Subscriptions started immediately, helped by the fact that we offered free issues to get people started, and we'd gotten the mailing list of Steve Beverly, who had just closed down *Matwatch*. The mail was incredible for a short amount of time. People would call up after the radio show was over, and we'd stay taking subscriptions for an hour or two.

★ ★ ★ ★ ★

The first major issue with Vince was in the initial issue of the newsletter. He positioned the radio show on the back page: "Announcing the *Pro Wrestling Spotlight* radio show on WEVD on Sunday night. Hear the news, with weekly interviews, with your hosts, John Arezzi and Vince Russo."

We had never discussed him being a co-host, ever. That was out of the blue, and I wondered what the hell was going on.

Now, Vince had been on the show on WGBB, first as an advertiser, and then he started coming to the station every week. I'd put him on the air here and there to talk about the store and new wrestling video tapes, and he integrated himself in the control room, usually screening calls. We also started discussing a video project with Jim Cornette, *The Best of the Midnight Express*, from their inception on through to that day.

But co-hosting? No way.

I sat down with Vince to talk about his assumption that he'd be co-hosting. "Vince, we never discussed this."

"Oh, I thought we did."

I told him I wasn't comfortable co-hosting with him, but that he could still be involved. He was offended by that, but we moved forward.

My guard was up.

★ ★ ★ ★ ★

With the steroid issue going on in pro wrestling, I was committed to covering it like a journalist would, seeking thoughts and opinions, getting both sides of the story. Vince didn't want us to cover it at all. He thought it would upset WWF and therefore ruin any chance for us getting big-name guests on the show, which had such a greater reach that it could now be heard up in Stamford, Connecticut, home of WWF.

It was the same in the newsletter. Russo was against covering the wrestling business the way that I had been and really wanted me to sugarcoat it all, to change the slant and the scope of the show, to make it more entertainment rather than news.

Yet it was the most newsworthy time in pro wrestling history, with the steroid trial approaching, followed by the WWF sex scandal.

The feedback on the newsletter was immediate, with the likes of Meltzer and Keller wondering who this guy was that I was partnering with. His writing was slammed and his juvenile humor questioned. We were like night and day in print, and we weren't gelling the way we should have been. I wondered how it would affect my relationships with other people, people I respected. That immediately began Russo's distaste for "dirtsheet writers."

We drove into New York City together every week to do the show, and we were always on edge, looking behind us, scared and nervous, the pressure of WWF on trial getting to us too. Each week, we got deeper and deeper into the coverage of the scandals, and we were frightened that someone might take issue. We were scared for our safety, let's put it that way, whether it was on the roads to and from the station, entering the building, or even in the building itself, where we'd have a quick look around before going in. Paranoid? Sure.

The newsletter was mainly Russo's baby. I didn't know how many subscribers we had, how the finances worked. All I thought about was selling ads for the radio.

Despite our growing differences, we still tried to do a newsletter each week. But I really wasn't into it. I enjoyed my Mat Memories column, since it was about my past, but there was stress writing about the actual news going on in the world of wrestling, especially news relating to the scandals. Vince was the opposite, totally into writing and gaining notoriety.

Vince did what Vince wanted to do. One day, he came in and said, "I'm going to Johnny Rodz's wrestling school and I'm going to be writing some stories about training to be a pro wrestler." I couldn't believe it. I didn't understand what the endgame was, other than that he wanted to be in the wrestling business, in any capacity. (Little did I know he would one day be world champion . . .)

★ ★ ★ ★ ★

Though we spent so much time together, I never felt we were friends, or partners for that matter, because we had such different goals. Vince never confided in me about personal matters, and that became an issue when his finances fell apart. He'd heard me complain about my own precarious money situation, but never thought to tell me that he was running low on dough, that his wife was on him to sell the store and find a new gig.

Unbeknownst to me, he started communicating with WWF and Steve Planamenta in PR. The office that we operated out of was in Coram, in the back of his video store. I'd come in a few times a week and work on the newsletter. One day, when checking the messages, I heard one from Steve at WWF.

Already paranoid because of what I was covering, and because of my finances—now I was wondering what my partner was doing behind my back. That killed my trust for him.

Our arguments grew, whether it was over the show, the newsletter, or money. He was writing checks that he couldn't afford, and his wife was on him a lot, thinking he was crazy.

While he didn't clue into my personal situation, I didn't really empathize with him as the video stores were falling from his grasp in the world of Blockbuster.

★ ★ ★ ★ ★

While it would be easy to dismiss Vince Russo as being totally pro-WWF, and therefore unsympathetic to the scandals that were unfolding around us, that wasn't the case. He was actually responsible for breaking a new aspect of the sex scandal.

He really enjoyed interviewing and was good at it. Vince was a fan of midget wrestling, and like me, their presence was an intriguing part of our initial fandom. The king of the little people at the time was Lord Littlebrook (Eric Tovey), who was based in Missouri, and trained a number of wrestlers, big and small. It was meant to be a routine "where are they now?" interview, but turned into something else when Littlebrook brought up how one of the wrestlers in his troupe, The Karate Kid (Chris Dube), claimed to have been sexually harassed. When Littlebrook brought it up with WWF management, they stopped using midgets altogether. To his credit, Russo then interviewed Dube, and it ran under the (cringe-worthy) headline, "Midgets Stand Tall."

★ ★ ★ ★ ★

After *Donahue* aired, WWF announced it was going to start testing for steroids and put a Canadian physician, Dr. Mauro Di Pasquale, out front as its lead face. It arranged for a steroid symposium, and Russo got an invite to go to it, with specific instructions not to invite me. Meltzer pointed out it was classic "divide and conquer" strategy, and he even went to bat for me, trying to talk some sense into Russo, but nothing worked.

The steroid symposium ended up being the last straw. Vince came back from that with an ultimatum: that we had to stop covering WWF the way we had. Russo met a bunch of the powers there, including Vince and Linda McMahon, and Shane McMahon, and was won over to their side. He told me that Vince McMahon said, "You guys don't know how much fun doing a wrestling radio show could be," insinuating that if we played ball, we'd have access to WWF stars.

He went and booked Di Pasquale for the next radio show, without consulting me, and he demanded time on the broadcast to rebut the *Post*'s Mushnick, and he accused me of telling Mushnick lies. Like with Meltzer, I set up a three-way call where Russo could talk to Mushnick— off the air. That didn't go well either.

I decided that I was done with him. I called up my brother-in-law and asked him to come down and have my back as I moved my stuff out of Vince's office. I wanted a witness at least.

With my brother-in-law behind me, I walked in and said, "I don't want to be in business anymore."

He lost it. "You're fucking broke and always will be broke. This is an opportunity for us and you can't get your head out of your ass." Vince ran out of his own video store, screaming in the parking lot, going berserk. I got my stuff and left.

As we were leaving, he threatened, "I'm going to take over the show. I pay for it, I'm taking it over. That's it."

"No, you're not fucking taking over the show, there's no way."

He immediately called WEVD to tell them that I was out and that he was in charge. The account executive that I was working with called me up to tell me that he'd gotten a call from Vince. He assured me that the contract was with me, so it was my show, that Russo couldn't take it over.

The newsletter was a little different.

★ ★ ★ ★ ★

On April 13, 1992, a new issue of the *Pro Wrestling Spotlight Newsletter* came out, compiled solely by Russo, and it included his "ten points of light" which explained the "creative, as well as business reasons" that "forced" us to "discontinue our relationship."

"I have been a wrestling journalist for some 90 days. In those 90 days the lying and deceit of my so-called colleagues, the 'inside' wrestling media, was too much for me to handle. When it came down to hurting innocent people, it was time for me to walk," Russo began. He took issue with all kinds of things, from Mushnick comparing Vince McMahon to Hannibal Lecter, to journalists digging up stories from the past, to talk of boycotting WWF. It was all over the map and didn't make much sense.

Russo claimed he owned the name of the newsletter, but he didn't. It lasted a couple of issues under that title, and then he stumbled along doing his own thing for a few more. Even worse was his radio show on WGBB. It was called *Vicious Vincent's World of Wrestling*. His show was filled with characters. He portrayed Vicious Vincent and had his friend Jimmy play the part of co-host "The Mat Rat," talking in a mousy-voice, and he brought in a rookie wrestler Vito LoGrasso or "Skull Von Krush" to be this Nazi-type villain. He'd answer simple questions from listeners and every so often he'd rant on me, calling me a fat pig and other things. At appearances, he'd have a big black hat and a cape, trying desperately to stand out.

★ ★ ★ ★ ★

The premiere issue of *John Arezzi's Pro Wrestling Spotlight* was published May 4, 1992, and it was my baby, but I didn't have the passion for writing a newsletter. I continued it more to make things right with the previous subscribers. Compounding the issue was that Russo had control of the mailing list and never shared details of subscribers with me. I had to start from scratch, announcing the newsletter on the show. I began with an editorial: "May I first give a heartfelt 'Thank You' to all of you who have rallied behind me during the past month, which can easily be considered the most stressful time I have ever had in the wrestling business. The phone calls, cards, and letters have cheered me up and made me more determined than ever to continue on in this crazy business. I cannot answer all the letters that have come in, so I hope this 'open letter' will serve as an appropriate response."

In all, I only published seven issues.

★ ★ ★ ★ ★

After the split up, I stayed on at WEVD but the pressure was too much. To be honest, the show was never secure again, and we were on and off for the remainder of its run. Since paying for the time was so tough, I moved around a lot. I went back to WNYG, then back to WEVD, and finally ended up finishing the run of the show on WGBB.

There were even a couple of weeks where I was hosting a *national* show. Sports Entertainment Network syndicated a wrestling show with Mike Tenay, *Wrestling Insiders*. For whatever reason, Mike had stepped away and they offered me the spot. Naturally, I jumped at it. Tenay and

**VINCE RUSSO AND I
REUNITE IN DENVER IN
2018.**

the people behind SEN made up and I was done. I never saw a dime from it either.

My show ended abruptly, without even so much as a farewell. One week it was on, and then it was done, and no one ever heard about me or the show again. *Pro Wrestling Spotlight* went off the air for good in February 1995.

12.

JUST CALL ME "BIG PORK BBQ"

While I was doing the *Pro Wrestling Spotlight* show, I began to have bigger aspirations.

Early in the days of the program, I fancied myself a manager, and given my Italian heritage and background, naturally I dressed up in a black suit with a white tie, wearing my ever-present dark glasses, as a Mob boss. I didn't really get into the action much.

The first guys I managed were the Power Twins and "Broadway" Sonny Blaze, in big Long Island high school gyms or Brooklyn community centers—so not exactly Madison Square Garden. I talked a good game on the show, trying to get the listeners out to watch.

The main thing I took away from managing was a hurt wrist and an appreciation for true up-and-coming talent.

That go-round, it was Sonny matched against Kid Krush, a short, intense newcomer trained by my old friend Johnny Rodz, looking somewhat uncomfortable wearing face paint in the ring. You could tell that he was really focused and was bound for better things; sure enough, he succeeded as Taz in ECW and WWE. But that night, Kid Krush did a spot where he came out of the ring and I took a shot and hit him. He retaliated by slamming my head into the ring post. I wanted it to look good, so I took a bump where I tried to protect my head with my arm, but my wrist hit full-force on the ring post. I hit really hard, tumbled back, and the people there from the state athletic commission really thought I got hurt. My wrist swelled up really fast and turned black and blue. I shouldn't have done it. In fact, "I shouldn't have done it" applies to my brief time as a manager.

By comparison, I thought that I was a pretty good announcer at ring-side, calling the matches on TV or offering color commentary. I did that at numerous indy shows and for the Savoldis on a bigger scale. Later, Joel Goodhart and Dennis Coralluzzo used me for their regional shows in South Jersey and Philadelphia. I called the famous Cactus Jack versus "Hot Stuff" Eddie Gilbert three-matches-in-one-night series for Joel. Another great match I announced with Chris Cruise pitted Terry Funk against Bob Backlund for Coralluzzo. Plenty of times, I used my radio pulpit to promote the shows that I was announcing on, knowing full well that I was being used. I always wanted that big wrestling company to call me up, but it never happened.

Another thing I did on the early *Pro Wrestling Spotlight* shows was play up a new Long Island promotion, talking about mystery backers and questioning talent on air that I had already made "deals" with about the potential of the non-existent promotion. My intentions were honest, as I intended to run some shows, but I just never did. The idea was presented to me by Sonny Blaze, who called the start-up East Coast Wrestling, or ECW (way before Tod Gordon formed Eastern Championship Wrestling).

When I did run shows internationally or in the U.S., it was under my IWAS banner, which stood for for International Wrestling All Stars.

★ ★ ★ ★ ★

In 1993, I helped put together a deal which made big news. While on WGBB and WEVD, with those stations having a bigger reach, *Pro Wrestling Spotlight* was heard by a lot of people, especially in the greater New York area, and one of them was an entertainment lawyer named Ron Skoler. He had made his name in the music business, mostly representing rap artists. He was really close friends with the managers of Salt-N-Pepa, Carol Kirkendall and Darryll Brooks. Ron was a fan of my show, and he had an interesting idea. He wanted help to break into the business as a promoter. He didn't want to promote traditional American wrestling: rather he was fascinated with lucha libre. He wanted to see lucha here in the U.S., and in particular, the AAA (Asistencia Asesoría y Administración, "Assistance, Assessment, and Administration") promotion from Mexico.

Ron saw me as the guy who could make the deal happen, but I didn't really know much about AAA, just about lucha libre as a wider concept in Mexico, and how its style differed from wrestling in North America, with its masked traditions and high-flying, non-stop action. I went right to Dave Meltzer and asked him if he could assist me with an introduction. Dave pointed me to Konnan (Carlos Espada), who was an emerging star in the just-founded AAA and who, since he had his roots in the U.S., spoke English and Spanish.

Naturally, when I talked to Konnan, he got really excited about the possibility of bringing lucha to the U.S. After some vetting, Ron and I got a call from Antonio Pena, who had started AAA in 1992, breaking away from the established CMLL (Consejo Mundial de Lucha Libre). Konnan was on the call as a translator. Everyone realized that it was a

★ ★ ★ ★ ★ ★ ★ ★ ★

ME AND ANTONIO
PENA.

serious play, and that the timing was right, as AAA was more ambitious and creative than the established promotion.

To make it work, Ron brought in Kirkendall and Brooks, for their experience with concert promoting. They all liked the idea, so there was financial backing and access to venues. What really sold the deal was Ron and Darryll taking a trip to Mexico City to see *TripleMania*, the biggest AAA show of the year—their *WrestleMania*. Based on what they saw, especially the crowd reactions, the two left there convinced it would work, and were all in on making it happen.

I was just the dealmaker, the person that set it up, the connector, and was given shares in the company when they formed the LLC. What I wouldn't be was a wrestling manager! When Pena first met me, he was taken with me for some reason, and he wanted to make a lucha character called Papucho, almost like Cupid. Papucho is the man every woman wants to be with and every man wants to be. I thought it was a rib, but it wasn't a rib, because Pena actually wanted to do it.

Ron wasn't just thinking about shows in the U.S., though, and had a dream of promoting internationally as well. He had aspirations to be the next Vince McMahon, and Ron sometimes acted that way. That happens when you turn away 8,000 fans from your first show.

★ ★ ★ ★ ★

La Revencha on August 28, 1993, at the Sports Arena in Los Angeles, drew a sell-out crowd of 17,500, with thousands turned away. It was unbelievable. We sure picked the right market to start promoting AAA shows. While it was primarily a Latino audience, there were plenty of gringos there too, lured by the spectacle and the hype for AAA, which had upset the apple cart in Mexico.

The double main event drew the people, but the whole show delivered. Having someone like Mando Guerrero, who'd been a star in the Los Angeles territory two decades before, in the opening match was one thing, but the high-flying lucha madness of a trios bout, with Psicosis, Heavy Metal, and Jerry Estrada beating Volador, Rey Mysterio Jr., and Misterioso in three falls, was out of this world. Those main events?

Octagon, El Hijo del Santo, and Blue Panther beat Love Machine (Art
Barr), Eddie Guerrero, and Fuerza Guerrera in two straight falls, and in a
triangle match, Konnan beat Jake "The Snake" Roberts and Cien Caras.

We were all excited about the huge success of this first event. Ron
was elated, as was I. Top insiders in the business like Dave Meltzer and
Mike Tenay attended and they were all congratulating us for this success.
Everyone left the arena with high hopes for the future.

We ran twice more in L.A., with lesser crowds, before I tapped out. I
missed out on the AAA-IWC show at the theater inside Madison Square
Garden in August 1994, and the famed pay-per-view *When Worlds Collide*
in L.A., in partnership with WCW.

The AAA shows in America were a huge success, even if the crowds
were never as large as the first one. But they made an impact and show-
cased the lucha libre style to the U.S. audience, and paved the way for
a lot of today's wrestlers. Many names got exposure that they wouldn't
have gotten otherwise.

There was incredible financial stress on me, and I eventually sold my
shares in Ron's promotion back to the company. I think I got $18,000 or
so for the shares. Ron likes to joke that I'm the only one that ever made

money on the deal as far as the American promoters were concerned. But that was solely based on my need to have cash to continue with day-to-day life, from the radio show to keeping a roof over my head.

★ ★ ★ ★ ★

Another venture with AAA took place in October 1995. I was the deal-maker for a joint show between AAA, IWAS, and Paul Heyman's ECW promotion at the New International Amphitheatre in Chicago, on October 21, 1995. John Regna and I promoted that show, and it did well, but we didn't make much money.

A TICKET FROM THE COMBINED IWAS/AAA/ECW SHOW IN CHICAGO.

The tapes are out there somewhere. Ron Buffone's crew, which shot all the ECW events, filmed, but I've never seen the footage. I didn't have the money to pay for the editing of the production, though some of it aired on ECW TV. And I'd love to see it, since it was the craziest night of wrestling that I have ever been involved with, which is really saying something.

It all built to the finale, with Konnan, Octagon, and Perro Aguayo, seconded by Terry Funk, facing Cien Caras, KGB, and Killer. In the end, Funk turned on his team and hung Aguayo with a rope outside of the ring. The fans rioted, throwing bottles and chairs. I wasn't sure that Funk would get out alive. We all waited until well after the crowd dispersed before leaving the building.

The wildness of the crowd harkened back to our international tours.

★ ★ ★ ★ ★

International Wrestling All Stars was the promotion that I put together to run shows abroad, due to the introduction Ron Skoler made for me with John Regna, who ran a talent agency called World Entertainment Associates. Our initial target was Southeast Asia, which we ran from June 25 to July 12, 1993.

A first misstep was bringing in Mike Appel, who discovered Bruce Springsteen, co-produced his first three albums, including the classic *Born to Run*, and was instrumental in getting Bruce on the covers of both *Time* and *Newsweek* in the very same week, unheard of for an entertainer, then and now. Mike was a friend of Regna's, who was interested in being involved. Right from the beginning, I had a funny feeling about Appel—a Russo-like feeling. I took Mike to an ECW show in Philadelphia. In the back, he was fascinated by it all and talked big about being partners and forming a company. His involvement didn't last very long, and I should have heeded my gut feelings, especially since I knew that he and Springsteen had had a falling-out and that Bruce had sued Mike. It was a famous and ugly lawsuit. Despite the big talk, he told me I was just the dealmaker, and that he would have all the power and run with it. So he's telling me he's going to fuck me right from the beginning. I couldn't and didn't tolerate the relationship so I went to Regna and said I wasn't going to be involved if Mike was. John listened and decided to stick with me.

★ ★ ★ ★ ★

With a local promoter on the ground in Southeast Asia who wanted to host wrestling, it all came together pretty quickly. They wanted headliners, wrestlers who had been visible on television, ideally WWF. Initial contacts included Jake "The Snake" Roberts, Greg "The Hammer" Valentine, Cowboy Bob Orton, and Wendi Richter. All my time hosting the show and getting guests, hiring people for personal appearances, and as a convention promoter paid off. I asked Paul Heyman if he wanted to help me, and he agreed. Initially Heyman was going to be the booker, but then Jake wanted to do it. There were internal problems right off the bat over who was going to be booking this thing.

At the end of the day, we had quite the lineup. With the permission of AAA, I got Konnan and the Mexican minis, Mascarita Sagrada and Expectrico. I had some local guys that I brought along—the Power Twins, Sunny Beach, and Ted Petty—and, just as importantly, Ted's wrestling ring. I brought my radio producer Bruce Jacobs along to serve as my assistant and ring announcer. For the marquee performers, I contracted names such as long-time friend Kevin Sullivan and his wife Nancy, who was a valet and manager, using the name Fallen Angel. I booked ex-WWF stars Warlord and Barbarian as the IWAS tag team champions. That was hypocritical on my part, since Warlord was always looked upon as one of the biggest steroid monsters in the business. When I was booking talent, I did ask them if they were "on the juice" and everyone said no.

The deal was for $250,000 for a two-week tour, which was pretty good money in 1993.

We submitted a bunch of names to the promoter as headliners, and they really wanted The Ultimate Warrior, Jim Hellwig. He'd done my radio show after leaving WWF, so I reached out about him appearing on the tour. The idea was that he'd headline against Jake Roberts, and Warrior would be the IWAS world champion. He agreed to it, and the initial figure that I guaranteed him was $25,000. Contracts were drafted by Skoler, who was acting as my attorney for the deal, and Warrior was going to be paid the most of anyone on the tour.

Our pay range went from $1,500 for two weeks for an opener like Mike Durham, $2,000 each for the minis, and $4,000 each for the girls, Medusa and Wendi Richter, all the way up to Warrior's number. Jake the Snake was getting $15,000 and he insisted that I bring Diamond Dallas Page along to babysit him and keep him out of trouble; DDP was $4,000—this was way before he was a star in WCW.

The problems started with Warrior, who had agreed but hadn't signed the contract. He called me up, complained about being away for two whole weeks, and demanded $50,000, doubling his payday. I was very distressed because that was going to come out of my profit. We had already told the promoters overseas that he was in, so we agreed to the new terms.

Fast-forward another few weeks, with the contracts drafted, and I'm at Skoler's office in New York City, and wrestlers who lived locally came in to sign contracts in person. At the same time, we were handling a deal between Jake Roberts and AAA to come in and be a top heel in Mexico, while we would run the U.S. shows. That meant that Jake was in the office that day, along with DDP, and they were in the waiting room while Warrior was on the phone with me and Ron, and it was all on speaker phone. It got heated and ugly, and Warrior now demanded $100,000 for the tour, the second time he had held me up for money, knowing that there was now some pre-publicity starting to happen about him heading to Southeast Asia.

When he demanded the extra money, I told him I couldn't do that. He said, "John, I need $100,000, or else I'm not going." I started yelling about how he agreed to $25,000, and then $50,000, and that there was no way he was getting the money. He said he wasn't going to go, and I told him to go fuck himself, and hung up.

Listening in from outside in waiting room was Jake. After I hung up, he stormed into the office raging. "You were going to pay that mother-fucker $50,000, and you're only paying me $15,000!" So I had to double his pay to $30,000, but not Dallas. That was the first time Jake held me up, a preview of things to come.

In fact, most of the big-name performers began to hold me up for more money. Talent talks to each other and they began to drive up their prices for this tour, of course after the overseas promoters had begun advertising. Greg Valentine agreed to an initial $6,000, and then held me up for another $1,500. Warlord demanded $8,500, which was $2,500 more than the agreed amount. I'm sure Jake had a hand in talking to all his fellow ex-WWF friends to hold me up. However, there was the honorable performers, like Kevin Sullivan, his wife Nancy, Bob Orton Jr., Konnan, Petty, Durham, The Power Twins, Sunny Beach, and The Barbarian, who all agreed to the original terms. Those who held me up took profit from me, and it still upsets me to this day.

Life as a promoter was not good; I didn't like it. The lesson I learned from all of it was that, except for a select few that I mentioned above, the wrestlers would bleed you dry if they saw an opportunity. They'd also try to position themselves to get to know people so they could do a run around you and take it over themselves. That meant a lot of people were kissing up to John Regna and Ron Skoler, and then the promoters overseas.

★ ★ ★ ★ ★

We spent two weeks overseas. It was a pretty cool experience. We had a great camera crew following us around. We went to Singapore and Hong Kong and had shows in the Philippines in Manila and Cebu City.

But there was trouble right from the start.

When we are all leaving through JFK airport in New York, Jake Roberts was just a massive troublemaker and had his personal demons in high gear. Singapore Airlines gave us our own private holding area, but Jake disappeared and could not be found. He realized that the airport was right near Jamaica, Queens, which was, at the time, a highly infested drug area and went out to score some drugs.

I was terrified about going to Singapore with some of these performers, since we'd all heard the stories about how the police dealt strictly with those who chewed gum, let alone what they did to those caught with hardcore drugs on them. We were presented with those rules at customs, including execution for narcotics. Did that stop these guys? Of course not.

The heat Jake created grew from there. Jake had with him a white albino cobra to use for his snake prop on the tour. He did not check it in through customs and kept it in his personal bag, which was cruel. At one point, he took the snake out of the bag and started chasing around our representative from Singapore Airlines, who then immediately reported him and the snake was confiscated. We had to find another snake for him when we got over there. (Admittedly, it wasn't as hard to procure a snake in Singapore as it might have been in, say, Chicago.)

A number of us were in the first-class section, and most of the plane was made up of wrestlers and the crew. Up front was me, Jake (who insisted on it as headliner), and DDP (Jake's babysitter, not that it helped).

The flight attendants came around with cocktails and Jake lit up a cigarette, but it wasn't a cigarette, exactly; he'd heat up a little bit of crack on a spoon and dip the cigarette into the liquid. The attendant asked me, "Would you like anything?" and I asked for a cocktail. Jake asked her, "Would you like some of this?" She was puzzled and politely declined. In short, Jake didn't give a shit and had no regard for anything.

At the back of the plane, some of the guys got drunk and rowdy. On the way to Singapore, we had a scheduled stop in Germany. As we were descending, I heard a commotion in the back of the airplane. Cowboy Bob had had a few too many and had misplaced his fanny pack. He was accusing the flight attendants of stealing it and getting really loud and obnoxious. People tried to calm him down, to no avail. When we finally landed in Germany, armed guards boarded the plane to deal with Orton. We'd been assigned a seasoned bodyguard, fixer, and tour manager, Eddie, who not only helped with the flights and customs, but also how to deal with situations like a drunk wrestler facing armed guards. As they were boarding the plane, Orton found the fanny pack in an overhead compartment. When the guards arrived, he got down on his knees and begged, "Please don't take me! I'm sorry! It was a mistake!" Eddie was able to diffuse the situation and we continued on to Singapore.

Others, like Warlord, were a problem in another way. Terry Szopinski is a nice guy, but it gets annoying real fast when he's always asking, "When are we going to get to the gym?" or "When am I going to be able to eat?"—sometimes with a menacing glare.

★ ★ ★ ★ ★

It was fun to see different parts of the world, and I quickly realized how good we had it in the U.S. In Manila, there were countless shacks with people living in really horrible conditions. It was the haves and the have-nots. We stayed at the Manila Hotel and it was beautiful, a true five-star hotel. The promoters arranged for us to have access to a private island for one day, with every amenity you could ask

IN CEBU CITY,
PHILIPPINES,
JULY 1993 WITH
SUNNY BEACH
AND THE POWER
TWINS.

for—beach, water skis, drinks, and a bevy of Filipina beauties. It was a paradise! We all had so much fun there.

Jake also insisted that his daughter, Brandy, be part of the tour, although I didn't have to pay her. However, I found it really strange to have to bring her along. They had a weird dynamic, and she was a young adult at the time.

Plenty of friendships developed on the tour, though, and that's when Greg Valentine and Madusa hooked up. I remember them buying Rolex watches there since they were so inexpensive.

And it was also a very beneficial trip for Paul Heyman, who ended up using many of the names later on his ECW shows. It was on that tour that he first put Ted Petty and Mike Durham together as a team, and they'd later gel as Public Enemy. It's where Paul E. hung out with Konnan for the first time, and he was in deep discussions with Kevin Sullivan and his wife, Nancy. Paul E. ended up leaving midway through the tour, going back to the States. I could tell he was getting bored, and he used the excuse that there was business he needed to attend to in New York. Paul ended up booking his own plane ticket back, and only asked for half of his guarantee, since he did not earn the full pay. I was grateful he was there, and happy to save a little money with him leaving early.

★ ★ ★ ★ ★

I was the figurehead of the IWAS, putting together matches with the guys, and I was front and center as the ring announcer, the Vince McMahon of the federation but without the money and power. When we did our press conferences, I was in the lead and introduced everyone else. As my assistant, I brought along Bruce Jacobs, who was my producer on the radio show. We shared the announcing duties.

DDP had an idea to draw a little heat. He wanted to take the microphone and introduce himself. So, every night when I was announcing him, DDP would push me down and I'd take a bump, and then he'd take the mic and give himself the intro he wanted.

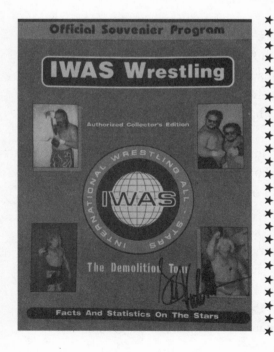

★ ★ ★ ★ ★ ★ ★ ★ ★ ★ ★

THE IWAS PROGRAM
FROM THE 1993
SOUTHEAST ASIA TOUR.

I also had to collect the money from the venues and pay the guys. All the wrestlers got 50 percent deposits before we went, and the balances were paid on the tour. Naturally, Jake Roberts tried to hold me up for more money again. On one day, we had a double shot, and both he and Dallas demanded double the pay.

★ ★ ★ ★ ★

Looking back on that tour, I learned things about professional wrestling that I didn't need to know, from the drugs and partying to the distrust and constant dissatisfaction from everyone. Wrestlers like to bitch and complain.

Listen, I'm not saying I was innocent, but with so much responsibility, I didn't get a ton of chances to let loose . . . I did one time, hooking up with a girl in the Philippines named Tess. My dalliance with her led to a lifetime of razzing from The Power Twins and Sunny Beach. She was a sweet girl, but tiny compared to me. When she was around the wrestling crew, she introduced me as her "Big Pork Barbecue." That's the nickname that the Twins and Beach call me to this day!

★ ★ ★ ★ ★

The last shows I promoted were separate from Ron Skoler, but still in conjunction with AAA. The 1996 shows were loosely attached to *TripleMania*, with a couple of shows in California and then a couple in Phoenix, at the Celebrity Theatre.

My final show was at the Arizona State Fairgrounds, and it was a fairly packed card, featuring mostly AAA guys and a few American heels. I brought Mil Mascaras in to headline, but he didn't have the cachet that he did back in his prime. I lost money on that show, and those last few shows in Arizona were the reason I finally got out of wrestling. I felt that too many people were taking advantage of me, like wrestlers who wanted reimbursement for plane tickets, which was a constant issue.

Mascaras, who was one of my wrestling heroes, was not the nicest guy in the world to work with. He upgraded himself, without my permission, to a first-class plane ticket, and then he showed up and wanted me to reimburse him for that. I didn't do it.

A year after I got out of the wrestling business, Mascaras was still calling me up asking for the money. On one occasion, my mom picked it up. She went, "Johnny, I don't understand what he's saying. He said Mascaras, Mr. Mascaras?" So I got on the phone.

"John, it's Mil Mascaras. I want to know about this plane ticket."

"Mil, I've been out of the fucking wrestling business for a year. I don't have your fucking plane ticket money, and I didn't even authorize it back then."

And I hung up.

★ ★ ★ ★ ★

One last Jake the Snake story.

I used to carry around a video camera, because I was always capturing highlights, backstage moments, touristy travel moments, things to add to our production. After a show in San Diego, I was in my hotel room getting ready to sleep, the phone rang, and it was Jake. He went, "Brother, do you have the video camera with you?" I said I did, and he asked, "I'm here with my girlfriend. I want you to film us having sex." I declined, but then he promised me an ounce of pot to do it. Hmm . . .

They came into my room, and his girlfriend was beautiful—but Jake was all drugged up and couldn't perform very much at all. *The Wrestling Observer Newsletter* would rate it a DUD. Jake took the tape, and I forgot all about it until a year later, when he called me and put his wife, Cheryl, on the phone.

"John, this is Cheryl Roberts. Is it true that you filmed my husband having sex with some whore in San Diego?"

I snapped at both of them.

"Listen, I don't know what kind of fucking bizarre world you two live in or what's going on in your lives. I'm not even going to enter this discussion with you, so you can both go fuck yourselves."

13.

THE WRESTLING
CONVENTION PIONEER

As a massive baseball fan, I'd been to a number of baseball card shows, where you got a chance to complete your sets and buy memorabilia. Often, there were retired players in attendance to sign autographs for a price. While I was doing my radio show, it occurred to me that something similar could work with professional wrestling.

I was right, even if the first convention I ran ended with me in jail.

It was called Wrestling Fans Fantasy Weekend; it took place on the weekend of August 25–26, 1990, and it was the first time that wrestlers and fans and merchants were all brought together in a convention setting. Previous conventions, like the WFIA events that I had attended, were aimed at fans who were deeply into pro wrestling, often doing newsletters or working on the periphery of the industry. Usually, a local wrestling promotion was involved and sent some wrestlers to the dinner, where awards were presented. It was all friendly and not-for-profit.

Whereas I saw the opportunity to make some money. The stars had aligned, as I had a wrestling radio show in a major market, plenty of contacts for wrestlers and vendors, and the time to do it. What I didn't have was the cash to get started upfront, so I needed investors. Enter the father-son real-estate team, Chris Liano and his son, Chris Jr. I met them through an ad call I went on. I told them about the plan, and they were fascinated by pro wrestling, big fans. They were interested in it right from the start. They were street-smart guys and good at the real-estate game.

They saw me as a conduit to working in the wrestling business. We formed a company called Bodyslam Sports for the first convention. I did the legwork and they financed it. They kept track of the money coming in and handled the payouts.

★ ★ ★ ★ ★

I wanted to make it convenient for people who would be traveling in from various places, and we tied it into WWF *SummerSlam*, which was in Philadelphia on the Sunday, and had a bus trip organized. Honestly, I don't know why I zoned in on the Royce Hotel, which later turned into the Ramada Hotel, across the street from LaGuardia Airport, though perhaps I'd been to a baseball card show there, since I went to them pretty frequently. It worked as a venue.

But now I needed names. It was a new concept for everybody, and I had to explain it. My main target was Sting, since I knew that he would be winning the NWA world title at some point in the near future. I figured that my relationship with the NWA would make that possible and asked them what it would cost. They presented a flat rate of $5,000.

★ ★ ★ ★ ★ ★ ★ ★ ★ ★

STING WAS
THE HEADLINER
AT MY FIRST
CONVENTION IN
1990.

From what I remember, you could sell photos, but they didn't want his autograph sold. I agreed to that since I knew he'd be a draw.

No one else cost anywhere near that much. Bruno Sammartino was the other name on my wish list, and he was around $2,000, but wouldn't let me charge anyone for an autograph. Everyone else was a little less, including Ricky Steamboat, who was a free agent, fresh off being NWA world champion; former NWA world champion Terry Funk; and, lastly, local boy "Cactus Jack" Mick Foley, whose career was just starting to take off. Big John Studd was booked but canceled at the last minute for health reasons.

Paul E. Dangerously just showed up, as did a number of other wrestlers, just to be a part of it and network, including a ton of indy guys such as Sunny Beach and The Power Twins. An older wrestler, Ox Baker, had a vendor table and was ahead of the game with T-shirts and other goodies for fans to buy.

Georgiann Makropoulos had a ton of connections, not only with Bruno, with whom she was really close, but also with people from the world of wrestling collectibles.

★ ★ ★ ★ ★ ★ ★ ★ ★ ★ ★ ★ ★

BRUNO SAMMARTINO
AND MY MOM AT THE
FIRST CONVENTION.

It was a big undertaking for me, and a real unknown, but it took on a life of its own quickly and just grew, to the point that I was already thinking about a second convention before the first one even happened.

★ ★ ★ ★ ★

Today, compared to wrestling conventions with close to a hundred guests, Wrestling Fans Fantasy Weekend is downright quaint. We had just six guests and around 25 dealers, but the place was jammed, with a few thousand fans making their way to the event from around the country.

The main thing that we should have done differently was the pricing structure. The admission charge was only five dollars and autographs were about the same, including photographs, and the bundle package was ridiculously low, ten dollars for everybody. It was way underpriced. My intent was not to gouge anybody.

There was no known market. It was a whole new thing for the wrestling business. You build it and think they will come. In the case of wrestling fan conventions, it was unique for the fans, because they'd never had the opportunity to meet a number of wrestlers at the same time. We drew a lot of regular fans but also the insiders, like Dave Meltzer from California.

I advertised it on SportsChannel. I did some radio advertising. I did *The Howard Stern Show* on K-Rock and *Mike and the Mad Dog* on WFAN. I definitely used my marketing skills to promote this in various ways, to create a lot of awareness for it. WCW had a TV show in the local market, hosted by Eric Bischoff, and they promoted it there. My own show was a great tool too, but was miniscule compared with the places I bought advertising.

There were two negatives from the event, and both involve (what else?) money.

Sting was late for his appearance, and barely interacted. It was obvious he didn't want to be there. I don't know how it worked between him and the office, or whether he got any of that money. Midway through his appearance, he got up and left. There were still a few hundred people waiting in line to get his autograph. I never found out why. I was really

★ ★ ★ ★ ★ ★ ★ ★ ★

**MY DAD DEEP IN
CONVERSATION
WITH RICKY
STEAMBOAT
AT THE FIRST
CONVENTION IN
AUGUST 1990.**

pissed off after that appearance. He had done the *Pro Wrestling Spotlight* show before the convention. I thought I had a good relationship with the guy. It was so upsetting. I was able to speak to him the next month and clear the air. I don't think he was fully informed about the terms of the deal. The Lianos contacted WCW and demanded a refund, and I believe that WCW agreed to repay half of the fee. But the aggressive way they handled the situation pissed off the powers that be in WCW, most of all, Jim Herd, who was the head executive there. Eventually, I was able to talk with Herd to smooth things over.

The other issue was the Lianos themselves. They had ulterior motives. They got these satin jackets made for themselves, with Bodyslam Sports embroidered on them. They made no secret that they wanted to be in the business: the kid wanted to be a wrestling manager, and the father thought he would become Vince McMahon overnight. Those were the egos that were involved there. I have no idea whether we made money on the convention—foolishly, I agreed to a three-way split—and I didn't work with them again. They tried to do another event in Connecticut later that year, which flopped when advertised performers cancelled or didn't show up. They faded out as quickly as they came in, and that was the last time I ever interacted with them.

★ ★ ★ ★ ★

During the run-up to the convention, Georgiann introduced me to an eccentric guy, a start-up promoter from New York, named Herb Abrams, who was planning on starting a wrestling company. Herb pitched me on the idea of doing a press conference to launch his UWF at the convention. No one knew who Herb was—but we sure did after the convention.

For whatever reason, I gave him the stage, and he talked up the debuting UWF, revealing his grandiose plans to take over the wrestling universe. He said he was fully funded, ready to take over the business as the number-one promoter, surpassing Vince McMahon and WCW owner Ted Turner rather quickly. Georgie had introduced him to Bruno, and Bruno introduced him to Lou Albano, and with those two credible legends aligned with the new UWF, it opened other doors for him. His press conference at the convention was memorable. Herb brought in Dangerous Dan Spivey and B. Brian Blair, who wound up having a pull-apart brawl to get some heat. But Herb doomed himself from the beginning in the press conference when he made the proclamations that Blackjack Mulligan would be his matchmaker (his booker) and that brawler Bruiser Brody would be wrestling for him. The only problem was that Mulligan was in jail at the time, and Brody had been murdered in Puerto Rico two years earlier.

For those who may have forgotten Herb or blocked him from their memory, he had grand plans and got UWF a spot on SportsChannel America. He hired a ton of wrestlers with name value like Paul Orndorff, Bam Bam Bigelow, Steve "Dr. Death" Williams, and even Colonel DeBeers with his pro-apartheid gimmick. Bruno was to be his color commentator, and Albano had his own interview segment. While UWF focused mainly on veterans, a few young stars, like David Sammartino, Stevie "Wild Thing" Ray, and Cactus Jack (whom he met at the convention), managed to make waves. That convention also introduced Herb to friends of mine, like The Power Twins and Sunny Beach, who played prominent roles with UWF.

He was a funny guy, small in stature but a larger-than-life personality, with a huge ego, and someone likable, if you could sift through his bullshit. His eccentricities were legendary, from his aversion to perfume, to his explosions of anger when he saw lipstick on a cigarette. Bizarre for sure! His downfall was the demons inside him that were caused by cocaine abuse. I remember many times speaking to him on the phone, and you could hear him snorting coke. He spent some money advertising on my radio show, and I had him and the UWF wrestlers on the air many times. I was later hired by him to run his UWF Convention in January of 1991 and help set up his live NYC debut at the Penta Hotel. I would guess that 75 percent of the crowd were *Pro Wrestling Spotlight* listeners. Overall, it went okay that day, but later the checks bounced to the hotel, so I had to repair the relationship before I did my own Weekend of Champions in 1991. Herb had left a sour taste in their mouth.

Out of plenty of outrageous Herb Abrams stories, this is one that takes the cake. A devoted listener of mine, a 14-year-old kid named Andrew Goldberger, had started a newsletter, called *Around the Ring*. Abrams sued him for libel, as Andrew had reported that Herb had bounced some checks. Though the newsletter might have been read by 10 people, that didn't stop Herb. Fortunately Andrew's father got him out of it. (On a related note, Abrams once had a jobber named "Davey Meltzer.")

UWF ran from 1991 to 1994, and its weekly show was called *Fury Hour*. The promotion put on one pay-per-view, before Herb died in 1996. He went out in a blaze of glory, naked, covered in cocaine and Vaseline, partying with two hookers while he trashed his office with a baseball bat.

In late 2019, I was interviewed for VICE's *Dark Side of the Ring* TV show about Herb Abrams, offering up my experiences. Sheesh, what a character.

★ ★ ★ ★ ★

Now, for the arrest!

We sold enough tickets to fill a bus to *SummerSlam*, which was at the Spectrum in Philly on a Sunday night, but not enough for a second coach. We had a wad of tickets leftover, as we'd bought 100. The plan was to sell them at the event, which was sold out. Naïve and optimistic, we arrived at the venue, and I got off the bus and immediately began selling tickets. Since it was a sellout, I sold the tickets above face value. The first person who approached me asked the price and when I told him, he pulled out a badge and said I was being arrested for ticket scalping! He was an undercover police officer. I was put in handcuffs and carted away. A few of the fans from the bus trip, including Fred the Elephant Boy from *Howard Stern*, saw it all unfold.

I was brought into the holding area in the arena, still in cuffs. Sgt. Slaughter was heading into the arena, and he saw me and just looked and said, "John Arezzi?" And he just started laughing and walked away.

Next, the other scalpers and I were put in a small van and taken to a county jail in town. It was a Sunday night, so I wasn't able to go in front of a judge until the next day. I was in a cell with five hardened men.

"What are you in here for, man?"

"I do a radio show in New York, and I got arrested for selling tickets." They all started laughing. There was a famous late-night TV personality, Joe Franklin, and they started calling me Joe Franklin in the cell. I spent the night on the hard concrete floor, and it smelled of piss.

After the *SummerSlam* show concluded, my fans on the bus found out where I was being held, so a bus filled with wrestling fans tried to get me out of jail—and, of course, they didn't release me, since I had to see a judge.

The next day, I saw the judge and was released on my own recognizance. I had an appearance ticket and I had to go back about a month later to pay a fine.

I had just moved my radio show to WBAB-AM, a bigger station, and my debut on the station was the Sunday after the convention. Callers teased me, "John, what happened last week? You didn't get on the bus with us!" I didn't hide it: I told them what happened.

The Lianos didn't want any part of it, wouldn't help pay the fine, and left me in the lurch, and they were upset that the tickets had not been sold. Guests like Paul E. Dangerously would bring up the arrest on the air, which I just laugh at now, but at the time it was embarrassing.

★ ★ ★ ★ ★

Even after the sour taste that I had with the partnership, I definitely saw the value of doing another event, and started thinking about what that could look like the following year. I did want to hold it around the same time as *SummerSlam*, which was at Madison Square Garden, meaning I didn't need to organize a bus trip again (and therefore avoid more jail time). I set the dates for the same weekend as the first convention, August 24–25, 1991. My financial partner for this one was Howard Kotlus, who was a listener of my show and was an accountant on Long Island, and it all went a lot smoother.

I changed the name of the gathering to Weekend of Champions to distance myself from the Lianos, and I liked the name better. The theme for me was literally bringing in former champions. I targeted real legends: WCW champion Ric Flair; former NWA champion Lou Thesz; former WWWF world champion "Superstar" Billy Graham; and two-time world champ "The Living Legend" Bruno Sammartino. The missing name from my wish list was "Nature Boy" Buddy Rogers. Once again, Georgiann came through. Rogers didn't really understand what I was asking him to do, but after speaking to him a couple of times and with Georgie's endorsement, he was on board. It all just fell into place and it became this amazing first-time event where all these champions were together. I added Rick Rude as a draw for the newer fans, and Woman who was making a name for herself in WCW, and I brought in manager Jim Cornette, to do autographs and photos and also because I wanted him to host the memorabilia auction.

Later on, I started getting calls from everybody, since they all wanted to be a part of it. I'd say I was actually besieged with calls. I had to think of my budget. I couldn't say no to Fabulous Moolah when she called, since she was the perennial women's champion. I added Johnny Valiant, former WWWF tag team title holder. Many others I allowed to come in and have tables in the ballroom. My dealer tables sold out pretty quickly, with 50 jam-packing the venue.

Flair's appearance was complicated by politics. There were plenty of rumors that he was leaving WCW when his contract was up. I reached out to Kevin Sullivan, who was a friend, and asked him to look into Flair doing a convention, with or without WCW's approval. Kevin said he'd help, and he did. He put me directly in touch with Flair. He asked for $5,000 fee to appear, and I agreed.

But it almost didn't happen. Just before the convention, Bobby Heenan appeared on WWF television with the WCW world title belt, indicating that Ric Flair was coming. I went, "Oh shit, he's going to the WWF." I was immediately worried that Vince McMahon would pull Flair from the show, and deep down, I knew it was going to happen, especially given all the negative things I'd said about WWF on my radio show and elsewhere.

Ric was the only performer that I had not signed a contract with—I'd sent it to him, and we'd talked, but he had never signed anything. After several calls, I got him on the phone and he assured me that he'd keep his word and would be there. In the end, he came and had a great time. He actually stayed longer than he had to, and even climbed into the ring that we had set up in the main hall with the dealer tables, to help the auction that Cornette was running. Performers got a 50-50 split on whatever was sold, and Flair got several thousand for a used ring robe.

Flair and I had known each other from backstage at WCW events dating back a few years. He shared a story: "A lot of you don't know this,

I'M WITH LEGENDS AT MY WEEKEND OF CHAMPIONS EVENT IN 1991;
FROM LEFT, LOU THESZ, BUDDY ROGERS, THE FABULOUS MOOLAH,
RIC FLAIR, WOMAN (NANCY SULLIVAN), AND RICK RUDE.

but I threw John out of the dressing room last year, because I felt our business was not being protected. But I have learned to respect him and I really am happy that I came to this. I've seen another side of the fans, and we're all in this together." He cut a well-received promo, and he genuinely had a good time.

Again, I underpriced it, with a five-dollar entry fee, and autographs and photos were too low. I couldn't help myself from thinking like a fan instead of a greedy businessman. We had a much bigger turnout, close to 5,000 people, so it wasn't a financial disaster, as my investor got his money back. But when it came down to the end, I didn't make much—certainly not what we could have made.

There's a famous photo of Bruno and Buddy Rogers together from the event, which almost didn't happen, since Bruno couldn't stand Buddy. Right from the start, Bruno said it would be a dealbreaker if he was even in the same room as Buddy for autographs. Once again, the amazing Georgiann made magic; she had run fan clubs for both men, and the two came together for two photos, one of the two of them together and one with Georgiann. I will label that photo as a bit tense and uncomfortable.

One special guest showed up from WWF, in a disguise just so she could be part of it, and that was "Sensational" Sherri Martel. She hung out with Flair and Rude and had lunch with the wrestlers during their break on Saturday.

The partying after night one was memorable. Everybody was in the bar that night, the two Nature Boys, Buddy Rogers and Ric Flair, drinking together; Flair being Flair, he's buying drinks, he's dancing around, and he's the center of attention. Rogers was in great spirits.

The fans came from everywhere, all over the world. It was just such a great time to have all these legends in the same room. There was really no backlash or anyone telling me they didn't have a good time. All the performers got paid, everyone made money. And I didn't get arrested.

★ ★ ★ ★ ★

What to do for an encore? There was no question there was a market for these conventions, and once a year seemed about right. For the event in

August 1992, I really wanted to have a gathering that would satisfy the hardcore fans with the legends, but I also wanted to try to bring in hot commodities that had never done similar signings.

My first idea was to reunite the Valiant Brothers with Captain Lou Albano, since it had never been done before. Another was having Sammartino and his student who turned on him, Larry Zbyszko. Through the process, I regularly consulted friends like Dave Meltzer, Wade Keller, and others, and Jushin Liger came up as a name that would be interesting and unique. He was a favorite of the hardcore wrestling fans, a Japanese wrestler who was considered one of the best in the world.

For the Valiants, I was confident, as I'd worked with Captain Lou many times, and he was open to the idea. Jimmy Valiant was completely on board. But Johnny, when I contacted him, said he wanted to think about it for a while. Eventually he said he didn't want to do it and never gave me a straight answer on why. At that time, I believe he was in discussions with WWF for a return as a manager, and he didn't want to piss them off if they found out he was appearing at an Arezzi event. After all, that was the year I had the most heat with McMahon and WWF. That disappointed me, as I brought him in the year before when he asked. I did bring in Albano and Jimmy Valiant.

Bruno was always great to work with, and he had his autobiography coming out, so came in for a third straight event—that's drawing power! Larry was surprised when I contacted him, but agreed to it. Unless I was getting worked, there still seemed to be some sort of issue between him and Bruno, something lingering there, a dislike that neither of them ever explained to me.

Liger I booked through a Japanese photographer, who shot often in the U.S. Liger had been in and out a lot in WCW, so he was a known quantity here. Filling out my lineup were names who had never done a convention previously, such as Killer Kowalski, Wendi Richter (and it was a bonus that Albano was there), Ivan Koloff, and Nikolai Volkoff. These were legends, but they were also cost-effective, since I'd learned from the overpayments to Sting and Ric Flair, as well as others like "Superstar" Billy Graham and Buddy Rogers. To my eye, there may not

have been a main eventer, like Sting or Flair, but there were so many moving parts that there was something for every fan.

I brought in Eddie Gilbert, who'd been a friend for a few years and who had pestered me about coming in for one of my conventions. Though we were pretty close, I was not aware of Eddie's personal demons and how they were taking over his life. At the end of the convention, I was really upset with him, as he was obviously on something, whatever drugs it was, and he was pretty out of it.

My money partner this go-round was one of regular listeners, who had offered his help and wanted a bigger role than in the previous conventions that he'd helped at. John Parker was a Long Island businessman, and a really sweet guy. It went well. John died in 2016 but his son Ian keeps in touch with me, and he told me that the convention his father ran with me was a memorable highlight they had shared together over the years.

As for the top moment of the third event, it was undoubtedly the reunion between Bruno and Zbyszko. It was a big deal. Bill Apter, in particular, was just over the top about the reunion happening. Zbyszko was injured and had his arm in a sling. We sat them beside each at the tables, and there was a key handshake between them that was documented by plenty of photographers. The interaction, including the handshake, was what I'd describe as cordial, not warm. I had hoped that placing them beside each other would rekindle something, but they didn't really interact much with each other during the event.

This was also the first convention where vendors brought in their own guests, and they included Kerry Von Erich, who, from what I saw, was not in the best of shape and was battling his own demons; people were definitely shocked to see him there since he hadn't been advertised.

"The Lightning Kid" Sean Waltman wanted to come in, but my budget was used up, so I comped him a table to sell whatever he wanted. He never forgot that kindness, and it helped get him in front of key people. A year later, he was in WWF as the 1-2-3 Kid.

Overall, I was much more experienced at running conventions, so I wasn't panicked at any point. More importantly, I wasn't working with partners who were in it to get into the wrestling business and take advantage of me. I didn't have the stress of wondering whether Ric Flair was going to show up.

Since I left with such a good feeling, there really wasn't any question that I was going to do a fourth convention.

★ ★ ★ ★ ★

The 1993 convention was very different because I was promoting wrestling shows at the same time, and had built a relationship with Mexico's AAA promotion and Konnan. So I was thinking the convention could help build the brand, IWAS, while still bringing in some unique names. I had confidence in my ability to pull it off and in my place in the wrestling world, as evidenced by my letter in the convention program: "Don't forget to have fun here. The lines may be a little long, but the end result will be worth the wait. The major wrestling promotions in this country don't seem to give a hoot whether you enjoy yourself or not these days, and when was the last time they allowed you to meet, greet, and socialize with the stars? I can't remember either."

The one name I wanted to get, but didn't know if it was possible, was the original Sheik, who had never, ever done anything like it before. On my side, I'd developed a business relationship with Sheik's nephew, Sabu, from shows I promoted, but it was Kevin Sullivan who made it possible.

During the weekend, other than shaking his hand, I had no contact with him. Everything went through Sullivan. Sheik's wife, Joyce, was there, and she got the money from me. He stayed in character the whole time, holding a large machete, banging it on the table occasionally to scare the shit out of anyone who was close. I wish I'd taken a photo of us together, but the fact was that he was a little intimidating and, in a way, I didn't want to lose the mystique that surrounded him.

The 1993 list of guests had many connections to shows that I had run previously. Jake the Snake was there to sign autographs, and he was an asshole, just as he always was. Other names were Greg "The Hammer" Valentine, Madusa, Cowboy Bob Orton, Jimmy Snuka, Sensational Sherri, Kevin Sullivan, and Woman. It was a hardcore fan's dream.

The new thing was a live wrestling show, which I promoted in the ballroom on the Friday night. There were some up-and-comers on this show, like Sabu, Konnan, Louie Spicolli, Chris Candido and Tammy Fytch, Tazz, and Bubba Ray as Mondo Klean. Terry Funk was a featured performer, and he worked against Kevin Sullivan. Sabu, with Sheik in his corner, worked against Konnan for the very first time.

Also for the first time, I used all my own money to promote the convention. I'd done the successful IWAS tour, and I made some money through the AAA shows that I was associated with alongside Ron Skoler.

I didn't lose money, but I didn't make a lot of money either, certainly not enough to live off for a year. Attendance-wise, it did okay, but nothing will ever come close to the numbers at the 1991 convention. Everyone left happy.

When I look back now, I wish I'd hired a professional camera crew to film the actual wrestling show. There is handheld footage of it that has been out there in the marketplace. It's not easy to watch though.

Going towards 1994, I had been planning another convention, but I was getting to the end of my rope with the wrestling business. It never happened.

★ ★ ★ ★ ★

It wasn't that hard to stop promoting conventions. They were a lot of work for not enough return. Plus, WWF took the idea of the fan interaction and made it another revenue stream for them. They were starting things like breakfast with the wrestlers and in-ring photo shoots on special pay-per-view weekends. That grew to the Fan Axxess events that take over convention centers now on *WrestleMania* or *SummerSlam* weekends. I didn't have the resources to compete with WWF, or even WCW, which ran some events for fans, like a cruise.

The legacy I created is obvious, with wrestling conventions dotting the landscape on a regular basis across the U.S. When you create something good, someone else will always be out there wanting to take advantage and trying to replicate the success. Tommy Fierro was a kid who followed me, and I mean a kid—he was only 16 when he put on a convention after I had thrown in the towel. Kudos to him. He asked my permission, and I had him on my radio show to promote it.

In 2019, after a self-imposed break to get a real job and start a family, Fierro ran another convention in New Jersey. He invited me to be a part of it and even presented me with an award, which was so nice. I'd been in hiding from wrestling and was only starting to reemerge. He was so gracious and appreciative to me for setting the bar, pioneering it all. That was a good moment for me, and it made me feel really good, even if only a very small part of the audience knew who I was. At the next convention Tommy ran, I got to interview Bob Backlund on the stage. And I plan on making more appearances for him and others I paved the way for.

14.

MEET JOHN ALEXANDER

As *Pro Wrestling Spotlight* was fading into the sunset, finally going off the air for good in January 1995, I started working with my IWAS partner, John Regna, at World Entertainment Associates out of New Jersey, to make ends meet.

Regna booked talent worldwide, from Jose Feliciano to LaToya Jackson and others. He also was the U.S. rep for the Peking Circus, which was one of my responsibilities while working there. John and I were still trying to drum up business for IWAS, but the shows were too few and far between.

Eventually, I came to realize that I had to put wrestling behind me. I had tried to make a living at it, but the money was not there.

I was defeated, both personally and professionally, and I really didn't like the person that I was becoming, in part because of how untrustworthy everyone was in the wrestling business.

How bad was it? I was almost 40 and made only about $12,000 in 1996. There were no savings to my name, no health insurance, not even a car. I was about to declare bankruptcy because I had creditors and people that were owed money. I was at the bottom of the barrel—and my weight had ballooned to a high of 388 pounds.

What I didn't expect was that my life was about to go full country, and that John Arezzi would be put in the rear-view mirror.

★ ★ ★ ★ ★

Scouring the newspapers for jobs—now there's a dated reference—I came across a small ad in *Newsday* for an account executive for WMJC-FM 94.3, Long Island's new country music station. I reached out and was invited in for an interview. But there was a problem: I didn't have any suits. Wait, that's not true. I had suits for wrestling, like a purple sports jacket, where you are aiming to stand out. Still, I pieced something relatively conservative together, and met with Barbara Ravinette, who was the sales manager. For some reason, she liked me, even though I wore dark glasses and was almost 400 pounds. I was invited back to meet the general manager, Tony Michaels. Finally: an in. Tony was an old-school radio guy, getting his start at WNYG and WBAB-AM years ago; he was a local guy, and I'd dealt with him previously when I brokered time on WBAB/WGBB. Plus, we shared an Italian connection; he had changed his name to a more generic-sounding one.

That was something I knew I needed to do too, to get distance from my pro wrestling background. I became "John Alexander." Why Alexander? I really enjoyed watching Jason Alexander as George Costanza on *Seinfeld*. He liked baseball too.

Barnstable Broadcasting owned a number of stations in the market, which could mean more possibilities for me. I really wanted the job, but Tony wasn't sold. He sat me down and said, "John, I like you, but look at you. I don't know if you can do this or not." I pleaded with him that I needed the job, that I knew country music, and that I knew how to sell. I asked him for 30 days to prove myself, and Barbara pushed him to give me a chance, reminding Tony how often the salespeople came and went. He consented.

That night, back in my apartment, I dropped to my knees and prayed. "God, thank you for this opportunity. From this day forward and for the rest of my life, I'm going to be a better person. I'm always going to be honest with anyone I do business with. I'm always going to under-promise and over-deliver and I'm going to change the way I operate in my life." I just decided that I was never going to try to take advantage of anyone—it was the wrestling business that I was trying to purge.

The goal was to travel a different path in my life, and be more faithful. I always believed in God, but I wanted to open up that line of communication deeper for the first time. In short, my life just turned around.

I borrowed some money to get a few new sport jackets, and I borrowed a car from a friend of my mom's. After a very short training period, I had my first appointment. It was at a nightclub that was about to open up on Long Island, in Farmingdale, called Tommy Knockers, and they were going to do some country nights and bring in some Nashville talent. I went in to talk to the person running the club, and who was sitting at the bar but wrestler Bubba Ray Dudley! Apparently, he was a friend of someone's from the club. I went into the manager's office, gave him my sales pitch, and got the sale.

Later that month, I made some more sales, so after my 30-day trial, I was confident, and sure enough, I was hired. In the second month, it was going gangbusters with sales and closing deals, and I was named salesperson of the month, as a part of a great team. I was mentored by legendary Long Island salesperson Charlie Cirelli, who showed me the art of dealing with nightclubs. Going into 1997, I was one of the top billers for Country 94.3 WMJC, and I got a chance to get really integrated in the country music business. I got the Matty T's Roadhouse account, and made lifelong friends with Matty and his staff. His club was a great place to showcase emerging country acts, which we promoted on WMJC, and everyone made money.

In a good example of how the world works in mysterious ways, the program director at the country station was Jim Asker. Twenty-five years later, he had an office down the hall from me in Nashville, where he was the country music editor at *Billboard* magazine. The music director was another Long Islander, Suzanne Borda, whom I'd worked with at WNYG years previously, when she was a newscaster, but she changed her name for broadcasting to Suzanne Alexander. We immediately connected with each other over the same fake last name. But she had a passion for country music. She's in Nashville now, and I helped get her a job at GAC television. Suzanne and Jim remain two of my closest friends.

In 1997, I made a living wage, about $35,000, and got out of bankruptcy. The borrowed car that I had? After the second month, the general manager, Tony, who was hesitant in hiring me, loaned me money to buy a car. He also allowed me to trade myself out some new suits (trading airtime for goods/services). I was so appreciative of people who believed in me and gave me the opportunity. As 1997 progressed, I got bigger clients, like larger car dealerships. My billing was starting to do really well. I won the award for the WMJC salesperson of the year.

One client, though, was very familiar.

The Attitude Era had just started to take off in the WWF. Because of my wrestling background, I was asked by the station to try to secure WWF as an advertiser, as it had been advertising with many competitors. I was really trepidatious; I didn't know if I wanted to do that, because of my history. Pete Anastasiadis, who was head of promotions for the station, talked me into it. A deal with WWF could provide the station with tickets to give away on air and at live remotes.

I set up a meeting with Hugo Maslich, who was one of the people that handled media buying for WWF, and his area was primarily New York but also the Northeast. I met him at the station, and I was John Alexander. He gave the station a shot with a little advertising buy, and we gave away some tickets. The station got a big response from the contest. I never told Hugo that I was John Arezzi, because I knew that if he did any checking on the name, the account would go out the window because of my past issues with the McMahon family. He saw that I knew a lot about the wrestling business, and he, Pete, and I would have breakfast once a month to secure the ad buys for WWF's local shows and arrange ticket giveaways.

★ ★ ★ ★ ★

Like WWF and its Attitude Era, country music was also hot, and New York City had launched its first country station in many years,

New Country Y107, owned by Big City Radio. Compared to WMJC, which reached about half of Long Island, WYNY was huge, with three towers, one in New York, one in New Jersey, and one in upstate New York. The owners also had stations in Chicago and Los Angeles, and in each, they'd arranged for an increased signal coverage. I was intrigued by the concept. When Garth Brooks played Central Park, they were a big part of it. WMJC considered Y107 the enemy as it began taking advertisers from it.

With my love of country music growing, I was seriously mulling a switch to this bigger station. But the difference maker was a new general manager that came into WMJC, Ron Gold, whom I didn't get along with at all and with whom I had an uncomfortable history. I didn't want to work for him. And many others didn't either. Barbara Ravinette left, and a new manager came in, a young hot-shot named Michael who was more interested in flirting with the women account executives than growing business. He left after a while, and as I didn't get considered for that job, I saw it as a slap in the face. I felt that I could run a sales department. I decided to reach out to the opposition, Y107.

★ ★ ★ ★ ★

It took a couple of tries, but I finally got in to meet with someone at Y107, Helene Wexler Gold, who was the general sales manager. She changed my life. Helene was impressed that I was getting money from the record companies, because they weren't getting a lot from them, even though the station had a much better reach and they were in New York City. It was all about relationships, really. At WMJC, Jimmy and Suzanne would take me into the meetings with the labels, including dinners with new artists like Sara Evans, Loretta Lynn's daughters "The Lynns," and others. I was given the opportunity to sell some advertising and work out some promotions. I was really starting to meet people in Nashville for the first time.

Helene took a shot with me, and I was offered a job in July 1998 to go over to Y107 in New York City. They had sales offices on 42nd Street, right across the street from Grand Central Station—what a great location. The studios were located in Westchester, New York, and we'd have sales meetings there as well.

At WMJC, there were some hurt feelings when I left, especially with Jim Asker, who had been very loyal to the station. He saw me as a traitor for going my own way. He didn't talk to me for about six months, but we eventually patched that up.

The move was the right thing for me, not just because my income doubled compared with the previous year. I became a really seasoned salesperson, and it helped to be at a big station that had a big budget for promotions.

And I became passionate and knowledgeable about country music. It helped that Helene sent me to Nashville to meet with people at the record labels, to try to figure out how we could generate revenue from them.

It was a real eye-opener the first time I traveled to Nashville to drum up business for Y107. I would meet with the marketing executives and the radio promotion teams. I learned that without the station's airplay support, the marketing dollars would be hard to get. My first meeting was with Sony Music, which included Columbia Records, Epic Records, and Monument Records. So that initial meeting was with some high-level people, and I went in there and said, "Listen, you guys aren't really spending any money with us. What can we do?" The executive across from me took a piece of paper, crumpled it up, and threw it at me. "You know why we don't spend any money with you? Because of your fucking playlist. You guys don't do what you're supposed to do." Later, I learned that was Jack Lameier, who was in charge of music promotion for all of Sony Music in Nashville.

Our program director was Darrin Smith, and he had been the station's program director before it flipped from New Wave to country. He didn't have a passion for country, and we'd butt heads on songs, so I understood the slap from Jack. Darren had a very conservative way of adding songs to the rotation—the opposite of what the Nashville music community wanted. Then I heard the same thing from every label on Music Row.

Y107 was a country station in the nation's biggest market, but it was not being programmed in a way to allow the new and developing acts to get airplay. In country, it's really important to help break new acts, and if a label needs a favor, you play ball with them—it's about relationships.

Back in New York, I sat with the president of Big City Radio, who was also the general manager of the station, and my sales manager, Helene, and I shared what I had learned. Essentially, our program director was not respected, but our music director, Shari Roth, was loved. The head of promotion was Jason Steinberg; he was a brilliant strategist and had great relationships with the labels. But Darrin was not one they warmed to.

One afternoon, I got a call from the top radio promotion guy in Nashville, Scott Borchetta, who at the time (before founding Big Machine Label Group and propelling Taylor Swift to superstardom) was the vice president for DreamWorks Records. He had a song that was moving up the charts all over the country, "How Do You Like Me Now?!" by Toby Keith. He told me direct that the station needed to get on this song. I told him I'd talk to my superiors, and I did. The song was added, and it changed everything: it was the breakthrough we needed. A week later DreamWorks marketing people called with a huge ad buy. And Toby Keith was given to Y107 to headline a huge Halloween party on the USS *Intrepid* in New York Harbor.

My bosses realized that I was now getting calls from the record labels in Nashville—because word spreads quickly there, as it's a very small, incestuous community. These were people that should have been calling the program director. From then on, I was included in the weekly music

★ ★ ★ ★ ★ ★ ★ ★ ★ ★

MINDY MCCREADY VISITS THE WMJC-FM STUDIOS IN 1998. SHE TRAGICALLY TOOK HER OWN LIFE YEARS LATER.

meetings, and I had a vote as to what was going on the air. One I know that I helped get played was Gary Allan's "Smoke Rings in the Dark." I was a lobbyist for music I believed in. And Shari was on the same page most of the time.

Before too long, I was going to Nashville every other month, and we were getting ad buys for the big stars' new releases and emerging baby acts. Then some labels would call to fly me in when they were introducing new talent. The record company revenue was not even my main business, since I had so many other accounts, but I just got so into it. I loved the music, I loved learning about new talent, I loved being respected by the record companies in town. My billing was going through the roof for all my other accounts, as they loved what I was doing, and so did I.

One of my main jobs was detailing with retailers on price and position programs—Walmart, Sam Goody, FYE, all the biggest record retailers. So there would be a Y107 section at a record store. FYE or Sam Goody would place the advertising buy with us, they'd get money from

A RECORD STORE SIGNING WITH DWIGHT YOAKAM IN 1999 WHILE I WAS DIRECTOR OF MUSIC MARKETING FOR NEW YORK COUNTRY STATION Y107 IN NEW YORK CITY.

the labels, and the labels got price and positioning in the store, which was key to them, especially with a niche market like country.

We'd do record release parties or meet and greets at retailers, and I dealt with the likes of Dwight Yoakam, Suzy Bogguss, and Deana Carter. I didn't mind taking a chance on a newcomer, even if it didn't work out. On separate occasions, I brought Kenny Chesney and Brad Paisley to the New York area for signings, and the turnouts were not great, but these two artists broke through in a huge way not long after.

The station was doing incredible things, including a deal with the World Trade Center with free lunchtime concerts in between the towers. A Top 40 station booked talent one day and Y107 got Thursday afternoons. I didn't put the deal together, but I was called in to get a music retailer sponsor for the concert series. That ended up being Sam Goody. We had CDs on sale at the concerts, and often a meet and greet with big-name talent, from the Dixie Chicks to Tim McGraw. There were other big-name sponsors too, like Chevrolet. The last concert there was the Thursday before the attack on the twin towers on September 11, 2001. I'd been at the towers every week for a couple of summers in a row and knew people working there, like security and tech people, all a part of the bigger community. To this day, I've never been able to go back. It was such a bright spot in my life, and I don't know who was killed. I knew many of them on a first-name basis, and still not knowing who survived the attack haunts me to this day.

★ ★ ★ ★ ★

Oh, as for wrestling at Y107? WWF and Hugo came with me and started advertising on the station. Promotions with WWF followed too, including events with advertisers and my old pal, Mick Foley.

★ ★ ★ ★ ★

It was a great ride at Y107, but all great rides come to an end.

In early 2000, we showed up at work, and all the upper management was gone. The station had been sold to a group with Hispanic

A 2018 Y107 REUNION DINNER FEATURED, BACK LEFT TO RIGHT,
ANASTASIA KAVALIS-MIANO, VINNY DEMASTRO, JASON STEINBERG,
JIM KERR, AND RAY ROSSI, AND FRONT, HELENE WEXLER-GOLD
(WHO ALSO RECRUITED ME FOR THE GAC JOB), JILL SCHLESINGER,
LISA SMITH, AND ME.

ownership. There was no notice, no warning. The programming team stayed the same, but I saw the writing on the wall immediately. I knew that it would not stay country, let alone broadcast in English. Sure enough, it later became a Spanish station in 2002.

I got a call out of the blue from my old sales manager, Helene. She'd quickly been hired by Jones Media America (the ad sales arm of Jones Media Networks), which had recently started Great American Country, a start-up music channel, to compete with the gigantic Country Music Television (CMT). They were looking for someone to do what I'd done at Y107, to grow ad sales but on a national level. She asked me about interviewing for the job. The catch was that the job was in Nashville. I interviewed and got the job, and 20 years later, Nashville is still my home.

15.

BIG COUNTRY

The idea behind Great American Country (GAC) was to have a cost-efficient TV network that would feature music videos of country music stars, since country music was so hot. Jones Media Networks wanted its piece of the pie.

It took several rounds of interviews, including a trip to Denver, which is where Jones had its headquarters, for me to be offered the job as director of music marketing. I started in July 2000. My list of references in Nashville, people I'd done business with, was rich and extensive. Everyone in Nashville loved me, as they knew I always tried to do the right thing for their artists, and went out of my way to try to get exposure for an artist or get a song added to a playlist. I believe I gave Jim Murphy, the liaison from Jones closest to the Nashville labels, about 20 names, and he talked to them all. All said I would be a great hire.

But it was not an easy decision to move to Nashville, as my heart was in Long Island. My nephew, Dominic, was three years old, and he and I had already bonded big time. I lived in the apartment downstairs from them, renting it from my sister Donna and brother-in-law Thomas DiBiase (no relation to Ted "The Million Dollar Man" DiBiase!), and our mother was in another apartment nearby. She needed constant attention. Dominic was the son I never had.

It had not been an easy ride, though. Dominic was often ill growing up. The house they were living in had mold, and he was always getting sick, he had seizures, he was in and out of hospitals. He was fragile, and I didn't want to be away from him.

Donna and I talked during the whole interview process. She was practical: "But Johnny, what are they going to pay you?" At Y107, I made close to $90,000 in 1999. So I told her that if I was offered $125,000, I'd have to take it. She warned me not to blow the job by asking for too much money.

Gary Schoenfeld was running Jones Media Networks, and he extended the offer, which was $110,000 plus commissions. I mentioned I had been thinking of more and asked for $150,000. He countered with $125,000. I'll never forget it; I took out a little piece of paper and wrote $135,000, a little bold of me but I felt confident that they wanted me. Deep down I didn't want to leave Dominic and have my sister Donna be the sole caretaker for Snooky. But the decision was made when, to my surprise, Gary agreed to the $135,000. Holy shit.

I asked for a day to talk to my family, which was fine. I called my sister after the interview, and she just went, "What is it? What's the number?" I told her, and she shrieked and said, "You have to take it."

I resigned from Y107 and moved to Nashville in July 2000, which was a very hard thing for me to do. But I kept the one-bedroom basement apartment at my sister's, because my brother-in-law was only charging me $500 a month, and that worked out, as I often had meetings in New York and could see my family. Before I moved to Nashville, I hunted around for an apartment and found a beautiful place for $580 a month.

For the first time in my life, I had a serious income.

★ ★ ★ ★ ★

The challenge for me was selling more than just local radio advertising for the first time. I had to quickly learn about national radio sales, and packaging the buys from Cathy Csukas, who ran the ad sales for radio. I also had to learn television sales and Internet sales. The Internet wasn't new, but it was only just getting to the point where ad sales mattered to companies online. I put together cross-platform packages: TV, radio, and Internet. Initially the website was CountryStars.com and then it turned into GACTV.com.

I had a wide variety of things to sell, especially on the radio front, as Jones Radio Networks programmed about 20 percent of the radio stations in the U.S., often in the smaller towns and cities. The programming was done out of Seattle and Denver, so I had to get to know the people who ran those offices. Jones Radio also syndicated programs, like country air personalities Bill Cody and Lia Knight. But their crown jewel at the time was Delilah, who hosted the number-one adult contemporary evening show in America.

Around Nashville, there were plenty of people to get to know too; even with those I had previous relationships with, I had to convince them that this little television entity, GAC, was going to be of value to them and their artists.

GAC was run on a shoestring budget. The production values were rudimentary, and the studios were in Denver. Everything came out looking low-budget, all the shows, so the labels were hesitant to put their artists on the station. Think *Wayne's World* (and it was called that by more than one of my label clients, partially because the president of GAC at the time was Jeff Wayne), something shot in a suburban basement, and you're not far off. One bad experience happened with Rascal Flatts, where they'd done a TV special, shot at the studio in Denver, and it turned out so bad that the label was embarrassed and didn't want it on the air. When I started going in to speak with the labels, their attitude was that GAC should just play videos and not do any original programming.

We were always being compared with Country Music Television, which was the major country station and way above us in ad buys, content, production values—everything. They were Goliath and we were David coming into the market in Nashville.

★ ★ ★ ★ ★

My solution to the labels was to propose partnerships on album launch specials or showcases, where the label paid for the production as a part of a package that I put together. In the end, the label retained the content, and GAC had permission to air or "license" it first. They liked that idea, and some traction developed with the labels because of the non-traditional programming that I was pitching.

Here's an example. At MCA, they were trying hard to break Allison Moorer, but it wasn't happening. I was a huge fan of hers for many years. They knew I was a big fan and they came to me: "Can we do something with Allison?" We did a cross-platform promotion with her—not for big dollars, maybe $20,000. But it helped her and it helped GAC. I put together a spot schedule for the release on GAC, across Jones Radio, and arranged interviews for her on both TV and radio. We also did giveaways of the new release across the radio properties. Allison remains a favorite of mine and is one of the most prolific singer/songwriters of our generation.

I was having lunch with Johnny Rose, who was the vice president of marketing at DreamWorks, and Toby Keith was coming out with a new record and everybody knew how I had helped with Toby when I was in New York. Johnny made a request: "I want Toby to own GAC for the month of July 2002, radio, TV, and Internet. So what can we do? What can we do that would surpass anything ever done for another artist?"

I came up with Artist of the Month, though I warned that I had to get approval. It got the okay, and it turned into quite the promotion. There were all kinds of announcements on the air, mini-billboards, "Here's another video from the GAC Artist of the Month Toby Keith." The label loved it and I was able to get a commitment of $50,000 for that campaign.

It took off from there, because as soon as we aired Toby Keith as Artist of the Month, the other labels—and it's a very competitive town when it comes to new music—saw the idea and asked, "Can we do that too?" Of course! Soon enough all the labels wanted meetings with me. It sold every month. Labels were very careful to not let their competitors know when a release was going to be—not now, but back then. It was very secretive. Usually the first tip-off was promotion in retail, through

Walmart, Best Buy, Target, and all those places, as those stores needed to know months in advance to price and position them.

Not to brag, but I still have records of my billings and earnings from those years. When I started, the GAC ad team had only brought in $150,000 or so from Nashville, whereas I turned that office into an multi-million-dollar annual revenue stream. And my deals were never "guaranteed." That meant that we were not on the hook to guarantee an audience. Most national TV buys are bought with audience guarantee. If your campaign didn't deliver the audience numbers promised, the client would get additional commercial inventory to get the audience promised. Not meeting the audience guarantees played a hand in GAC's downfall later on. My billing went from hundreds of thousands of dollars to millions pretty quickly. In 2004–05 my billings surpassed $5 million in revenue. While television led the way, radio wasn't that far beyond, and as the years went by, Internet revenue grew too.

The key was that I was never held back. If I saw an opportunity or came up with an idea, my superiors generally let me run with it. Jones Media Networks had expanded its base and it was doing a lot of things with outside programming. I was able to offer opportunities on the Motor Racing Network, a NASCAR-based platform, and more. But the biggie was Delilah. She had a massive audience, so the Trisha Yearwoods, LeAnn Rimes, and Shania Twains of the world—the crossover acts that were half country, half adult contemporary—did very well on her show.

★ ★ ★ ★ ★

Country music had truly gone from a regional genre to something far bigger when major advertisers like Home Depot and Bush's Beans wanted to find a country star to promote a product. We could now go to a label and say, "We have an opportunity with this national advertiser. Can we do a promotion with your artist?" That became another value-added proposition that I could offer to a label.

I can't say that Nashville itself was very progressive at the time, though.

Being Italian, I was unique, a minority. Actually, Southerners pronounced it "*EYE*-talian."

Not long after I moved there, I was invited to join the board of the Williamson County Council for the Arts, as my home was in Franklin. After the first meeting, the board adjourned, and an older Southern belle, who obviously came from money, started talking to me. "Well, we're about all ready to go get a glass of wine, and you're welcome to come with us." I responded, "Yeah, I'd love that. I'm Italian, so I love wine." She was like, "You're *EYE-talian*? Your last name is Alexander. Let me think about this for a minute, because that's an Anglo name. What did your Mama do, marry a white man?"

I was like, "Huh?"

When I got my bearings, I asked, "What do you mean a white man? Where do you come from?" I was offended.

She said, "Well, I'm from here."

I said, "Everyone comes here from somewhere. My ancestors came here from Italy. Where did your ancestors come here from?"

"Oh no, we've always been from here."

I said, "Well, I really don't think I want to be on this board and be a part of this." I didn't call her prejudiced to her face, but I wasn't going to be denigrated in a situation like that. I didn't want to be associated with that kind of backward thinking.

I was puzzled and bemused more than anything else. "Where the hell am I?"

★ ★ ★ ★ ★

In 2004, GAC obtained the rights to broadcast the Grand Ole Opry, which was a huge thing, so I could sell spots and sponsorships. People wanted to be associated with the Grand Ole Opry, and it's always a thrill to go see a show there. It really is the foundation of country music. Getting to play the Opry was an honor, and getting the broadcast rights elevated the status of GAC in ways we had not seen before—not just to the advertisers, but to the managers and to the artists. I got to know the people behind the scenes, including Steve Buchanan, who was executive vice president; Pete Fisher, the vice president and general manager of the Opry; Gina Keltner, who helped book the artists with Pete; and Dan Rogers, their marketing executive. A great team that looked after the iconic brand.

★ ★ ★ ★ ★

Don't get the impression that I could do no wrong. I almost got fired in 2004.

The Department of Tourist Development in Pigeon Forge, Tennessee, wanted to do something big for the holiday season, to promote its annual Winterfest, and I suggested a very elegant Christmas show in Pigeon Forge, headlined by Lee Ann Womack (who had one of the biggest hits ever in "I Hope You Dance"), since she had a holiday album coming out. I put together the package and sold it through. It was a huge deal and included participation by the record company, MCA, via its marketing director, Tom Lord. I had to put together a production budget, which the label was underwriting, and the ad buy was big, not only from the label to promote the Christmas album but also from the Department of Tourist Development; all told, it was a high six-figure revenue generator on the promotional side.

We didn't have our own big production staff, so I met with various production companies and secured one to work with us, with top director Steve Angus. The budget was pretty high, more than anything GAC had ever spent on anything before. I faxed the budget to Denver for approval, for GAC's head of marketing, Scott Durand, but that fax was read first by the president, Jeff Wayne. About a half hour after I sent the fax, I got a call from Jeff, who was screaming at me.

"What did you just do?"

"What are you talking about?"

"This budget! What do you think this is, the fucking Academy Awards?!" And he hung up on me. I was stunned. I'd done everything right, and it wasn't our money that was paying for the production; the outside parties were paying for *everything*.

Then Scott called. He wasn't yelling, so I was able to explain that GAC wasn't paying for it, with the label paying the production cost and money coming in for the ads from both Pigeon Forge and the label promoting the album. That cooled it down.

I added a few more acts to the show, including Rebecca Lynn Howard, who had a number-one hit with "Forgive," and then an up-and-coming artist, Steve Azar. We brought in GAC personality Suzanne to host the show. The show was taped at the beautiful Louise Mandrell Theater with a full orchestra. We put Louise on the show as well, because she had a big fan base, she was a great musician, and it was *her* theater. In the end, it was a spectacular show which really elevated GAC, and not only was it the best Christmas show we had ever done, it was also the best-looking show, period.

★ ★ ★ ★ ★

The better production values attracted better shows. I took a call from one of the top video production guys in town, Greg Travis, who immediately complained that no one in Denver ever returned calls. He had a show ready to go, *Country Music Across America*, with host Storme Warren. It was designed to be a weekly newsmagazine show. I fell in love with it, because in the 10-minute sizzle reel, all the A-list stars were in it—Garth Brooks, Reba McEntire—promoting it. I thought to myself, "We have to have this show."

I overnighted it to Denver to look at, and the call came in: "Hey John, what do you think it'll cost a week to do this?" They had told me it would be about $20,000 to $25,000 a week for a full show. Immediately, it was "We can't do that. We don't have the money to do that. Will they give it to us? Maybe with a revenue split?"

When I got back Greg and Storme, I had to say there was no budget for it, but then I asked them how they had funded the awesome sizzle reel. They said that the City of Nashville had put the money up, the tourism board for Music City. It turns out that Butch Spyridon, the president and chief executive of the Nashville Convention & Visitors Bureau, did the deal. I'd heard Butch's name often, as he was a powerful man in town, maybe with more pull than the mayor, but we'd never met. We toyed with the idea of approaching Spyridon for the funding and set up a meeting.

Butch is a real dealmaker, and talks in a low voice, and he was interested in sponsoring the show, but as always he had bigger ideas in mind. He brought up the annual Fourth of July concert which the NCVB promoted and asked if we'd consider airing it live. That was huge. Before long we were putting together a deal which formed a great partnership between GAC and the biggest promotional arm for Music City. Our deal came together, to my surprise; it turns out there was a special one-time grant out there from the state that helped facilitate it.

It was a multi-year, $3-million deal to put *Country Music Across America* on GAC, with the City of Nashville sponsoring the show and GAC airing the city's Fourth of July celebration.

★ ★ ★ ★ ★

As much as I was a salesperson, my title as director of music marketing gave me a little more creative weight, and I wound up getting producer or executive producer credit for many shows on GAC. Again, creativity came in handy. There wasn't a lot of money available for a Billy Ray Cyrus music video, so we shot some of it at my house in Franklin, just outside of Nashville, which I had bought in 2003. It was dizzying at times, bringing money in, doing specials and meetings to set things up.

As GAC's importance was growing, along with our acceptance as a force in country music, we were ambitious in wanting to be involved with bigger artists. One meeting I set up was with the one and only Dolly Parton. Glenn Jones, owner of GAC, wanted to honor Dolly for her lifetime achievements at Ford's Theatre in Washington, DC. I got a call from Scott Durand to see if I could help facilitate a meeting with Dolly. I contacted and set up a meeting with Dolly's manager, Danny Nozell, who liked the idea. And with some back and forth, I was able to get the meeting with Dolly set up for Glenn, Scott, Jim Murphy, and me. We met at her compound off 12th Avenue in Nashville. Glenn flew in on his private jet with Scott and Jim. I met them at Dolly's office, and we had the meeting. Dolly was pure business with lots of questions. Everything had to be spelled out in minute detail. It was an amazing experience for me. Dolly agreed to be honored and it was one of the finest hours at GAC.

Not only did I set up meetings, but I took meetings with everybody. I had an open-door policy, as you never know who would show up at your door!

One afternoon, likely in 2001, there was a knock on the door, and there was a kid outside with her mother. This shy girl had long, curly

★ ★ ★ ★ ★ ★ ★ ★ ★ ★

IN 2006, GREAT AMERICAN COUNTY HOSTED TAYLOR SWIFT IN A SUITE; IT'S ME, JERI RICE, TAYLOR, AND JACKIE MCDONALD.

blonde hair. She was handing out her CD. It was Taylor Swift. She had not been signed yet. I did take the CD, and I wish I had it today. Taylor was only 11 or 12 at the time.

Taylor came into the GAC picture again years later. It involved Scott Borchetta, who had recently started Big Machine Records. Scott saw Taylor play at the famous Bluebird Café at a label showcase and signed her. Scott was backed by a financial investment in his company (initially 3 percent of Big Machine for $120,000, rumored to be the first of almost $4 million he eventually invested in the company) by Scott Swift, Taylor's father. Borchetta set up a meeting with the GAC brain-trust. "What can we do with this kid? She's only 16 but will be a huge star." GAC came up with "Short Cuts," a series of brief clips designed to show off the personality of an artist. The very first artist was Taylor. For the advertisers, we brought in Dairy Queen and Oscar Meyer hot dogs to sponsor the story of this 16-year-old kid who was recording her first single ("Tim McGraw") in a recording studio and hanging out with her friends after school. It was initially a three-part story edited into vignettes. We wound up doing several with Taylor during the first few years of her stellar career. Those videos were spearheaded by Scripps Networks' Jim Zarchin (whom I still do business with) and Jim Rink (who worked as a freelancer for GAC).

Everyone was happy, with the sponsor tie-ins, with the product placement, with the music. It was her first national TV exposure, and it worked: it created awareness for this newcomer who is now world renowned. No matter what happens, we can say that GAC gave Taylor her first taste of national TV exposure.

At the same time, I worked with the label and their head of marketing, Kelly Rich, to make Taylor the GAC Artist of the Month (now tied in with music retailer FYE), and every person ordering a presale would get a CD autographed by Taylor. So her debut blew up huge, between "Short Cuts" and FYE and Artist of the Month.

Later that year, in 2006, I ran into Taylor and her mother at LaGuardia airport, going back to Nashville. I said hello, and we sat together on the plane. She was such a super nice person, and they were so happy with what GAC had done for them, all the exposure. I told them I'd come up with the Artist of the Month program and helped with the ad sales.

Our paths crossed again later with the City of Nashville, when we were broadcasting the Fourth of July concert in 2007. She wasn't a big star yet, so she was on early in the show, which also included Rodney Atkins and the Van Zants, Donnie and Johnny, who were brothers of the late Ronnie Van Zant, former lead singer of Lynyrd Skynyrd.

In my home office, I have an autographed framed poster from a GACTV.com promotion with Taylor Swift, given to me by Big Machine, a real collector's item. Nearby, there are plaques given out by labels and management companies to recognize executives who have helped them on their way to successful releases. I received my first gold record with *O Brother, Where Art Thou?* from Mercury, because I had put together a cross-platform campaign for the soundtrack on GAC television and Jones Radio Network, where the top prize was a trip to New York City for the movie premiere. We also highlighted the soundtrack with extensive marketing, promotions, and contests. It went on to sell more than

12 million copies. There are others from Toby Keith, Sara Evans, Brad Paisley, and Miranda Lambert.

★ ★ ★ ★ ★

Another time, Mike Borchetta invited me to see a new video by Shawn King, whom he had just signed to his label, Lofton Creek Records. Mike was a legend in the business, and Scott Borchetta's father. Mike was responsible for signing Tim McGraw to Curb Records. Mike was a great guy, and since he was also a baseball fan, we'd often talk about the sport for hours. Mike mentioned that Shawn was married to talk-show host Larry King of CNN. My first thought was "How old is she?" But he talked me into it, and he promised to bring in Shawn and Larry. She was much, much younger than Larry, very pretty, and, it turns out, his seventh wife. We sat down to watch the video together and I shut off the lights in the office. It was pretty good. When I turned the lights back on, I realized that Larry was slumped in his chair, sleeping. Mike suggested I wake him up. As a joke, I said, "Hey Larry, that's the first time anyone has ever fallen asleep during a meeting with me." He looks at me and goes, "Well, call me when you're 72." It was sarcastic but right on the money.

★ ★ ★ ★ ★

Up in New York, my nephew kept getting sick, and my sister would call, "Dominic's in the hospital." I would stop whatever I was doing and fly up. Fortunately, I had the financial means at the time. And I began flying Dominic, my sister Donna, and my mom to Nashville for visits. My sister would come with a bag filled with medicines, nebulizer machines, and inhalers for Dom, who had asthma as well. The remarkable thing was that Dom would come to Tennessee to visit and get better physically while there. My sister also found Tennessee beautiful, but it was the improvement of my nephew's health that convinced her that maybe they should move there with me.

Donna made an incredibly hard decision and left her husband Thomas. She moved to Tennessee with Dominic in mid-2003. We then moved our Mom down into an apartment later that year. Thomas visited often, keeping a close bond with both his son and my sister. To this day, Thomas is very much a part of both of their lives and sees them several times a week. I call him my brother.

I admit that I have spoiled Dominic since he was born. I still do. I turned him into a Mets fan when he was still in the crib, and his father was a die-hard Yankees fan. Whether it was buying him a motorized car or a video game system on his birthday, or taking him on adventures and road trips to see our beloved Mets, nothing was too much. We also went to several MLB All Star Games and many WWE events. We always sat in the first row for wrestling and got great seats for baseball, even staying at the same hotel as the Mets so he could meet the players. Around the time Dom was five years old, he said, "You're like a genie, 'cause you grant wishes!" So, from that day forward, I became "Uncle Genie." It has stuck, and it is what my sister and nephew call me. I feel fortunate to have been able to take care of my family.

★ ★ ★ ★ ★

Family is not always blood. Lindsay Walleman was a shooting star that blazed into my life and was gone way too soon.

I met Lindsay through Donna, as she was moving to town from Chicago and wanted to know more about Nashville. She was bubbly and

ME AND DOMINIC WITH LINDSAY WALLEMAN AT ONE OF MY CHRISTMAS PARTIES.

enthusiastic. You were taken in by the twinkle in the eye and I knew she was a real go-getter. I networked and got her a job at a local modeling agency, initially working doing paperwork. But Lindsay wanted to get into the music business, and I introduced her to John Ettinger, who was in radio promotion at Mercury Records, which was a part of the Universal Music Group family. John loved her right away and hired her. Immediately, she was a success in the radio promotion side. Lindsay worked for a few labels but eventually settled in at Warner Brothers, where she is now a legend.

Lindsay was family to us, hanging out at the house with my sister and my nephew. We just laughed and had a lot of fun together. In retrospect, I was mentoring her, but I didn't necessarily feel that at the time; she was just a friend that I wanted to help. Lindsay was a beautiful girl, further enhanced by her personality. She had a posse of friends, so I'd often go out with them. They kept me young.

One time, in April 2007, I took her with me to Atlanta to see the Mets, since Dom was sick. We were at the Westin Buckhead, in downtown Atlanta, where the Mets were staying. New York had just beaten the Braves, and announcer Ron Darling, Moises Alou, and Carlos Beltran were at the bar. I bought them drinks, in celebration of the Mets victory. We all chatted for a bit. They then invited us to go out with them to another bar not far from the hotel. It was really cool talking to the players, and the rookie Lastings Milledge met us there. We were having a great time, and I was getting off on talking to my Mets heroes, really enjoying my conversation with Carlos. Then it turned ugly.

I went to the men's room, and when I came back, Lindsay was standing up with her finger in Beltran's face, and she hauls off and hits him in the mouth. She was a feisty girl. I couldn't believe it. Beltran's going, "Why you hit me? I do nothing wrong!" She and I left, and she told me that when I got up and left to the bathroom, Beltran had asked, "Why a young, pretty girl like you with a big, fat guy like that?" She immediately defended me, and that's what I walked back into. I was blown away that she hauled off and hit a Met, defended *my* honor, hurt because of what Beltran said. It was bad enough that Carlos had taken a called strike three to end the 2006 playoffs in favor of the St. Louis Cardinals, but to put me down, that was his personal strike three to me. He will always live in infamy for his part in the cheating scandals that tainted the 2017 World Series–winning Astros, which continued into the 2018 season. The Mets hired him to manage the 2020 team and fired him because of the scandal before he ever managed one game. I was not in the least bit sorry for him.

Lindsay and I stayed in touch, but her rocket ship continued to soar to great heights in the music business. Warner Brothers Nashville head John Esposito said she was destined to run a label someday. But, as fast as her shooting star was across the industry, she developed a rare form of cancer and died on April 9, 2013, six years to the weekend after she had defended me in Atlanta. She was only 28. The greater music community set up the FTL ("For the Linds") Sarcoma Fund in honor of her, with a fundraiser every year. She lit up the sky in her short time here and made an impact which will be remembered in Nashville forever.

★ ★ ★ ★ ★

On the personal side, I really enjoyed Nashville, as there was always an event or a concert to go to, and I had plenty of friends. I never dated a ton—or, more correctly, I never dated anyone for very long. I don't let many people get really close to me, and when they do, I push them away. When I was a young boy, I saw the volatility in my household, and the mental illness of my mom and my older sister Linda, and I vowed then never to get married.

The other complication has been my weight. When I initially moved to Nashville, I was about 325 pounds. I have managed to get it down to 280, give or take 15 pounds, since then. It's not easy, especially when life continually throws you curveballs. Sometimes I feel like the weight is a self-defense mechanism for me, not letting women get close to me.

★ ★ ★ ★ ★

On the home front, my dad was going through rough times. He was diagnosed as a diabetic as an adult, and then he developed a very rare affliction that eventually caused the loss of his legs, Charcot syndrome.

My dad never really took care of himself, that's the thing. He never went to doctors. He might have lived a lot longer had he taken care of himself. By his early 60s, he was very disabled and went on disability benefits. His problems walking led to a nursing home in New York—he couldn't move to Nashville—because of his fragile health. That was difficult for Donna especially, as she worshiped our father.

In October 2004, my dad was in failing health in New York. We were told that he had taken a turn for the worse, and it was time to say goodbye. Simultaneously, my nephew had gotten sick, and given his own past health issues, my sister didn't want him to get on a plane right away. We got a call in the middle of the night that Dad had died.

While I was making arrangements for us all to go up to New York, I get an email notification that GAC had been sold to Scripps Networks, which owned other specialty stations like the Food Network and HGTV. No one knew that it was even for sale, let alone that a deal was close. I pushed it aside to focus on my dad. We arrived in New York for my dad's wake and funeral. I was in awe of the number of friends and associates that came to give their respects to "Big Sam." So many people were crying. I stayed strong, as did my family. It was a true testament to those my father had touched in his life, and I gained a new perspective on the man that had been my father.

After getting back to Nashville, I had to deal with the fallout of the sale of GAC. The deal was only for the television network GAC and its website. Scripps bought it for $140 million. Owner Glenn Jones spread the wealth around a little, with employees getting bonus checks from proceeds of the sale. I received $25,000, which was appreciated. With the sale, I was immediately assured that my position was safe. Although I was no longer a part of Jones Media and its radio networks, I would continue to be part of GAC. There were meetings going on that I wasn't a part of. Many of those in Denver were let go, including President Jeff Wayne. Scott Durand, the vice president of marketing, was relocated to Nashville, which I was happy about, as were Jason Mease, vice president of online, and Kelly Kamm, our business manager. I could have gotten the ax, but the GAC people said, "We want John. He's got a great relationship with Nashville. People love him."

★ ★ ★ ★ ★

There are two words that separate Jones Media Networks from GAC: unlimited resources.

When I started there, the GAC office was one room, and then it was a little bit bigger, with a few more people. We recorded all of our little shows across the street at Reba McEntire's building, Starstruck Entertainment; they had TV and radio studios in there. Then we moved into our own facility, because the revenue that I had been bringing in allowed us to grow. Every year was getting better. All the money that I brought in, which was label money, was used to grow the infrastructure in Nashville. But with Scripps, they had big ideas and a lot of money, so I was in one way excited for the new resources, but wary of the changes that Scripps had in mind to grow the brand.

★ ★ ★ ★ ★

And, as always, there was pro wrestling.

One afternoon, I got a call from our receptionist out front, and she said there was a woman on the phone named Dixie Carter who wanted to talk to me. She introduced herself and explained that she was running a wrestling company in Nashville, in partnership with Jeff Jarrett. She laid it out there—her promotion, Total Non-stop Action, or TNA, was looking for a new home for its TV show. We arranged to meet, but I was John Alexander, not John Arezzi, and I was excited to talk about wrestling. Dixie and Jeff arrived, and I might have met Jeff a couple of times in the past, but he didn't remember me. They talked up TNA and Toby Keith's involvement. They were amazed at my knowledge of wrestling.

I pitched the show, but the powers at GAC didn't want anything to do with wrestling. TNA ended up on Spike TV instead.

I did become friends with Dixie, and since TNA ran shows in Nashville, Dominic and I started going to the shows, often hanging out backstage. Fortunately, none of them ever figured out who I was. I enjoyed it because my nephew got autographs from A.J. Styles, Kurt Angle, and Abyss.

★ ★ ★ ★ ★

By early 2005, Scripps Networks fully took over GAC, with these high-powered executives coming into our little home, and new upper management being hired. Our existing team was just a handful of close-knit people, a real team which could handle just about anything: my sales apprentice, Travis Hensley; Scott Stilley in production; cameraman Jonathan Greer; Shanna Strassberg in artist relations; producers Tamera Saviano and Lonnie Napier; and on-air personalities Suzanne Alexander, Nan Kelley, and Bill Cody. Scott Durand was our Denver liaison and is one of my best friends to this day. We were creative and worked our asses off on a tiny budget to get things done. We met with the new executives, and next thing you knew, the changes began. After the Denver office was closed, and the select few were transferred to Nashville, the growth began. The team grew rapidly, they moved us out of our office, they rented an office space with a huge TV studio, and they pumped millions into the new space. Our little team became a big office, with 40 employees or so.

My existing sales manager for GAC was Norma Taylor, and she was a real New York seasoned veteran of advertising. She never really got me, other than that I was this maverick that kept busting down doors and bringing money in. I was not your traditional salesperson and had my own style. In our meeting, she told me that I had to change my image. I usually wore jeans and a Tommy Bahama shirt, and rarely wore a suit. "The culture is going to change now that Scripps is coming in," she warned.

I tried to explain to her that I didn't need a suit to meet with the labels, where people dressed similarly. She asked about the cost of my shirts, which I found weird, as was the vibe. She was ultra-paranoid about Scripps, which was a company that billed hundreds of millions of dollars a year in advertising. In its best year before Scripps, GAC did maybe $10 million annually across the board.

The culture at Scripps was amazing. The sales teams were the best in the TV business. Each year there was a national sales meeting made up of all the Scripps salespeople, sales planners, and executive assistants.

It was mandatory to go. And it was first class. There were hundreds of people there. Norma warned me to stay away from Jon Steinlauf, who was the head of ad sales and one of the most brilliant analytical thinkers, like Rain Man in a lot of ways. He was a top sales guy who'd come from Turner Sports and built huge revenue for Scripps, into billions annually.

"Why do I have to be afraid of Jon?"

"Jon's really conservative, and if he hears you talking, it's not going to be good for you. Be on your best behavior."

At the meeting in Florida, I was paranoid and worried, wondering why my good life had to change. A few people I was with pointed out Steinlauf, who was about six feet tall, not the imposing figure that Norma described. He wore glasses and was impeccably dressed, and everyone wanted a bit of his time. And not being shy or intimidated by anyone, I decided to be pro-active.

I just walked up to him and shook his hand. "Hi Jon, I'm John Alexander from the Nashville office."

"Oh, John, I've heard a lot about you." Then he noticed the ring on my finger, which I wear every day; it had the New York Mets logo on it. He commented on it and admitted to being a huge Mets fan himself. We just hit it off. He was a brilliant guy, and he started picking my brain a little bit. Jon was impressed with my non-guaranteed revenue deals, and he let me do my thing for the most part. After all these years, we're still friends, but he's also a mentor. We go to Mets games together a couple times a year, and every time I'm in New York, we meet up for lunch or dinner. Recently, Discovery Networks bought Scripps in a multi-billion dollar merger, and Jon is now president of the ad sales division. He has 16 networks under his umbrella and brings in billions in ad sales a year, across the U.S. He was the ultimate boss that I had to report to. And he is someone I respect as much as anyone I've ever worked with or for.

A couple of weeks after that sales meeting, Norma Taylor was fired. The new sales manager was Susan Leigh. Susan was a personable, nice, great politician, a great salesperson, and she loved what I was doing, loved my entrepreneurial spirit. She said, "You are going to be such an asset to the company because of all the salespeople that are here that I've inherited, and the new ones that are going to be brought onto the team, you need to educate them on country music, so we know how to sell it." A lot of different people were weeded out or fired, and a lot of new, sharp, young salespeople were in, and they started taking trips to Nashville. I would take them around to the record companies to teach them how they worked. So I started to develop relationships with co-workers in Detroit or Atlanta or Los Angeles. I immediately became the guy who was the connector. I'd get a call: "Listen, this advertiser wants a country music artist. What can we do?" I would go around and find out the new releases, who needed promotion from the labels. It became a cool situation.

My problem was that I was a maverick, that I cut deals that were not cookie cutter, and basically I was as much a part of programming as I was of sales. That changed with the hiring of the new president of GAC, Ed Hardy, and the new head of programming, Sarah Trahern, who had been at CMT for years and had recently worked at the Home Shopping Network, another Scripps property. I'd had one experience with her a couple of years before that, when there had been a car accident in front of the office, and the woman who was hit by the other car had come into our office. She was shaken up, so we sat her down as we waited for the ambulance. But she had her wits about her too, and she introduced herself as Sarah Trahern and mentioned that she was looking for work.

Sarah and Ed were the two people responsible for the direction and programming of GAC. With Scott Durand as their head of marketing, and Jason Mease heading up online, the four of them were the leaders. Sarah and Ed immediately wanted to separate ad sales from programming. As they planned things out, I knew that I'd need to sit down with them. So much of the money that I brought in was non-traditional revenue, doing TV specials or producing something, super-sized deals that often involved programming.

At the sit-down, I was told that I couldn't make those programming deals any longer, because Scripps wanted to own its own content and not let the labels get the shows back. I explained that was the only way we'd been able to afford it to this point. "Well, we can't do that anymore."

From there, I was less and less involved with the programming part of the business, meaning that I mainly was doing advertising sales. My

Artist of the Month program was still rocking, bringing in the $50,000 a month, then it was upped to $75,000 a month. I did a big deal with Best Buy, which was a price-and-position deal. So I was doing innovative things, creating opportunities, but not doing anything on the programming side, which was a disappointment to me.

In 2005, even without radio, I did $1.6 million in billings, and another $300,000 in online. In 2006, it was even bigger, $2.5 million in ad sales on GAC and more online. I'd build these relationships and these labels were spending more with me than they did with even our competitor, CMT, because I was innovative and super-served them.

The labels asked me about doing something for younger artists, the other end of the Artist of the Month deal, which was for big names. Scripps had experience with creating smaller vignettes, which looked like programming but it was actually a paid spot. They were usually two minutes in length. I went to Scripps and talked to my people in New York and put together this thing called "Fan Focus," which was a spot that told a story about an artist. That allowed for promotion of the artist and their new album, and I arranged a deal with Best Buy for price and positioning for that artist. My billings skyrocketed again. Then I created the "Get to Know" series, which was for newbie acts and resulted in more billing increases.

I still had to help the labels with exposure for their artists. When the performer was the Artist of the Month, you're expected to play their videos on the network. The music director they hired, who screened the videos and decided what videos would be played, was an Italian guy from New York, Tony Travato. He was programming the TV network like a radio station, like a Top 40 radio station, and that was not the way to break an act—you couldn't get the exposure. So labels were paying for the Artist of the Month and Fan Focus deals, and a lot of times I had to fight to get their videos played. It created tension between me and the record companies. I was constantly being told by the new "powers that be" at GAC, "You're an ad sales guys, you don't dictate what we play." It was tense and I was getting frustrated by the whole thing.

The only saving grace for me was my people in New York, who allowed me to work with the other sales executives to bring artists in and do deals. The biggest deal that I did during my time at GAC was as part of a team putting together a $15-million deal with Bush's Beans. Many cable TV networks wanted that deal, including our competitor CMT. It was going to be huge for whoever landed it. The client wanted an artist to be a focal point of the campaign. After searching throughout Music Row for an artist who fit the criteria for the campaign (an outdoors person who loved to cook out and loved beans), I was able to secure Craig Morgan to be the spokesperson. Scripps won the buy, and we got a lot of money. I was the hero.

★ ★ ★ ★ ★

As a part of a bigger company, I was networking, doing well, but there was something missing for me inside. I missed the programming part of the job, and I was now out of the loop when it came to the creative side of GAC.

In the latter part of 2008, my billing began to decline. The Internet had become more prominent, and budgets were being splintered: I saw erosion across the board.

After a few years, Scripps really didn't know what to do with GAC. Ratings were down and it wasn't generating the revenue that was projected. We were not hitting our audience guarantees for our advertisers, which meant less and less inventory to sell as we were giving make goods to everyone, and the costs for programming were skyrocketing. Here's the reason why—on the deals I used to do with the record companies, they would retain ownership of the shows. When Scripps decided it wanted to own the shows, it didn't take into account that there were publishing fees that needed to be paid; if you put a song on TV, someone's got to pay the publisher, that's part of it, that's where artists and songwriters make their money. Scripps, Ed Hardy, and Sarah Trahern soon discovered that Scripps was not in a position to pay these enormous publishing fees for a network that was not generating the revenue that all the other networks were. They started doing the same deals that I had done, with the labels paying for production and retaining ownership, but I was cut out of these commissions.

In 2007, I was able to do a huge deal with concert promoter Live Nation, working with William Morris and Brad Paisley's management to promote the Paisley tour. I got $250,000 and the naming rights to the tour for GAC. So we'd have our logos on their trucks; we'd promote their whole tour. We cut in a separate advertiser too, an insurance company. Midwest promoter Brad Garrett gave us a similar deal with Martina McBride. These were new relationships I was developing and were bringing in significant billing, but a year later, after the Paisley tour, I got cut out of the deal by upper management. They still sponsored the tour, but no money was exchanged: it was all in-kind marketing back and forth, promoting each other.

I realized that I was no longer happy; I was still making great money but not feeling fulfilled, and I missed the programming input. And if programming continued to cut deals with labels that took away from ad sales, then the writing was on the wall that my income was going to suffer before too long.

One of the last straws occurred in 2009. Susan Leigh, my sales manager and a great individual to work for, was transferred from GAC to one of the other networks that was struggling a little bit, DIY. In her place, we were assigned a Scripps veteran, an older, cantankerous (putting it politely) man named Bob Calandruccio. Bob was running ad sales for DIY, but his team hated him, so instead of firing him, he and Susan traded places. Bob was bully-like in his management approach; a tough, old-school guy who didn't understand country music at all. But he was an Italian guy, I'm an Italian guy, so I figured we'd get along—but it was the opposite. He would be on the phone, yelling and screaming, "What are you doing down there? We've got to bring more money in." I was not into his techniques at all, and I didn't want to be a part of it.

I kept my head down, put in my deals. Everything seemed to be falling apart around me, and I wasn't enjoying my job, so I began to look for my next opportunity.

My fate turned at a Halloween party in 2009.

16.

THE DARLING OF MUSIC CITY

Halloween has never been a big thing for me. Growing up, I was not a Halloween fan, except for getting candy. We didn't have the money for elaborate costumes. I don't think I dressed up more than once or twice after turning 10 years old, with the exception of Halloween 1999, when Y107 had a huge party, featuring Toby Keith, on the historic *Intrepid* battleship in New York Harbor. I vowed not to dress up again for Halloween.

So what made me dress up for that party in 2009? It was out of character. I made the decision to go on the day of the party, as many of the co-workers I was friends with at GAC kept asking me to come.

The party was at Mike McCall's house. He was one of the freelance stylists at GAC and had become a dear friend. I called myself the Ghoulfather, done up like the Godfather but as a vampire, with a white face and blood dripping down onto my black pin-striped suit. I'd forgotten how much easier it was to have a different personality when you are dressed up. All the girls wanted photos with me.

Michael invited an eclectic group of people to that party, including many industry people. He was the stylist for several country artists in the business, one of which was recording artist Sarah Darling. Sarah was dressed in a little sailor's outfit, like she jumped off a box of Cracker Jacks. She introduced herself, along her boyfriend Jack, who was dressed to match as a sailor. I knew her from a few visits she had made to GAC. The network was playing one of her videos, "Jack of Hearts." She came into our conference room to sing once—I hadn't been there, since I was so fed up with the network, and I wasn't even going in to see the new artists.

Sarah and I started chatting. She was signed to a relatively new label, Black River Music Group. They were the one label in town that I could never get a meeting with. It was run by producer and renowned session musician Jimmy Nichols and his wife, Tonya Ginnetti, who was the business manager for the label. Beyond that, I didn't know a lot about them.

After a few cocktails, Sarah and I began talking about her career. When she mentioned Black River, I was blunt: "Your label sucks."

Naturally, she was defensive. "What are you talking about?"

I said, "No one ever returns a call there. They're the only label in town I can't ever get a meeting with." She proposed that we have lunch to talk about it, and I agreed.

★ ★ ★ ★ ★

We met for lunch the following week at the Palm Restaurant, where I was considered a VIP. I tried to arrange most of my business lunches there. The Palm is famous for its steaks, but also notable because of the caricatures hanging on the walls. If you were a local celebrity, politician, or high-profile Nashville executive, most likely you got honored by having your face on the wall. I was one of those faces.

Quickly, I learned that Sarah was an incredible person. She was very nice, had a deep faith in God, and had a vulnerability about her, which made you want to help her. It was a good first meeting. I remember leaving lunch and getting in my car for a concert I was going to in Tunica, Mississippi (about four hours from Nashville). I put her debut CD *Every Monday Morning* in my car stereo, and by the time I finished listening to it, I was hooked. She sounded a tad like Mindy McCready (more on her in a bit). I listened to it end to end several times during that trip, and called Sarah from the road, telling her I wanted to help. I was impressed with her songwriting and vocals and felt I could assist the label and create awareness for her via GAC.

★ ★ ★ ★ ★

Sarah went back to Black River, and I finally got a meeting set up. The meeting also took place at the Palm, this time with Sarah and John Gusty, who was overseeing marketing at the label. John had a vast background in the industry and was a musician himself. He also had a few cool side projects, one of which was being involved with Jon Bon Jovi, helping with his e-commerce and website. John was quirky, almost hippie-like, and a brilliant guy.

After meeting with John and Sarah, Gusty then set up a lunch for me and the rest of the Black River team, where I presented a large marketing plan to run on GAC, including a video series called "Get to Know." The concept was a three-part video, paid for and sponsored by Black River. They had a lot of video footage of Sarah—in the studio, recording her first record, on the road, and visiting radio stations. Lots of B-roll of her as a kid and teenager, and interviews with the label, her parents, and grandparents were all included. The package, including Artist of the Month exposure, cost the label $75,000. They bought it.

Not long after, Sarah was all over GAC, and her record sales started rising, but the label had stopped promoting any new singles from it, concentrating on putting together her second album. The debut album had modest sales, nothing to be impressed by. Jimmy began playing new songs for me to get my opinion.

But I was impressed with a cover video I saw on YouTube. Sarah and her guitar player at the time, Mike Noble, were captured performing U2's classic "With or Without You." I saw it on the streaming site and felt it could be a breakthrough song for her. Jimmy decided to record it for the next album.

What I didn't know at that point was that there was potential big money behind Black River.

★ ★ ★ ★ ★

In early 2010, Sarah and I went to lunch. She made her pitch. "You're doing so many things for me, and you really believe in me."

I agreed, "Yeah, I think you're a star."

"I don't have a manager," she said, leaving it dangling. I had mentioned managing Patty Loveless years ago. She asked me point-blank, "Will you be my manager?" I was flattered.

I said that I had a job, albeit one I wasn't happy with, at GAC. Artist managers generally work on a percentage basis, so I asked her what she had made in 2009. She said she didn't make any money. We both laughed. Then I got serious, and I asked how it would be possible, since managers work on commission.

"Sarah, I believe in you. I know how to market and all that, but I can't work for nothing."

Then she said, "I think you should meet our investors."

"Who, Jimmy and Tonya?"

"No, they are partners in the label, but they don't finance it."

"Who are the financial people?"

When she said Terry and Kim Pegula, it did not mean anything to me. I had never heard of them. I did my research and discovered Terry was a major player in the natural gas business. Their fracking company, Eastern Resources, was about to be scooped up by Shell Oil for a whopping $4 *billion* before the end of 2010.

Sarah arranged for us all to have lunch; of course, we met at the Palm. Tonya was at that lunch with Sarah and the Pegulas. They asked about my background. I found them to be warm and engaging, and very cautious because of their status.

After the lunch, I wrote them an email, outlining suggestions on what I would do with Sarah if I were calling the shots—I was so brash that I even told them that the planned single, "Wrapped in Moonlight," was weak and wouldn't succeed. I wasn't pitching for a job, or maybe I was on some level, but I was saying what should be done. I got a thank you back from them, but nothing substantive.

From that point on, Jimmy, Tonya, and John all did their best to recruit me to Black River. But there was resistance because of my income.

I told them what I had made through Scripps and GAC, and it had been my biggest earning year, something like $250,000 in 2009. I did know, however, that I wasn't going to hit that figure again in 2010, because my billing was beginning to free-fall due to the change in sales managers. GAC programming was also taking more label-marketing money than ever before, not that it filtered through to me. But, as it stood, Black River could not afford me.

Black River was operating under a strict budget at the time and still considered a start-up. The Pegulas gave them a fairly small budget, with Jimmy and Tonya trying to stretch that money the best they could. At that time, Terry and Kim were not all in—unbeknownst to their partners, Jimmy and Tonya. It wasn't until they closed the deal with Shell that they decided to give the label significant resources.

In the summer of 2010, the Pegulas convinced a family member to temporarily go to Nashville. His name was Gordon Kerr. Gordon was the brother of Kim Pegula. Kim was a Korean girl that the Kerr family, from upstate New York, had adopted as a toddler. Gordon was an associate assistant superintendent of a high school in Ocean Park, New York, and had dabbled in music, as a horn player, himself. Gordon was to be a liaison between the Pegulas and the president of Black River (Jimmy) and the vice president (Tonya) Once he made his way down to Nashville, he was given the title COO. He was to have no say over the day-to-day functioning of the company, outside of financial considerations. Overseeing the finances at Black River was initially a short-term project for him. He didn't even bring his family to Nashville at first.

It took me a long time to get a meeting with Gordon to talk about any potential opportunity, and when we did meet, he only gave me five minutes. But I had to meet with him as he was overseeing the money. He was dismissive and abrupt. "Jimmy and Tonya told me all about you. I know who you are. Everyone here at the label has been wanting me to meet you. But there is a problem. My family doesn't like you."

I said, "What?"

He said, "They think there's an ethics issue with you."

"What are you talking about?"

"They don't like you" he said again. I was upset. But at the end of our talk, he looked at me and said, "There's something about you, though. I want to have another talk with you. I'm driving home to Buffalo tomorrow. Why don't you call me while I'm driving and we can get to know each other more?"

Even though I was pissed by the unfounded accusation, I did call him in the car at the time we planned. Right from the start, I said, "I'm doing this call with you just to clear my name with you and your family. I've been in this town for 10 years now, have an impeccable reputation, and so what you said to me yesterday affected me greatly. I need to tell you who I am and give you a little insight on my background. I am not pitching you for a job, I just want to clear my name." It ended up being a two-hour conversation.

At the end he said, "I think my family might have misjudged you. I will talk to them. No promises, but I think you will be a good person to bring into Black River." A couple of days later, I got a call with Jimmy, Gordon, and Kim on the phone. "We want to bring you in to be part of our team. We can't pay you what GAC is paying you, but we can give you $125,000 to start. Black River will pay half the salary and we own a sports agency called Ayrult Sports out of North Carolina, run by sports agent Brian Ayrult, and owned by Terry and Kim. You can help Brian with their NFL clients in football."

I took the offer. When I left GAC, the entire staff autographed the original sign from our 16th Street office, as I had been instrumental in generating the revenue that kept us growing. It was bittersweet to leave on a new adventure.

★ ★ ★ ★ ★

My title at Black River was vice president of strategic marketing. The learning curve was more concerned with the people I was working with than the job itself, which was well suited for someone as connected as I was around town.

Jimmy was a great creative guy and Tonya was the businessperson. It was interesting watching them work when I got there. There was not much distance between the husband-wife team. They were joined at the hip.

Even the story of how the label started is pretty epic. Years earlier, Jimmy had been in a band called the Nichols Brothers. Jimmy and Tonya were based in Ohio, but they were mostly on the road with the band. During a road tour in 1991, their bus broke down in Olean, New York, the same town where Kim and Terry lived. By chance, they went to a donut shop, where the owner just so happened to also own a company called Blue Bird Coach Lines, a bus company. He fixed the bus, and Jimmy agreed to come back to the town to do a show for him as a thank you. That show took place on December 23, 1992. Fatefully, Terry Pegula was there with his wife Kim and literally a handful of people. The Nichols Brothers played and Pegula was impressed. He introduced himself to Jimmy and a friendship was formed. By 1993, Terry offered to move the Nichols Brothers to Nashville.

Although the Nichols Brothers did not make it big, Jimmy began making inroads on Music Row and became the keyboard session player many big artists wanted on their records. He also became the music director for some huge names, including Reba McEntire and Faith Hill. Jimmy also started producing artists, including Mindy McCready. Mindy had exploded onto the scene in 1996, having been signed by BNA Records. They had great initial success with her and the debut album, *Ten Thousand Angels*, which yielded several hits, including a number-one song. Mindy had a very public romance and break-up with Dean Cain, who played Superman in the popular TV series *Lois & Clark: The New Adventures of Superman*. After her initial success and public break-up, Mindy battled personal demons that kept derailing her. She bounced around, landing deals with other labels, always ending with tabloid-like drama. But she was an incredible singer, stunningly beautiful, and people kept taking chances on her. Jimmy was one of them. When Jimmy produced a new album for Mindy, and her bills remained unpaid, Jimmy reached out to the Pegulas for help to cover the debt. Terry and Kim came to Nashville for a meeting with Mindy, but came away not wanting to be in business with her. But they did want to be in business with Jimmy and Tonya. That's how Black River Music Group came about. Mindy violated the agreement she had signed with Jimmy, and he released her. Her star burned out for good with her suicide in 2013. It is one of the more tragic tales of Music Row. To this day, if you mention Mindy to Jimmy, he gets very sad. He believed in her so much.

Each month, Jimmy and Tonya were given a certain amount of money to run the label, but it was a struggle to establish themseles without a flagship star. Gordon was brought in to see how the money was being spent, though he was not a savvy record guy. He was conservative and his teaching background was a big part of who he was, very buttoned up, and also very religious. He was parochial in almost everything he did. Gordon made it a point of preaching his credos, like "Always hire better than yourself," and "Always leave a place better than when you found it." And he was like that in the way he handed out discipline. In short, he treated everyone like they were students.

It was a small staff. The day I started, so did a new director of business affairs, Emily Hungate. We were encouraged to invite people in who might be a good fit, as Black River began to expand. There was the radio team, tasked with getting Black River acts on radio stations across the country, as well as the attorney, the online and video people, and the folks who ran the studio.

Black River also owned a publishing company, headed by Celia Froehlig, one of the most respected publishing people in town. Her division was really strong and had hit records with various artists. They also owned two recording studios, one called Sound Stage, which was doing well, and the other other called Ronnie's Place, bought from Ronnie Milsap. Each were excellent, historic studios, which they had poured money into, and were robust businesses.

The one thing that didn't happen was working with Ayrult Sports in North Carolina. I had a couple of conversations with them, but that was about it, even if half my salary was coming off its books.

★ ★ ★ ★ ★

The first signee was Jeff Bates, who was a traditional country artist. He had had some hits with RCA, but he had a substance abuse problem and that caused him to be dropped from the label. Jimmy signed him to Black River to make a splash on Music Row. Based on Jeff's cachet as a name artist, and the fact that he had a large, loyal fan base, made the decision easy. Jimmy felt that his signing would be something that would give Black River the credibility it needed.

But it was Sarah Darling who had the potential to change things around. Jimmy actually found her through MySpace. They had some interns looking for artists, and Sarah had this nice MySpace following. She was originally from Mitchellville, Iowa, near Des Moines, and came to Nashville as a teenager. She worked hard over the years to raise her standing in town.

Two things helped elevate her profile. She was involved in the E! reality show *The Entertainer*, which Wayne Newton hosted for national television, and she made the semi-finals. Wayne told her, "You're really a country artist from what I'm seeing from you, so you're not going to win." He encouraged her to go to Nashville, and she did.

She landed a role in the breakthrough music video, "Save a Horse, Ride a Cowboy," with Big & Rich. She played a mannequin in the video, and there were discussions on whether it was a person or a real mannequin. CMT even ran a contest to guess if she was real or fake.

Sarah was very sweet and also someone who would never give up the dream, a dream she had as a little girl. People gravitated to her naturally. Hers truly was, and is to this day, one of the most beautiful voices in the entire music business. She was a hard worker, an aggressive networker, and kept attending songwriter rounds, learning to write better songs.

Black River immediately started putting money behind Sarah. The first album was produced on a budget, and the other expenses like the wardrobe, music videos, and radio promotion cost the label significant capital. But she was not yet making money. When her car broke down, Jimmy and Tonya approached the Pegulas to help, and they bought her a brand-new Mustang—Jimmy went to his brother and got a family plan discount at the dealership he was affiliated with.

For all her talent, Sarah didn't break through with her first album. The fault was with Black River's radio promotion team's inability to get her single releases added to key reporting stations on terrestrial radio.

There are two main charts, *Billboard* and Mediabase. Those charts run the music industry. Without songs on those charts, nothing else matters. They were dominated by the big distribution companies like WEA, UMG, RCA, and Sony. The big radio stations didn't really look at Black River as a force. They were a tiny independent label. The stations didn't really give too much credibility to the Black River promo team. It was my job to create a huge buzz surrounding Sarah, so the radio promotion team would have a better story to tell about her. I knew Sarah was a star that deserved the chance to compete, but it was an uphill climb for me without the radio story. It was a catch-22.

★ ★ ★ ★ ★

My first day at Black River was on Sarah Darling's birthday, October 4, 2010. But my set-up work began long before that, as I began opening doors with the bigger strategic partners which I had developed during my years at Scripps Networks and GAC.

Annually, I would go to the Academy of Country Music (ACM) Awards in Las Vegas. In 2010, while I had had initial conversations with Black River about jumping over, I was invited to a private Sarah Darling performance in the suite they had at the MGM's residence property, owned by the Pegulas. In that suite I met John Marks, who later became the program director for SiriusXM's *The Highway* and is now running Spotify Country. He loved Sarah Darling. There were other important radio people there too. I was able to invite some guests as well, one of whom, Lou Raiola, became an early believer.

Lou ran Warp Speed out of Minneapolis and was associated with many huge brands. His company was focused on strategic-cause marketing initiatives. His client base was impressive, and he was very respected. Warp Speed worked with many national brands, spearheading cause marketing efforts with organizations like CARE, General Mills, United Health Care, the Starkey Foundation, and his largest client, the NRA. Lou was involved with many fundraising events, hooking up brands and charities. Lou and I had met through Best Buy, which was trying to do something with music already downloaded to new cell phones. He was also a huge supporter of hockey and knew of the Pegulas, who were in the process of buying the Buffalo Sabres NHL franchise and had just given an incredible gift of $88 million to Penn State to build a new hockey arena.

I brought Lou to the Pegula suite in Vegas to see Sarah perform. He immediately fell in love with her and started to help. Lou booked Sarah for a private fundraiser at his home for a collegiate hockey team. The event was during my first week at Black River. I made a real good first impression. Sarah opened up for Lee Ann Womack. Lou had big players there at his party, and we networked with all of them. Sarah blew everyone away with her acoustic performance, and doors started immediately opening for us.

In my second week at Black River, I had a meeting with Teresa George, the senior vice president of brand integration and strategic partnerships for the Academy of Country Music. We spoke about having Black River and the Pegula family come in to help sponsor some of the ACM events, including the red carpet (which would be changed to the yellow and red carpet for Shell Oil, which I wanted Terry to bring to the table). If I could put together the deal, the ACM (on the other side) could help Sarah and Black River. Teresa promised lots of opportunities for Sarah if the sponsorship could come together.

It's a good example of how things work on the big stage in Nashville. Everything is always about relationships: you scratch my back, I scratch yours.

At the same time, Sarah was in the studio, working on a new album with Jimmy. It would end up being called *Angels & Devils*.

A huge rift in the company came with Sarah's song "Bad Habit." Jimmy, in his role as producer and label president, started playing it for some people, including Vince Gill, who was one of the biggest stars around. Vince loved it. Jimmy thought it would work best as a duet with Sarah, and even though Sarah was a relative unknown, Vince agreed to sing with her—and he did. The original title was "I Want to Be Your Cigarette." The concept of the song is that this girl always wanted her boyfriend or her lover to be as addicted to her as he was to cigarettes. It's an amazing song and it opened up tons of doors for her. But the Pegula family, conservative as they were, hated cigarettes, and they didn't want to be associated with a song that had cigarettes in the title, and a big argument took place. Jimmy changed the title to "Bad Habit," hoping it would take some of the heat off Terry and Kim. Jimmy wanted to put it out as a single, but it was not a song that the Pegulas wanted any part of, and they wouldn't let Jimmy release it, even with Vince Gill singing on it. That caused tension internally.

After a couple of weeks, I went from wide-eyed and puppy-tailed to recognizing many of the challenges, especially regarding internal politics. The main issue was Jimmy and Tonya, who had run the label since its inception, and Gordon, who was put in place by his family to oversee everything. The tension between them was obvious and escalating each day. It made for an uncomfortable working environment.

Initially, Gordon and I had a great relationship. He saw me as his right hand. One of the first big things that happened was that the Pegula family wanted to meet with Gordon and me, privately, in Boca Raton, Florida. I agreed, but Gordon said he would drive down, as he'd never been on an airplane before, and he was deathly afraid of flying. But the Pegulas insisted on sending their private plane to pick us up in Nashville. Gordon had had opportunities to fly before but had never trusted anyone to go with, but he trusted me. On October 27, 2010, we went down to Florida. On the plane, Gordon panicked, and my job was talking him down. Me helping him there and back strengthened our relationship and deepened his trust in me.

★ ★ ★ ★ ★ ★ ★
BLACK RIVER
CEO GORDON
KERR AND I
HEAD ONTO
THE PEGULA
FAMILY JET.

The Pegulas were the nicest people, and eager to make Black River a legitimate force in the entertainment business. And they were billionaires. We had dinner with them and I talked about some of the ideas that I had on the marketing side to elevate Sarah. But they were also interested in other media, in other opportunities in the entertainment space—and they were even interested in buying GAC, because they felt they wanted to buy a television network. I even set up a meeting for them with Scripps corporate. But they were told that at this time GAC was not on the market. I was excited by the dream opportunity, as I wanted to develop television shows and explore the multimedia landscape and all the opportunities in it. But more than anything, I wanted to break an act, big. The dinner went very well, and we stayed at the Pegulas' home, which was incredible.

The flight back to Nashville was a lot easier than the flight there. Gordon was less nervous, but still had a look of extreme anxiety until we touched down. He has never flown again to this day.

In November 2010, things came to a head, just four weeks after I was hired. Jimmy and Tonya were forced out, leaving Gordon Kerr to take over leadership of the company. I felt terrible about them leaving, since they went to bat for me to get me hired, after John Gusty had recruited me.

It changed my relationship with others in the company. Some of the older radio promotion guys saw me as a threat, in part because I actually expected results from them, whereas Jimmy hadn't been all that hard on them.

After the departure of Jimmy and Tonya, we'd have group meetings every week to try to figure out what to do with Sarah, what the single would be, and everyone had a vote—except her, which I found very odd. The choice was "Something to Do with Your Hands." It was a good song but certainly wasn't as powerful as "Bad Habit," and "Bad Habit" was the song that later got her on the Grand Ole Opry.

★ ★ ★ ★ ★

With the single for Sarah's "Something to Do with Your Hands" nearing release, I knew we had to do something special to help her break through. I was assigned the task of executive producing her music video. I met with video directors and chose Stephen Shepherd, who'd worked with many artists, most notably Gary Allan, and was creative and quirky but cost-effective. I wanted a celebrity tie-in, someone to portray her love interest in the video, someone to play the role of a handyman. To start, I considered Hollywood types, from more minor shows, but then I thought about how Cyndi Lauper's early videos had featured so many wrestlers. My first thought was Mick Foley, but Sarah vetoed that. I then thought of TNA and A.J. Styles came to mind, and it was a bonus that he lived a few hours away in Atlanta. TNA was headquartered out of Nashville. I reached out to Dixie Carter and she put us in touch. We shot the video in January 2011, and it was quickly evident that it worked. They had some chemistry and A.J. fit the role of "Mr. Handy," fixing things up around her retro kitchen. It turned out to be a great video because the colors really popped and everything looked great. I showed it to the team and they all agreed it was good, so I asked for the resources to get it out there. That meant a publicist who knew not only country music but also pro wrestling, so I called Don Murry Grubbs of Absolute Publicity, whom I knew from my days at GAC.

The video got some good traction immediately and debuted on CMT in January. The station had a voting system for new videos added to their playlist, and it was a hit there, shooting up to number one on CMT.com. Both GAC and the Country Network added it too. We got

SARAH DARLING AND A.J. STYLES ON THE SET OF HER VIDEO FOR "SOMETHING TO DO WITH YOUR HANDS."

Sarah in *People* magazine, on countless radio interviews, and I even took her up to New York for a media tour.

★ ★ ★ ★ ★

Every country artist has a dream to play the mecca of the industry, the Grand Ole Opry. Sarah was no exception. I had a good relationship there with Pete Fisher, who booked all the talent, so I set up a lunch with him on January 11, 2011. At lunch, Pete did not embrace the idea. He said to me, "John, sometimes the team is just as important as the artist, and Black River doesn't have the team in place for us to get behind an artist. They are just not very respected in town." I shared with him what I knew about Black River and encouraged Pete to meet the owners. He knew Sarah and had seen her perform, and loved her voice. As I left, I gave him an advance copy of the album, which was coming out on Valentine's Day, and mentioned that Sarah had a duet with Vince Gill on the album, "Bad Habit." His ears perked up. He promised to listen and get back to me. The very next day, Pete called me. "John, 'Bad Habit' is an incredible song. Sarah is undeniable! We'd like her to be part of the Grand Ole Opry!" Pete then called one of our publicists, Erin Morris Huttlinger, to work out the details. There was one other big surprise. When an artist makes their debut on the Opry stage, an official Opry member does the honors of introducing the act. Vince Gill had agreed to introduce Sarah and sing the duet "Bad Habit" with her!

Her Opry debut was February 26, 2011. During my association with her, she played the Opry more than 80 times. You present Sarah with an opportunity and she usually hits it out of the park, she's that talented.

★ ★ ★ ★ ★

Due West was a new act on Black River. They were three Nashville musicians, Matt Lopez, Tim Gates, and Brad Hull, who had joined the label a few weeks after I started there. They were an independent act, managed by Nancy Tunick, and they ended up on Black River. They had some great songs and wonderful harmonies. They could have been another

Rascal Flatts if the Black River radio division had been up to par, and since Gordon was only just coming in, he was still learning the business.

Everything comes down to how strong your radio promotion team is; if they are not good, without deep relationships with programmers and especially if they are not respected, then you're not going to get anywhere with your acts. Multiply that tenfold if you're with an indy label. Jimmy could be a little headstrong at times, in part because he knew that he had a big backer. A lot of the radio stations no doubt looked down on this start-up, which had not established any credibility or track record.

Personally, I really liked the Due West guys and helped them when I could, including getting them onto the Grand Ole Opry for the first time.

Every label has stories about the ones that got away too.

Ayla Brown had been a finalist as a singer on *American Idol*. She was the daughter of Republican Senator Scott Brown from Massachusetts,

ON A RECRUITING DINNER TRYING TO LAND *AMERICAN IDOL* FINALIST AYLA BROWN. LEFT TO RIGHT, GAIL BROWN AND HER DAUGHTER AYLA BROWN, KIM PEGULA, RADIO CONSULTANT AND GROUP OWNER JOHN MADISON, AYLA'S MANAGER JIM MCGREGOR, TERRY PEGULA, SENATOR SCOTT BROWN, AND ME.

and had been a star basketball player at Boston College; she is in its hall of fame. I had been introduced to Ayla through the charity Songs of Love Foundation, when its leader, John Beltzer, set us up. To me, Ayla had star potential, and I felt that she should be a part of Black River. We met while I was at GAC, and she had aspirations to move from pop to country music. I convinced her to move to Nashville. She was also well connected through her father. But Ayla also had the "it" factor.

Terry Pegula was a big conservative and liked the tie to Scott Brown, so Terry, his wife Kim, and I went to Washington, DC, to meet with Ayla, her mother Gail, who was a TV news anchor in Boston, and Senator Brown. Ayla also brought a mentor, John Madison, who was huge in the radio business, one of the biggest group owners ever. Ayla's manager was there too, Jim McGregor. He was a novice and didn't have a lot of experience managing, and although a nice guy, tended to push a little too aggressively, which led to deals falling through. Ayla was loyal to him, even if he was out of his depth. With the Pegulas' blessing, we did offer Ayla a deal, for a test single. McGregor didn't like the terms and wanted a full album commitment. In a conference call, Gordon got agitated with him and pulled the deal off the table after the call.

★ ★ ★ ★ ★

As I had experienced with my own Straight Up Management years before, it can be difficult balancing acts, and in a bigger environment like Black River, everyone had an act that they championed.

Rick Bumgartner ran the radio promotion department and was an old-timer with dated ideas. He didn't like me right from the start, as Gordon gave me his office and asked Rick to move to another spot in the building. This was not my doing but it soured Rick on me. You can just tell when someone doesn't like you. Rick was really big on Due West, and he had the ears of the Pegulas, since his wife was the Pegulas' real estate agent in the Nashville area. Rick sabotaged a huge deal I was working on, set up by my contact with the ACM, Teresa, who wanted to help me since I was trying to get the Pegulas to convince Shell to sponsor the red carpet at the ACM Awards. She set me up with Bob Romeo, a huge talent buyer in the business, and Starstruck Entertainment, the company owned by Reba McEntire and her husband, Narvel Blackstock. Narvel's son Brandon (who would later marry Kelly Clarkson) was Blake Shelton's manager, and constructed a potential deal that would have put Black River on the map. He also helped Due West and developed relationships with three of the biggest players on Music Row.

Blake was going out on tour in 2011, and the Blackstocks were looking for a sponsor. I suggested to the Pegulas that they reach out to Shell to underwrite the Shelton tour. Shelton's tour would be "powered by Shell." The buy-on would get a Black River act on the tour, and Shell would spend $20,000 or so per date for the title sponsor rights. It was perfect!

At the same time, Kenny Chesney was gearing up for a tour, and Rick had concocted an idea with a local radio program director in Palm Beach. They would have the Pegulas buy sponsorship and have Due West involved on the Chesney tour. There were not a lot of specifics offered up, other than that Due West would be involved, for $350,000.

In the end, the Pegulas chose the Chesney tour for Due West, and not Blake Shelton with Shell as sponsor. However, it wasn't a real opportunity for Due West, as they weren't on the same show as Kenny Chesney; instead, they would appear at off-site radio station parties to promote the show and didn't play at the concerts themselves. So it really didn't mean shit: it was not near anything close to Due West opening up for Blake Shelton.

I couldn't believe it when Gordon told me and got really upset. I said, "Not only is this messing up my relationship with the ACM and Bob Romeo, but it's also hurting my relationship with the Blackstocks and Blake Shelton. This is not the right decision to make." You only get one chance, sometimes, with gatekeepers on Music Row, and when this deal blew up, it hurt us, badly.

The Pegulas decided to meet with Rick and the radio programmer in West Palm Beach to hear more about this supposedly great deal for Due West with Kenny Chesney. They went to a show promoted by the local radio station, where Rick's program director friend worked. Due West and Sarah Darling were both performing there, but there was a slight problem. Hardly anyone was there. Rick had them on a side stage next to the food trucks. It just wasn't a good situation. They were never given the whole truth and then they sniffed out that it was not the right thing, so they pulled out altogether. It seemed so small-time to them, so they distanced themselves from other opportunities after this misstep orchestrated by Rick. It made all of us at Black River look amateur to its owners.

In the coming months, I did my best to restore the company's reputation, including making a deal with the Grammy Foundation, where Black River would sponsor and host Grammy Camp, with more than 100 students from across the country coming to Nashville for a music business camp. I also did a deal with the City of Nashville Tourism Board to sponsor its Walk of Fame.

★ ★ ★ ★ ★

After the mess with the ACMs, I pleaded to Gordon to allow me to salvage the relationship, and he gave me his blessing, after talking to his family. At another meeting with the ACMs, I asked about doing something on a smaller level, and maybe tying Sarah Darling into it for the 2011 awards. Teresa George put together a deal where Black River sponsored parts of the ACM Awards and, in return, Sarah Darling would get to perform at a concert on Freemont Street, a free show a few days before the ACMs in Las Vegas, and attended by thousands. She also got some autograph opportunities and was on the main show, albeit during a commercial break, singing "Something to Do with Your Hands." She got that exposure and that rub in front of the huge crowd and it cost Black River about $70,000, to sponsor a few events during ACM week.

My next pitch was a lot more complicated.

★ ★ ★ ★ ★

Through my first year at Black River, I'd tried to get Sarah a manager. After each meeting with a potential manager, she would come back and tell me she didn't like him (no women pitched themselves for the role). It always came back to "Why can't you manage me?"

Internally, Black River didn't want anybody to manage an artist under the roof of the record company—it just wasn't done in the industry. It was a potential conflict of interest.

But she insisted, so I made the pitch to Gordon that it could and should happen. His idea was to make me vice president of strategic marketing and artist management, and that Black River would sign Sarah to a management agreement, meaning that I would not be on the paperwork. Essentially, I was her day-to-day contact at the company, her manager, but not in writing.

Unfortunately, the rest of Black River was never totally on board. The radio promotion department was worthless, with the exception of one guy that worked in the Midwest territory, Joe Carroll, who was a respected seasoned veteran and who worked on many big songs during his career. Joe loved and really believed in Sarah. Most of the rest of the team didn't give a shit. Every one of the publicists working with us at the time just didn't like Sarah. There was an internal struggle and I was trying to weed out some of these people that really didn't believe in her.

Getting a job at a label is very, very hard. But, once in, you tend to stay employed for a long time, which makes it harder to break in. And poaching good employees was just as hard.

★ ★ ★ ★ ★

Gordon knew that he needed someone to run the label, the music side of it anyway. I was directly responsible for the hiring of Greg McCarn.

When I was GAC, Greg was the vice president of Lyric Street Records, which was owned by Disney. He wasn't just a client but a friend. He'd left there in the fall of 2009, going to work for a start-up digital distribution tech company, one of the first in the nation. I actually set up a meeting with him and the Pegulas in the summer of 2010, before I was hired. He was not impressed. When I said I might try to work there, he pleaded with me not to. "John, they will be out of business in a year! You're my friend, don't go there." His tune changed once I got hired and he saw the way things were beginning to turn around. In February 2011, he called me up, asking me to join him for breakfast. He was basically fishing for a job with Black River. In a way, it was a lot like the wrestling business, where people wanted to get into Black River because they saw the Pegulas as money marks they could take advantage of.

Greg was a brilliant guy, who'd gone from publicist to head of marketing for Lyric Street. He had a sharp, analytical mind and knew the business. He wanted to meet Gordon and wanted to run Black River. I set them up. After Gordon met with Greg, Gordon came by my office and said, "He's the guy."

A couple of weeks later, Greg McCarn was hired as the general manager of Black River Entertainment. In hindsight, that was the beginning of the end for me, even if it didn't come until two years later.

He may deny this, but in my heart, I know that Greg didn't believe in Sarah Darling, who was the reason I was there and the reason I'd been hired in the first place. He just didn't think she had what it took.

At the core of the issue is that Greg did things in a very traditional way, and I was an out-of-the-box thinker. For Sarah, I was doing everything for her other than getting her on terrestrial radio, with the exception of one station. WJVC My Country 96.1 had just gone on the air on Long Island, and I knew the owners from my radio days in New York. I made fast friends with Program Director Adam "Phathead" Zuckerberg and took Sarah to New York to meet him and their team, and to celebrate my 54th birthday. I got a great birthday present, as Phathead immediately began playing Sarah's single on heavy rotation and made her a star on Long Island. Sarah had a believer in Phathead and WJVC. Unfortunately, there were not enough Phatheads.

I decided to put my head down and my marketing cap on, and called upon many of my deep client relationships in Nashville and the brands I had worked with at GAC.

Sarah liked to cook, so I set her up with Jarden, the large company that owned the slow cooker Crock-Pot. Sarah and I flew down to their headquarters in Boca Raton, Florida, and met with their marketing team, headed up by my close friend Susan Selle. This led to a partnership surrounding the single, "Something to Do with Your Hands." Sarah was featured on the packaging of more than a million Crock-Pots. They launched a new Crock-Pot with Sarah as the spokesperson. We also gave away more than a million free downloads. It was a great promotion.

In 2011, I opened up many doors for Sarah, and we developed incredible relationships.

To capitalize on the single's name, I created a promotion called "Something to Do with Your Fans" and took Sarah to ballparks around the country. Radio stations would give away tickets to meet Sarah in a luxury suite at a ballpark, she'd sing the national anthem, and we'd present tickets to local radio stations to give to their listeners. We worked with the New York Mets, the Cleveland Indians, and the Atlanta Braves. In Atlanta, there was a rain delay right before the game, so we were put in a holding room. In walks Scotty McCreery, who had just won *American Idol*, along with his mother, who was managing him at that time. We had time to talk during the delay, and his mother was impressed with what I'd done for Sarah. That was a first good connection.

We had four major entities all wanting to help. I called them our "Core Four," consisting of CMT, SiriusXM, the Grand Ole Opry, and the Nashville Convention & Visitors Bureau. CMT gave Sarah video support, SiriusXM gave her satellite radio airplay, the Opry made her one of its regulars, and the NCVB, run by Butch Spyridon, called Sarah the "Darling of Music City" and even wrapped her tour bus.

We also signed with a booking agency who began to get her paid gigs, Buddy Lee Attractions.

But one of the highlights of 2011, going into early 2012, was a close encounter with former Beatle Sir Paul McCartney.

Andrew Eisner, who had worked with me at Scripps Networks, called me one afternoon and said a friend of his, David Ross, wanted to

★ ★ ★ ★ ★ ★ ★ ★ ★ ★

SARAH DARLING SEES HER TOUR BUS FOR THE FIRST TIME.

meet with me. He had a project that was associated with ex-Beatle Paul McCartney. My ears perked up. It was a benefit album called *Let Us In Nashville: A Tribute to Linda McCartney*, where the profits went to the Women and Cancer Fund. David had been looking for artists to cover various McCartney songs for the project and was having a hard time getting people to take him seriously. We hit it off, and I offered up Sarah for the project. She chose "Blackbird" as her cut on the album. It was stunning. Credit goes out to the producer, Dann Huff, who was one of the elite talents in the business—and who was a friend of Greg's. Dann also agreed to produce Sarah's next album, which was a huge get for her at that point in her career.

David Ross then organized an amazing benefit show for the charity at the historic Ryman Auditorium and asked Sarah to play three songs, including "Blackbird." It was her first time on the Ryman stage, and it was pure magic.

I gave the CD to John Marks during an event right before Christmas. John was the programmer of *The Highway* at SiriusXM. Over the Christmas break, I started hearing "Blackbird" being played on *The Highway*. He just took that song and started running with it. It was a great way to end 2011.

When we resumed work, I suggested we use "Blackbird" as the bridge single until Dann Huff and Sarah finished the full album. We needed a video for "Blackbird" and we were fortunate that the organizers of the project had filmed the making of the song and the benefit show at the Ryman Auditorium.

We put the video together, thanks to their work, and I took it over to CMT, as I knew that they liked to review new videos before airing them. They suggested a few tweaks. Thinking about the other possibilities in town, like GAC, I thought of doing something really out of the box. I went back to David Ross of the McCartney tribute and asked him whether they could make three separate videos, one for each of the country TV networks. David loved the idea, and in the end, we had one in black and white, one in color, and one of a live performance. All three videos were picked up and all three rocketed up the playlist, enhancing Sarah's visibility even more.

Then something crazy happened, and if it had actually come to fruition, it would have been a game changer. David Ross and his partner Dennis D'Amico brought in a third party, Dennis's friend, attorney John Rago to be the intermediary in a very unique idea. Through my Academy of Country Music contacts, I pitched the idea of having Paul McCartney appear at the 2012 ACM Awards, and have Sarah sing "Blackbird" with him. McCartney had actually heard the cover of "Blackbird" and was impressed. The idea got legs as everyone was on board, the ACM, and even producer Rac Clark (son of Dick Clark) and the TV partner, CBS. John Rago went back and forth with McCartney's manager Lee Eastman. Sir Paul also wanted the involvement of Willie Nelson or Vince Gill, if he was to do it. He would sing "Blackbird," and Willie or Vince would be there, and Sarah would join them, until it grew into an all-star tribute, with Sir Paul performing with a dozen or so people. With the awards taking place in April 2012, months of work were being put into this idea. "Would McCartney agree to do this?" It was a daily gut-wrenching wait.

I went to the Grammy Awards with Sarah in February. Paul McCartney was honored with its MusiCares Person of the Year award. Since we were still in the middle of talking to his team, and felt we were close to getting a deal with him, the label authorized us going out there and bought up premium tickets to the charity event.

The next night, at the actual Grammy Awards, the show ended with the very concept that we had come up with—McCartney came out with an all-star rock band and jammed out. While I was sitting there, seeing this unfold in front of me, I started getting texts from Gordon Kerr, saying they were sorry that my idea wouldn't be happening at the ACMs. I later learned that it was the same production teams behind the scenes, which explained it. There is no other way to put it: it was a crushing blow to me at that time. A week later we got the final word. We were told that Sir Paul decided to take a gig in Uruguay and would not do the ACMs. My heart still aches when I recall that time period.

★ ★ ★ ★ ★

After that, we focused on the new album, with Dann Huff. We were excited that this could be the project that launched Sarah's career nationally.

The first single was chosen. It was a song written by up-and-coming songwriters Caitlyn Smith and Bobby Hamrick, called "Home to Me."

I immediately went to my list of potential strategic partners and landed a huge deal for Sarah with the snack cake MoonPie. I had been trying to affiliate Sarah with them for a year. I sent an email to their head of marketing, Tory Johnston, which simply said, "Biting into a MoonPie feels like 'Home to Me,'" and attached a copy of the song. That did it. Tory reached out and we worked out a huge "Home to Me" promotion, partnering with the Grand Ole Opry for a trip giveaway and a meet and greet with Sarah. The promotion was nationwide and was on three million boxes of MoonPie. It was everywhere!

During the summer of 2012, Butch Spyridon and his wife, Sunny, got Sarah signed to the prestigious CAA booking agency, which got her more, better paying gigs.

"Home to Me" was an amazing song and should have been a Top 10 hit. Instead, it only hit number 34 on the *Billboard* Hot Country Songs chart.

★ ★ ★ ★ ★ ★ ★ ★ ★ ★ ★ ★ ★ ★

THE SARAH DARLING MOONPIE PROMOTIONAL PHOTO.

Greg McCarn was slowly changing the label, bringing in new acts like Craig Morgan (whom I'd worked with on that huge Bush's Beans deal at GAC) and Kellie Pickler, and rebuilding the radio promotion team. The new acts surpassed Sarah on the priority list. Early on, Greg also canned John Gusty, who had recruited me, so I lost a true ally.

It was all so puzzling to me. Black River had spent an enormous amount of money on Sarah, but it had all started to fall apart by late 2012. I could tell, I felt it, and I fought with nearly everyone internally, and often my Italian temper would come out. I was obsessed with breaking Sarah, but I was turning into a maniac trying to do it, and, in retrospect, I probably didn't play it right, politically. But I was her champion, albeit an obsessed one, and I felt alone in the fight.

From Sarah, I was constantly hearing, "They're ruining my career."

And causing more internal fighting between the label and me was the fairy-tale romance Sarah was in the middle of, with a suitor from the U.K.

James Muriel was his name, and Sarah had sung demos for James's father, Andrew, who was a big-name aviation finance lawyer and a songwriter. He often told her, "You would love my son, you should meet him." They finally met in 2010, at Andrew's funeral in England. James had called Black River to say his father had died suddenly and to ask if Sarah would sing at the celebration of his father's life, performing some of his songs. They were both in other relationships at the time, but a connection was made at that sad event. They communicated via email for a year, until early in 2012. James invited Sarah on a first date in Paris, which she'd never been to, on Valentine's Day. They fell in love.

With Sarah traveling a lot more, going to see James, I was put in the position of protecting her at the label, but not revealing where she was at times. I was stuck in the middle, dealing with the demands the label made of her, which were becoming more time consuming. I had to cover for her and would get caught when they needed her. One day, I was brought into a meeting, and it was like the Spanish Inquisition. I finally blurted out, "She's in fucking England visiting her boyfriend." Then it was "Ah-ha, we knew there was something going on!" It was very difficult to navigate through all of this.

Meanwhile, "Home to Me" came out, getting traction, and the label was spending some money to get some interesting opportunities for her. They got her on *The Bachelor* and she sang the single on that popular show on ABC. She was on Conan O'Brien's show. But they failed again with her on radio.

This isn't just in country, but in order to elevate a song to the top of the charts, hundreds of thousands of dollars need to be spent on promotion. Black River wasn't willing to go all the way with this one. That failure meant that Sarah had had four singles that didn't break, and that meant that radio pretty well looked upon her as damaged goods, and as though she would never make it.

It was all so incredibly stressful, and I was losing my mind with frustration and distrust with people in the company. I was not the easiest person to work with, because I was just so angry at everyone.

It was around that time that I began to realize that my tenure at Black River might not last.

At the end of 2012, Scotty McCreery came back into the picture, as he was about to go on tour. He had a single that had started to break, so he was hitting the road to support it. Greg McCarn knew McCreery's manager at the time, Todd Cassity, and also knew they were looking for an opening act on the tour, which would hit 25 to 30 cities in 2013. Everyone thought Sarah would be great to open. There wasn't a lot of money involved, maybe $1,000 a night on a bigger show, and the caveat was that some of McCreery's staff would have to be on Sarah's tour bus. It was costly, but the label and the Pegula family agreed to it, as they thought it was a good opportunity for her.

Sarah had what they call a 360 deal with Black River, which means she was signed to the record company, to Black River Publishing, and she gave them percentages of the merchandise and tour revenue. In return, Black River did everything a record company is supposed to do, like pay for her recordings. And remember, they also were her *managers*. But they also were supposed to give her tour support if an opportunity like this came up. The idea is that the money is recouped through royalties down the road.

Gordon didn't like one of Sarah's band members and didn't think he was good enough, and he wanted him out of the band. Personally,

I didn't think it was the place of the head of the label to dictate to an artist who they should have as their musicians. So I stood up for Sarah and it caused tremendous amounts of heat between me and Gordon. It eventually led to my termination.

The guitar player was Scott Hundley, who was a loyal player for Sarah. He was good, but he wasn't the best vocalist. He'd been on the road with her for quite a while. There were internal discussions and it was Gordon's decision to let him go. However, Gordon played it up like it was a joint decision and that Sarah and I were on board with the firing. Gordon met with and fired Hundley. Scott called me up and asked why I had thrown him under the bus. I just told him that it wasn't my decision and that Sarah and I weren't on board with the call. Scott confronted Gordon, calling him a liar, which resulted in Gordon going batshit on me, saying that I wasn't a team player.

In all of my life, including the chaos of pro wrestling, that period from the end of 2012 into the middle of 2013 was the most stressful I had ever experienced. I was being mentally tortured in a lot of ways. Upon my eventual exit, I signed a non-disparagement agreement, and I can't reveal everything else that happened during those last tumultuous months.

Another catalyst in the eventual departure of me and Sarah from Black River was Sarah's relationship with James in England. The two of them decided that James was moving to the U.S. to be with her. Gordon was livid when he heard James was coming to the States.

I was called into yet another meeting to discuss the Sarah–James situation. Gordon put together this calendar where Sarah would be on tour with McCreery and visiting radio on days off. This meant she would be booked up seven days a week, with time in the studio or writing built in. He presented it as a fait accompli. He then set up a meeting with her, me, and other members of the Black River team. It ended with her losing her ever-present composure.

She balked: "I can't do this schedule." She stood up, and I'll never forget it, because I'd never heard her say it before. "This is fucking crazy! I don't have to take this fucking bullshit!" She stormed out, crying. There were always a lot of tears at Black River.

What led to my departure was an explosion during auditions to replace Scott Hundley. Scott's best friend was Jason Cheek, the drummer in Sarah's band, and when Gordon showed up at the first audition, Jason didn't say hello to him. He ignored him. Gordon gave me one of those sideways looks and pointed to my office, which was right next to the recording studio. In my office, he asked, "What's his problem?"

"Well, Gordon, you just fired his best friend. He's not very happy with you."

"Well, maybe I'll fire him too," he said. I then had my biggest explosion ever at Black River.

"Why don't you just fire him then? You're the CEO and the hatchet man, so fire whoever the fuck you want. Fire me, too! Now get out of my office, because I am fucking tired of this bullshit!"

He started turning purple, because he was a devout Christian and he hated the "f-word," and I couldn't stop saying it in our conversation. His eyes were bugging out of his head, and then he started crying. And to be honest, I did as well. I was emotionally spent.

The very next day, I was called into his office and pulled off the road. "From here on in, you're going to fill out these forms if there's any opportunity that comes in for Sarah; give it to Emily"—who was in charge of business affairs—"and I'll decide whether to proceed or not."

I said, "What, are you kidding me, you're cutting my legs out from under me now?"

"This is the way it's going to be."

I immediately went to my doctor and asked for medical leave. I felt I was close to a nervous breakdown. Then I presented the doctor's note to Gordon: "I'm too stressed to work. I'm going to take some time off." My nephew and I went down to Florida, where spring training was underway. I knew my time was almost over.

Sarah's attorney, Denise Stephens, entered to negotiate an end to her management deal with Black River, which I knew was coming. At issue wasn't just the ridiculous schedule but also the conflict of interest of her being managed by the president and attorney for the label (remember, I was not on the paper contract, but in reality acted as her personal manager). Another issue was the way Black River had bailed on promoting "Home to Me."

In the end, Black River agreed to dissolve the management agreement, contending that it had been thinking about releasing her anyway. But she was still on the label.

While in Florida, I had to take a call from Greg McCarn to talk about the plans Black River still had for Sarah. He said they didn't have any. When told that, she wanted off the label. Gordon went to the Pegula family, who loved Sarah but agreed to let her go from the label.

As soon as I got back from Florida, the first week of April 2013, I was called into a meeting with Emily Hungate and Rush Hicks, the company lawyer, where I was terminated. Sarah was gone and my role had been eliminated. Gordon was not even in the meeting. I had to sign a non-disparagement agreement to receive my tiny 12-week severance package. I got to keep my medical benefits for the remainder of the year.

John Alexander, a high-ranking Nashville music mover and shaker for more than a decade, was now unemployed at the hard-to-bounce-back age of 56.

★ ★ ★ ★ ★

At the end, as everything was falling apart, I wrote a letter to the Pegula family, laying out everything that had happened over the last year and a half, the things that had been said, the incredible mental stress that both Sarah and I had been put under. I also laid out the challenges facing me ahead, re-entering the marketplace at my age, knowing it would be very difficult to get a job back in the business, especially a well-paying gig. I put it in a FedEx envelope and I sent it. My mistake was that I told Sarah that I sent it. She started panicking, worried about all the repercussions, as the deals had not all been voided yet. She begged me to try to get the letter back. I tracked it and they retrieved it, and it never got delivered. I still have that letter, sealed in that FedEx envelope.

Somewhere in my mind, I thought the right route would be to sue Black River Entertainment, and that Sarah should as well. I knew there were so many things that they wouldn't have wanted to come out in court that it would have been settled quickly.

Terry and Kim Pegula were always good to me, and I have the utmost respect for them. They simply didn't know most of what was going on at the label after giving Gordon his reign. Their purchase of the NHL's Buffalo Sabres and then the NFL's Buffalo Bills took up all of their time. They always treated Sarah like a daughter and they treated me well too. Sometimes I think Gordon made up the quote that they didn't like me before he hired me.

It's hard for me to write negative things about Gordon, as we were most definitely friends at one point. Sarah and I went to church with his family, and his kids called me Uncle Johnny. He was really into loyalty, so there would be a lot of people that came into the inner circle, they'd come to his house for dinner, and then all of a sudden they're not there anymore. That happened many times, with people that got close and were then gone. His reputation in Nashville is not great, and he has never been fully embraced by the Music Row community.

★ ★ ★ ★ ★

After everything that went down with Black River, Sarah and I continued to work together. It was not easy, as we didn't have enough resources to move forward. One private investor came when we left the label to assist in a single called "Little Umbrellas," which got some traction during the summer of 2013.

But here's the thing about how Nashville operates, and I'm not going to say who the record executive was. When we left Black River, I thought we were well known enough for Sarah to get another record deal immediately. It didn't happen. There was one label that expressed interest. I was driving in my car and I got a call from one of the top executives in town to talk about Sarah. He said, "You know, John, Sarah's great and all that, and we think she really has potential. But you know this is a million-dollar investment." What I took that to mean is that if we went into their office and put a million dollars on the desk, we'd have a record deal.

We actually had a good 2013. We had CAA as the agent. I think we had income of around $400,000 in bookings. My commission was 15 or 20 percent, whatever it was. We had expenses from travel and paying the other musicians. Sarah continued to open for big names like Alan Jackson, Tim McGraw, Little Big Town, Lady Antebellum, and Carrie Underwood. I got her a deal for a line of boots with Durango (Crush Sunflower Slouch Western Boots), which brought in some money for her.

But things were nearing an end.

★ ★ ★ ★ ★

A new network TV show was launching in 2014. *Rising Star* was a hit in Europe and ABC bought the U.S. TV rights. The casting people reached out to Sarah on social media, and she wanted to go for it. Unfortunately, the show was a flop, and Sarah was eliminated early on, leading me to believe it was not on the up and up. These talent reality shows are cast in a way that the producers have a good idea of how it's going to turn out.

Rising Star also cost us significant income in 2014. We had to cancel all of our summer engagements, as ABC required Sarah to be in Hollywood from June through August (or as long as she was an active contestant). We lost roughly $300,000 worth of dates, and I had to start borrowing money again after many years of being solvent.

Up in New York, Sarah and I met with a potential investor. Later, I sat her down with my attorney, and she said, "I don't want another investor. I want a record deal. I don't want another bridge single before I get another deal." She turned that down.

A short while later, in October, Sarah and I had lunch at a restaurant in Brentwood, Tennessee, not long after I had back surgery. She dropped the news: "I'm really not happy."

"I know. Things aren't going well, but . . ."

"No, I'm not happy."

I knew what was coming. "Are you firing me?"

"I don't really want to put it that way."

"How else can you put it? You're firing me, is that what's happening?"

"Yeah, I'm going to change direction."

I got up, left a $20 bill on the table for a lunch which we didn't even have, and walked out, hurt and angry.

She had a three-year contract with me, and I immediately knew I wasn't going to let her out of it. My attorney, Wayne Halper, got involved. Basically, I had opened up every door in Nashville for her.

There's never any real loyalty when it comes to this business, which I understood. But this was still a shock to me in many ways.

I told her that I didn't think it was right to let her out of the contract. She tried on her own for a couple of months, and nobody in town offered to help her on the management side. Everyone knew how much I had put into her career. Just before Christmas 2014, she agreed that I should continue on as her manager.

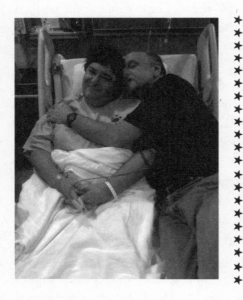

★ ★ ★ ★ ★ ★ ★ ★ ★ ★ ★ ★ ★ ★

MY ATTORNEY AND FRIEND WAYNE HALPER PAYS ME A VISIT AFTER MY BACK SURGERY.

★ ★ ★ ★ ★

Throughout 2014, when Sarah was hot, I tried to convince her to do a crowdfunding project, PledgeMusic, IndeGoGo, or Kickstarter, to raise money to do a new album and to fund the marketing. I tried to show her how it was a new trend. I learned about crowdfunding by researching for a project for her. She dismissed the idea for many months.

Finally, in 2015, she decided to do a PledgeMusic campaign, and we raised significant money through her fans, just under $40,000, to put an album out. It was called *Dream Country*.

One of her new songs was "The Girls of Summer," and I thought it was beautiful. I believed in it and took it to my friend, John Marks over at SiriusXM's *The Highway*. He helped us with every single thing she ever did, gave her a lot of airplay, and loved Sarah. He heard it and said, "Yeah, I think I can give this it a shot, but it needs to be shortened a little bit, and it's mid-tempo. But shorten it and I'll give it a chance." When I told her that, she said, "I don't want to shorten the song, and I don't want another bridge single." She was frustrating me because that song could have gotten some airplay, it could have gotten some traction, but in the back of her mind, she wasn't happy—and I wasn't happy any longer. I could not get my passion back after she had let me go the previous October. But I still believed in her.

At that point, I had Wayne draw up a release agreement and presented it to her. We both realized that our business relationship had simply run its course.

It was the right time to split, as without a manager going balls to the wall for you, it's difficult for an artist to generate and maintain progress.

I had put everything into Sarah and we came so damn close to breaking her huge nationally, had Black River just done the right thing by her. She could have been a superstar, because she had everything.

★ ★ ★ ★ ★

There is a happy ending for Sarah though.

She finally found an audience . . . in England. Her husband proved to be a brilliant marketing person and found the funding Sarah needed to really get rolling. The missteps and failures in Nashville didn't matter overseas.

Her album *Wonderland* hit number one on the official U.K. country album charts, with "Call Me" being the hit song off the record, and she continues to be in demand as a touring performer.

★ ★ ★ ★ ★ ★ ★ ★ ★ ★ ★ ★ ★ ★ ★

**SARAH AND ME AT
HER WEDDING.**

We're still friends, have met for a meal or cup of coffee occasionally, and stay in touch, mostly via social media. She is like a dear old friend, and I wish her continued success.

17.

STARDOM STARTS AT THE MELLOW MUSHROOM

For all that I did to help the careers of Patty Loveless and Sarah Darling, perhaps the biggest crossover star of them all turned out to be someone who introduced herself to me in a pizza parlor in Franklin, Tennessee.

The place was called the Mellow Mushroom, and I was there for lunch with my nephew, Dominic, and my friend Suzanne Alexander. A young blonde girl a couple of tables over kept glancing over to us, and I thought I recognized her. She took the initiative and came over to say hi as we were getting ready to leave the restaurant.

"Do you manage Sarah Darling?" I said I did. "Well, my name is Kelsea Ballerini, and I'm a singer/songwriter here in Franklin." I made some pleasantries, and then she added, "We're friends on Facebook, you know."

"Well, how many songs have you written, Kelsea?"

"I've written about 200 songs."

I was floored: "That's amazing." I gave her a business card and suggested she call me to make an appointment to play me a few of them. I asked her to bring her guitar and play her three best songs, and added that I wanted not the one that her mother liked or that her boyfriend liked, but the songs that meant something to her.

A few days later, she came into my office. She told me her story up to that point, how she had moved to Nashville from Knoxville when she was 15, and researched people in the country music industry through sites like Facebook, to get a leg up, to show off her work.

Then she sang for me.

The first song blew me away, and the second one was equally good. I stopped her. "You're really good." I called over to Gordon's office and asked if I could bring her over to sing for him.

She did the same thing, told him a little story, and went into her songs. He didn't overreact or anything, though. Sitting in the conference room with us was Robert Carlton, who worked in our publishing division, and one of Gordon's sons, Mike.

After she left, I asked Gordon what he thought. "Oh, she's okay."

"Gordon, I think she's a star."

"Oh, she's okay. We've got Sarah anyway. We already have a girl on the label. We'll keep an eye on her."

That wasn't what I expected or wanted to hear.

I waited for Celia Froehlig to get back from whatever meeting she'd been at, then went into her office and shut the door. "Celia, will you take a meeting with me and this very cool kid, Kelsea Ballerini? I just brought her into see Gordon, but I'd like your take on her." She said okay, and a couple of days later, Kelsea came back. After playing for Celia and me, Celia just started glowing. She saw it too. This girl was a star, albeit a diamond in the rough, and Celia saw enough to realize Kelsea had unlimited potential. So she was all about helping develop her. I was happy.

Celia and I were the champions of Kelsea at Black River.

★ ★ ★ ★ ★

In the music industry, there are people who sparkle in person, and others who can't cut it live but who come through terrific on a recording. Kelsea's first CD, a self-made effort, was a case in point. "Was listening to your CD today. It does not compare to you LIVE. Hearing you sing live just blows the recorded stuff away! I can only imagine what a top producer would do with you in the studio," I texted her in July 2012.

"That's why I'm so cautious on handing out my CD, I would *so* much rather play in person," she replied. "Plus, the producer I worked with for those songs wanted to give them a really retro sound which ended up sounding a bit dated."

"Totally hear that," I replied. "Just be assured that the Kelsea I've heard in the past week and a half is the *real deal*."

★ ★ ★ ★ ★

On the one hand, there's chaos with Sarah Darling, with everything falling apart, and on the other, there's Celia and I starting to help Kelsea Ballerini.

I was navigating her through appointments at the label, introducing her to everyone there. I set up a big meeting with her and the head of A&R, Doug Johnson, and another with General Manager Greg McCarn.

Kelsea got to sit in with some of the staff writers at Black River, one of whom was Gordon's other son, Josh. The two hit it off, and not only began writing together regularly, but after time, they began dating as well. Kelsea was also hanging with one of the brightest young writers and aspiring producers in town, Black River's Forest Glen Whitehead.

Kelsea was so likable that everyone wanted to help her. And she was really starting to learn the business. At the same time, I was also meeting with her and her mother, Carla Denham, on a regular basis to hear songs and to strategize. I wanted her to succeed and was a cheerleader and adviser, but I was also working on the business side with Black River, with my job being to do what was best for the company. I actually wanted to help her more than I was doing, but I had my obligation to be on the road with Sarah, and that was already a full-time job.

Kelsea was truly authentic and real. She'd sometimes come into my office crying because she wanted it all so badly. Her talent was undeniable.

★ ★ ★ ★ ★

Kelsea's mother was there every step of the way for her daughter, who she just called "Kels." Carla was also a talented marketing executive. Very smart. She was inquisitive, trusted my advice, and listened. She was a bit impatient, but that was natural. The music business is a marathon, not a sprint. I'd get thankful texts from her: "I really appreciate your belief in and guidance with Kelsea. She (and we) need that," or "Well Kelsea and I believe in you—and trust you, which is huge. Really want to have you work with Kelsea." Carla knew enough to look out for their best interests, but saw in me the champion that had the best of intentions for her little girl.

And aside from working on crafting her songs, Kelsea was still in school. I dropped her a hello on August 27, 2012: "Hope school is ok (know where you'd rather be!)." Her reply: "School is school. Enjoying friends and going to class (mostly on time) . . . would rather be exercising the other side of my Hannah Montana double life. Ha."

Later that year, in November, she texted me during a seminar at school with one of the producers from the hit ABC TV show *Nashville*, wondering if it would be appropriate for her to introduce herself to him after it was over and pitch him her songs. I shared Black River's experience with the show; up to that point, we had only gotten Sarah Darling a cameo appearance on *Nashville*, during the first episode. "I'd love to have a song on that show," she noted. Although it didn't happen, she more than made up for it in the future, doing many shows for ABC.

In January 2013, I was awkwardly placed between mother and daughter. "Quick advice: I'm getting a tattoo on my wrist that I've wanted for a while now that says, 'let it shine.' Just small and quaint. Mom's biggest worry is that it will affect music stuff, but I didn't think so. Do you?" asked Kelsea. I was diplomatic: "Haha! You are asking the wrong guy. Very conservative when it comes to tattoos especially when they are noticeable. Will it affect music stuff? It won't affect your talent. And don't think it would prevent anyone from doing business with you. Just a matter of taste. It's your body."

★ ★ ★ ★ ★

As 2013 began, Kelsea was getting quite frustrated with the lack of progress with Black River, and I began asking everyone what was happening with her. Even with all drama with Sarah, and with my status at Black River getting more tenuous, I still felt I had an obligation to find out as much as I could for her.

On January 9, 2013, Josh and Kelsea played the famed Bluebird Café together, a song they co-wrote. Playing the Bluebird was a big deal. It is the premiere singer/songwriter venue in Nashville, even though it holds only 100 people. If you talk too loud as a customer, the staff place a "SHHHH!" card on your table. It was all about respecting the art of songwriting. When Kelsea got the booking, she texted me about the gig: "You were the first person I thought to invite." I happily accepted the invite. "Glad you are able to be there. See you then!" I sat with the very proud Carla, who was beaming, watching Keslea. Gordon was also there, as was his wife, Kim, and Black River had most of their staff there as well.

After the Bluebird gig, Carla asked to have breakfast with me and Kelsea, and we met at a little restaurant called Dotson's in downtown Franklin. At that breakfast, I agreed to ask Gordon to call her to set up a meeting with him. At the office that week, I gave him Carla's number, but he didn't call her. At the end of January, Carla reached out to me again via text. "Hey John, just checking in. Had anticipated hearing from

Gordon . . . haven't heard anything. Suggestions?" I gave her his cell number. She called him that day and reached back out. "Thank You John. Kelsea and I are having dinner with Gordon on Tuesday night." Gordon never told me about the dinner meeting, which took place on February 5. Kelsea reached out to me right before the dinner meeting. "I am just looking for clarity. I've been so conflicted with it, and no matter what he has to say, I will leave with a lot of peace."

After the dinner, the wheels were set in motion to offer her a development deal as a writer with the publishing company. Terms were not the best, but starting out sometimes you get what you can. On Valentine's Day, Kelsea texted me with news: "Just left Black River with mom, told them I would accept the deal and after this semester will do it full time. GOD IS GOOD. So excited to be part of the BRE family."

I was cautiously optimistic for her. But I also had to tell her that I felt I was on my way out the door, and that any thoughts we might have had of me managing her were unrealistic.

After my departure from BRE, Kelsea, Carla, and I stayed in touch. Kelsea and I would get together for coffee now and then, and her mother would continue to reach out to get advice.

By the fall, Kelsea had proven herself as a writer for Black River and they offered her a record deal. Her mother immediately reached out and asked me, "Need a favor—we need to find a heavy hitting entertainment attorney who can negotiate for Kels. Who's the best in town?" I sent her to Denise Stevens, who was Carrie Underwood's attorney. And Denise represented Sarah Darling as well. Three days later Carla texted me, "Met Denise today, great referral! Thank you—you do good!" However, Gordon and the BRE legal team did not want any part of Denise, which I assume stemmed from her negotiating on behalf of Sarah Darling and her recent departure from the label and management company. On November 8, Kelsea reached out to me: "Turned down BRE record deal offer today. Holy cow. I'm just so disappointed. And frustrated. Went on a wild goose chase for a new attorney for a deal that was 'non-negotiable.'"

With Kelsea now in a serious relationship with Josh Kerr, things changed. At the 2013 Black River Christmas party, with cameras on,

Gordon gave Kelsea a record deal she accepted and launched the career of a star.

Black River invested an enormous amount of money to break her, and now she is the face of the company. She elevated Black River to respectability. I left them one hell of a parting gift . . .

Kelsea had her debut single, "Love Me Like You Mean It," go number one on the *Billboard* country chart, which hadn't happened since Carrie Underwood's "Jesus Take the Wheel." She followed it up with "Dibs," which also hit number one, making Kelsea the first female country artist since 2001 with back-to-back number ones. But she did it again, with her third single, "Peter Pan," making her the first female artist to accomplish that feat. Her debut CD, *The First Time*, got plenty of praise, and *Billboard* magazine chose Kelsea as its 2015 Top New Country Artist.

Kelsea has won several major awards, including the 2015 Billboard Women in Music Rising Star Award, the ACM's New Female Vocalist of the Year in 2016, three Radio Disney Awards, and another ACM award in 2017.

My role in the whole Kelsea Ballerini story has now become revisionist history. I'm never acknowledged as the one that brought her in.

KELSEA BALLERINI PERFORMS AT THE RYMAN AUDITORIUM ON VALENTINE'S DAY 2018.

During her early interviews, she mentioned me, that I was the one that found her and believed in her, but my name no longer gets mentioned. Even when I met Gordon recently, he brushed off our relationship: "You guys were friends on Facebook or something, right?" I have three years of text messages and emails detailing all that I did. She kept in touch up until her first single came out.

I have not spoken to Kelsea since February 2014. I met with her mother several times over the years. She wanted advice from me on a start-up company she was considering. I last saw her on Valentine's Day in 2018, when I ran into her at Kelsea's headlining show at the Mother Church of Country Music, the Ryman Auditorium. I bought my ticket on StubHub.

18.

ALWAYS HUSTLING

There's a special feeling when you are watching an unknown talented act perform their music. It feels like getting hit in the head with a sledge-hammer, and you know in your heart, "That one will make it."

It's the music, the voice, that indelible "it" factor. It's the presence on stage, their charisma, the charm that they have in their everyday interactions with people. It's that thing that draws people to them.

I felt that way with Patty Loveless, with New Kids on the Block, with Sarah Darling, with Kelsea Ballerini. If it was baseball, I'd be batting .800 with that lineup, though I was not there beside any of them when they hit stardom.

Really, I should have been an A&R guy, just looking for talent, rather than managing them and dealing with all the personal stuff that goes along with it. It's really a no-win situation when you're working with emerging and developing acts.

And even when you discover someone, you need to have a finan-cial commitment behind them, which was always my issue, and it's why big-name managers scoop emerging stars away from the little people. That's the feeder system of the music business. I was always the one with no money trying to push my acts, until I was at Black River, which was owned by billionaires.

It's always a roller coaster. I always put too much out for the artist and have gotten too deeply involved in trying to do everything for them.

There is no such thing as loyalty in the music business. The vast majority of artists will drop you on a dime no matter what you've done for them in the past. You have to keep making constant progress, building constant momentum. Once that starts to trail off a little bit, even with a temporary setback, then all of a sudden you've got to watch your back.

But I had to do something after leaving Black River Entertainment.

★ ★ ★ ★ ★

In April 2013, not long after parting ways with Black River, I founded Alexander Music Marketing & Management. Essentially, I was doing what I had been doing: artist awareness campaigns, content production and development, sponsorship and endorsement deals. I knew tons of people in the town and found work, but it was tough being on my own. My main client was Sarah Darling, until we parted ways.

The end days with Sarah coincided with some of my darkest days, health-wise.

In September 2014, I woke up and couldn't get out of bed. I couldn't walk, my legs were dragging. I was in excruciating pain, all in my lower back. I bailed on a gig I was supposed to go to with Sarah. My personal doctor, whom I've had since moving to Nashville, wasn't available, so I went to a clinic. Eventually I got some painkillers to get through a few days until I saw my primary care physician, Dr. Charles Marable, who set me up for an MRI. It turns out that I had a ruptured disc in my back that was affecting my spinal column.

Without any income, I started to sell things off, including my Rolex watch, my Beatles memorabilia, whatever I had to, in order to pay my bills. Of course, I'd had a nice lifestyle earlier, I'm not going to say that I hadn't. I had a great 401K for a while. When I went over to Black River, I took a drop in income. But I was still helping my family financially and had my own high personal expenses and hefty tax bills. I was penalized for early withdrawal from my retirement funds and my taxes changed significantly, meaning I had an IRS problem one year, and I owed them close to $150,000. I then had to re-finance my home to pay off the IRS, leaving me to get by paycheck to paycheck, and I was no longer getting a steady wage.

After the diagnosis, surgery was next, and Dr. Marable introduced me to several surgeons. I went with one of the best . . . I thought. We went ahead, just an overnight stay after the operation—but when I tried to get out of the hospital bed, I still couldn't walk. "Don't worry, it'll heal in three or four days, you'll be fine, and will feel uncomfortable for a week" is what the surgeon told me.

I got home and was still immobile, and living by myself. My neighbors brought me groceries, but I was housebound and could barely move. And it was getting worse.

The surgery didn't correct the problem, so I went back to see the surgeon, and he looked at the new MRI and said, "Ever hear of that Britney Spears song, 'Oops! . . . I Did It Again'? Whoops, you did it again, it's ruptured."

"What do you mean I did it again? I didn't do anything—you did the surgery and you didn't do it right."

The second surgery corrected it, and physical therapy followed. To get around, I had to rely on a cane for support.

After promoting so many gigs that raised money for charities, I was now the one who needed help. I reached out to the Music and Health Alliance in Nashville and met an angel who I'd known for many years. If it were not for Sheila Shiply-Biddy, I would have lost my house and gone bankrupt. She got me new affordable health insurance through Obamacare, contacted the Grammy Foundation and ACM Lifting Lives for me, and assisted me in applying for hardship grants. These organizations allowed me to keep my house, to give me money to pay my bills. Believe me, it was embarrassing; even writing about it now makes me uncomfortable. I had been making tons of money, and through it all, I always helped my family: I paid my sister's mortgage; I gave money to my older sister; I paid for our mom's room at the nursing home. The money came in, and even though it was big money, it also went out, primarily to help my family.

★ ★ ★ ★ ★

With Sarah gone, I took a couple of gigs, freelance consulting for artists that I tried to help, but I was not able to get the doors open as easily as I had in the past. And my passion for giving it all for an artist was beginning to sour. Paid consulting just wasn't my thing.

I had great relationships with people in Nashville and on Music Row, but once you're out, once you're no longer in the inner circle, you're out. The people you did business with, and who you thought you were friends with, you'd see them at restaurants, parties, and shows, they would look through you and not at you.

Here's an example. At GAC, I worked with Sarah Trahern, who programmed the station. She saw the writing on the wall at GAC and landed *the* job in town, becoming chief executive of the Country Music Association (CMA). She was and still is the Queen of Nashville.

I applied for the job of vice president of strategic marketing at the CMA. I couldn't even get a face-to-face interview, couldn't get past a human resources phone call, couldn't get a meeting with her. That's the kind of thing that goes on in this town. That's why I'm so disillusioned with the current state of Nashville.

The town is a have or have-not town, cliquish and incestuous, and when you're down and out, no matter who you were in the past, you're not going to get help from anybody.

But if you have even a little bit of something going on, then you get all the congratulatory emails and calls, and they all want to take meetings or have lunch.

It happened with Bandtwango.

★ ★ ★ ★ ★

When I was up in New York, I met with my fellow Mets fan Jon Steinlauf, who was still running the ad sales at Scripps. He has been a mentor to me and has always been straight up and honest. GAC was still operating, and I asked about work there, but he said the plan was for the company to get out of country music altogether. There were also rumors of a merger between Scripps and Discovery (which did happen in 2019). I left that meeting depressed, wondering what I was going to do next.

Up next was a lunch with Carl Allocco, the same Carl from Carl and the Passion. We had found each other again when he came to Nashville to live for a while and worked for Songs of Love. But he'd since moved back to New York.

CARL ALLOCCO AND I GO WAY BACK, FROM THE STRAIGHT UP MANAGEMENT OFFICES IN 1986 UNTIL TODAY.

Ironically, I found myself ranting to someone who had caused me so much grief when I was managing him: "Is it over? Am I fucking done?" He had his own frustrations with the music business. We started talking about crowdfunding, as I'd done with PledgeMusic, and he was fascinated by the potential of it all. I saw a business opportunity.

I shared my view that crowdfunding companies were glorified listing services and that no one was actually trying to help the artists. I saw it as a void and Carl agreed. We batted around ideas for a company that did crowdfunding differently, helping and nurturing artists. It didn't happen at that lunch, but it wasn't too much longer before we created Bandtwango. Carl stayed in New York to do the creative and I was in Nashville, armed with my knowledge of marketing and ability to spot talent.

Bandtwango opened an office in December 2016, and it was a struggle from day one, not only from a financial standpoint but also given how much the music business has changed over the years.

There have always been incredibly talented people coming to Nashville, chasing a dream, often without any money or connections. They can't get in to see anybody.

Then you have the kids that come into town that are marginally talented (if that), with wealthy parents who can open doors and who have an illusion that their kid is going break big. They're sucked in by bottom-feeders who are paid huge amounts of money to advance their kids' careers.

It's really not fair, it's not a level playing field, and it's only gotten worse in the last 10 years.

When I was at GAC and Black River, I'd take meetings with anybody, because you never know. I mean, a kid who introduced herself to me at a pizza place ended up being Kelsea Ballerini. My thought was always "Why not? Come sing for me."

That's definitely not the norm here in Nashville. You can't get to people unless you're well connected or you have some sort of buzz going on from something else.

There's a hundred new artists arriving every month, and they play these clubs, up and down the Broadway strip, very few get paid, they all work for tips, and most of them are incredible musicians. They think that record company guys are hanging out there waiting to discover the next star. But they don't get anywhere. I doubt that an A&R person has walked into a club in downtown Nashville to find somebody in the last 20 years. It just doesn't happen.

So think of Bandtwango as a bridge to get doors open.

It's artist development in a non-traditional way. Because of how corporate it's all gotten, the labels are petrified of signing anybody. The revenue streams are not as robust as they used to be. Streaming is now starting to make huge money for the record companies, but the money doesn't trickle down to the artist.

The idea for Bandtwango is to meet with anybody and try to decide if they can raise money through crowdfunding and their fan base. We look at it as mining for gold, where we have a pan, and it's going into the riverbed, and we're pulling it out, shaking it. After the water, debris, and silt is gone, there's a little piece of gold that's nice and shiny. Those, you set to the side and then try to help them open doors.

Bandtwango exists to mentor, to educate, to teach, to show these kids that arrive how the town really operates.

I've been marketing music for 20 years now. I know the town, I know what they look for, I know how to get things done here. Bandtwango has rarely turned anyone away, and in the early days, we did launch campaigns for just about everyone; more recently, we've been more selective on the process.

We're not getting a lot of help from the community, and it's really sad, because Bandtwango could be a feeder system for the industry. Nobody else does the artist development anymore. When they put a single out, if it doesn't fly, then a lot of times that artist is not going to have a second single.

To use a wrestling term, we're a developmental system, or in baseball, we're the minor leagues.

And just like my time in baseball and wrestling, there was little money for me. When Bandtwango was my main focus, I received no salary. The goal was to convince potential investors that this is the business model of the future, that you can develop an act and catch fire with it. You don't need to hire an expensive radio promotion team.

The labels today are just looking at streaming numbers. They are getting their artists from publishing companies—and the publishing companies are doing more of the artist development than the labels are. The publishing companies are nurturing the writers.

The sound coming out of this town is not what it was. Country music all sounds the same today, ever since Florida Georgia Line broke. Everything is this bro-country stuff, closer to rapping than to Hank Williams or Johnny Cash.

Women don't get equal treatment or opportunities. I saw it with Sarah Darling and have seen it with many others. Most labels didn't want to have more than one female artist on their roster. I am hoping that is beginning to change since there is now a unified outcry by women executives and the media, who are focusing on the disparity in the industry. The industry is long overdue for an overhaul.

Bandtwango goes against the grain.

★ ★ ★ ★ ★

On the Bandtwango front, and with the exception of a very few, I do not enjoy working with today's artists. I don't know it's a generational thing or if it's the way social media has changed people's perceptions of what they should be doing as an artist. There's a disconnect, and maybe it's because I'm a much older guy in the music business. I don't see a lot of artists coming in here that are doing it for the right reasons—most of them want to be stars and not artists. Most of them are more concerned with shooting a picture of their next lunch for Instagram than a recording session.

By the beginning of 2020, I realized that I had lost the passion and desire to continue on in the music business, and decided to turn the management and operational direction over to my friend and co-founder

Carl. Although I owned a fairly large equity position in the company, my lost enthusiasm was not good for the long-term health of the company, nor my own health. Carl and I have always had opposing viewpoints on many aspects of how to handle artists, and this led to tension. I had slowly developed severe hypertension since forming Bandtwango, and the daily stress of dealing with the artists and daily interactions with Carl was leading to a health crisis I felt was imminent if a change was not made. I hoped Carl would take Bandtwango to great places, and help the artists that reached out to him, but in the horrific year that was 2020, it was not meant to be. The music industry was decimated by the COVID-19 pandemic, which affected everyone in it, and Bandtwango was no exception. The company closed in September 2020. It was a great idea, but sadly, without new clients in an uncertain industry, its fate was sealed.

★ ★ ★ ★ ★

People rise, others fail. It's not just a Nashville thing.

There are good people, one of which is my friend Pete O'Heeron, whom I met when I was at GAC. He started Cold River Records, which is not to be confused with Black River. He came into town as an outsider and had made his money developing patents for the medical industry, some really high-tech, innovative, state-of-the-art patents. He would work with patent-holders and then market those patents to surgeons and hospitals around the globe.

At a family gathering, Pete heard a second cousin, Katie Armiger, sing, and he thought she had potential as a country artist, so he started a record label around her.

Being new in Nashville, no one would meet with Pete. Except me. Pete was just so grateful that I took a meeting with him at GAC, and then I got behind his artist and helped her get her videos played.

So we developed a friendship that continues. He's like a brother to me. He went through a lot of trauma as a kid and has shared some deep things.

I stood behind him as the problems began between him and Katie. He probably put close to $5 million into her career and she never broke through. He persevered. His attitude was "Screw you, Nashville, I'm not going away!"

In the end, Katie just decided she didn't want to do it anymore, after they had recorded an album and put out a new single.

In 2020, Pete folded the label. He's still someone I'll go out of my way to help, because that's what friends do. And he's been there for me, time and time again. He's the brother I never had. Pete is now at the forefront of several major medical breakthroughs that could literally change the way people are treated for spinal injuries and chronic back and neck problems, and even repair tissues and organs damaged by viruses.

★ ★ ★ ★ ★

Another example of the rise and fall is Cyndi Thomson. She made a big splash when she debuted in 2001 with a number-one song, "What I Really Meant to Say." Cyndi was this gorgeous, syrupy-sweet girl from Georgia and she set the country music world on fire. As fast as she skyrocketed, she crashed quick, quitting right in the middle of her fame, and no one could understand why. She had a failed attempt at another comeback, and there were rumors about her returning to country music, but that never happened.

She had a Facebook profile and posted a photo of her on *The Tonight Show* with Jay Leno. I commented on it, something like, "That should be you again." Within a few minutes, she messaged me on Facebook and said that she had heard a lot about me and wanted to meet, so we did. Cyndi not only wanted to get back into the business, but she had already recorded a whole album. It turned out she lived really close to me, so I went over to her house one morning, and I listened to it over coffee. It was incredible! The album blew me away, sounding progressive with a mix of Appalachian, Native American, and country influences. The production and songs were great, and I thought it was destined to be a platinum album.

After consulting with a few people I trusted, and being familiar with her husband, Daniel, from his freelance work at GAC, I confidently entered into a management agreement with Cyndi. We started to look for funding since she didn't want to go the major label route again.

Since Sarah had turned down Michael Nasti in New York, who was going to put significant money behind her, I approached him with Cyndi's latest project, and he immediately fell in love with it. We flew up to New York and met with Michael.

That's when I first noticed that there was something amiss with her. We met at a cafe in Babylon, New York, and the meeting dragged on, and I had a family obligation that I was running late for. I tried to wrap up the meeting a few times, until finally we all got up, and I said I'd go bring the car around. Ten minutes later, she got into the car and was angry at me. "He wasn't done with our conversation," Cyndi said sternly.

I said, "Yeah, I think he was done with our conversation, Cyndi."

She said, "This is more important than your family. They can wait."

It was a whole different side to her.

Michael wanted to invest. He came down to Nashville but asked to meet with Cyndi privately first, which I was okay with. Later, I had a dinner party at my house to reintroduce her to industry people. Before the dinner, though, Michael and Cyndi arrived and told me that they were going to do something on their own, and I'd get a piece. I felt I was being cut out and was unnerved and upset.

After Michael went back to New York, she decided she didn't want to do business with him because of the terms and instructed her attorney to pull the plug.

Looking back, it's my feeling that Cyndi finds a way to sabotage relationships with people that want to help her, with some inner fear in her that doesn't allow her to reach her goals and achieve her potential.

We ended the short-term management relationship. My lawyer, Wayne Halper, who was the head of business affairs with Capitol Records Nashville when Cyndi was there, and later went on to become the general manager of DreamWorks Records, hammered out the details of the dissolvement with Cyndi's high-powered attorney, Michael Milom.

A year and a half later, I ran into her at the supermarket, and we made chit-chat. She asked what I was doing now and I discussed Bandtwango. She asked to come in for a meeting, which I agreed to. But she decided that the Bandtwango model was not something she wanted to do. She is still an enigma in Nashville.

★ ★ ★ ★ ★

Out of the blue in March 2016, I got a call from John Gusty, who was my first champion at Black River. He had a vast resume in the music business, including running the website for Bon Jovi and working for the innovative Echo Music before they were purchased and screwed over by Ticketmaster. Like me, he left Black River under poor circumstances, and there were bad feelings there. We hadn't kept in touch, other than running into each other at events.

He wanted to have lunch to discuss a project. John told me about working for two sisters, Pearl Barrett and Serene Allison. They were a Christian singing duo, who were very health-conscious. Their father was a pastor.

They had a self-published book entitled *Trim Healthy Mama*. It was more than a diet book and more about lifestyle change. They developed a lot of their own products and supplements. It had been marketed to friends and family through Facebook, but had grown organically to the point that they had been offered a multi-book deal by Random House.

John had been hired to build out their website, including the e-commerce side and wound up becoming president of their publishing division, Welby Street Press. He wanted my help as a multimedia connector, because I knew not only how to market but also how to put deals together and connect people with like-minded goals. Their hope was that I could help them explore television, radio, and whatever else we could, making mass media opportunities, maybe even a weekly show.

There were really four people running the company: Pearl and Serene, and their husbands, Charlie and Sam. At our first meeting we hit it off, since they were so genuine. They saw my credentials and the things that I'd done in my career and gave me a shot as a consultant.

I went to work leveraging old relationships. Two colleagues from Jones Media Networks, Cathy Csukas and Gary Schoenfeld, were now running AdLarge, which represented tons of national radio shows to sell advertising, as well as developing programs and podcasts.

David Sams was another meeting, through his cross-country radio platform Keep the Faith. He was also the king of infomercials, successfully marketing products that made hundreds of millions of dollars. Before that, he'd been a television executive at King World Syndication, managing *Wheel of Fortune*, *Oprah*, and *Jeopardy*, among others. He fell in love with the girls and their mission right away.

Contrast that with Scripps Networks, which ran the Food Network and the Cooking Channel. They didn't really get what the girls were trying to do, since they were talking about lifestyle changes and losing weight, and the Scripps channels were really all about indulgence.

It wasn't long before *Trim Healthy Mama* was a successful podcast. Later, we launched a national radio show, which has had a difficult time clearing stations, since a lot of stations haven't understood what the sisters were trying to do. We thought we had a deal for them to appear regularly on the Nashville-filmed *Pickler & Ben* talk show, but Scripps pulled back at the last moment, considering the lifestyle change they were advocating was akin to an unproven diet, unlike, say, Weight Watchers. *Trim Healthy Mama* is not a diet but a lifestyle change, eliminating sugars and damaging carbs from your food choices. It teaches when to eat proteins, fats, and carbs.

Everyone liked working with me, my innovative approach, and the fact that when I said I was going to do something, it got done. They started asking me about some of the other things that I do, and they ended up investing in Bandtwango.

Unlike Black River, where I clashed with so many higher-up people, I love Charlie and Pearl, and Serene and Sam, and their family-first ideals. It's fodder for a reality show. The two sisters have 17 or 18 kids between them, maybe more. Serene adopted children from different parts of the country, and Pearl has kids, and now they have grandkids. The clan is a tremendous, eclectic group of people. It's a tight-knit group, and I was happy to be integrated into it.

We've had our ups and downs. The company grew too big, too fast in 2018, so they had to cut back on extras, like me. But when it was time to place their infomercial, they knew who to call—me. I set them up with my former Scripps Networks colleague Jim Zarchin, who had worked on those early Taylor Swift vignettes. Jim's team from Z Media Ventures produced a great 30-minute program on them. So now, with my new company Alexander Media Services, I used the years I spent working in ad sales to place media for them. They promoted a new starter kit as a part of a *Trim Healthy Mama* lifestyle. But, as most have discovered in the midst of a global pandemic, nothing was easy. A robust ad budget was allocated, but uncertainty in the landscape during COVID-19 led to the curtailment of the campaign.

So, I went back to that old love/hate relationship, where I started this ride, pro wrestling.

19.

PRO WRESTLING, THE CRUEL MISTRESS I CAN'T SHAKE

Other than a few interactions with TNA Wrestling, which was based in Nashville, I had dropped all contact with my friends and colleagues in pro wrestling. I went cold turkey.

Oddly, it was an appearance on the NBC game show *Deal or No Deal* that revealed for the first time to many of them that I was still alive! When I disappeared without a trace, many thought I was in witness protection.

It was in early 2007, not long after my mother died. I was watching *Deal or No Deal* and there was an ad for an open audition for the show in Nashville. I immediately thought my sister Donna would be a great fit. She had been seriously contemplating moving back to Long Island with Dominic, so this would be a distraction from both her grief and the potential move.

She scoffed when I presented the idea, as she didn't watch the show. But I persisted, selling her on the idea that she was a thousand percent New York, yet would show up at an open audition in the South. Donna made lots of excuses not to go, like Dominic having a Little League baseball game. "He hasn't had a hit yet. What if I miss his first hit?" I suggested that he might get a hit because she wouldn't be there. (Ironically, he did get his first hit.)

During the audition, she spent a ton of time waiting and kept calling me with updates: "I've been here for three hours!" It took forever to get in, for your 20 seconds in front of a casting agent. She spent the time making friends with people who were in line. When she did finally get in, her patience had been spent. They asked her why she wanted to be on *Deal or No Deal*, and she let loose after the long wait: "Wait one second, before I answer anything, I've been standing outside for 11 hours! There's no coffee, there's no bathroom! You just wait in line like a bunch of animals!"

When she finished her rant, they just told her to stay, getting her into another area where she was on to the next round of auditions. There she really got a chance to talk to the casting people, and they liked her enough to bring her back for a second audition, which was the following day. At the second audition, it was a mock game of *Deal or No Deal*.

For those unfamiliar with the game show, essentially there are 26 briefcases with money, ranging from a penny to a million dollars. Cases are eliminated during game play, the Banker offers periodic "deals," and the contestant has to decide what to do. They are allowed to consult with pre-arranged friends and family on decisions.

All animated and excited, Donna did great at the second audition, and a few weeks later she got the call that she would be on the show, the season opener for the fall of 2007.

Unbeknownst to Donna, the producers contacted me with an idea. They pitched making it a New York–themed show for her and surprising her with friends and family. And how do you do that without tipping off the contestant? Well, you go through the contestant's brother. It was a lot of work for me, since I had to figure out how to contact all these people without her knowing . . . and Donna keeps in touch with everybody she's ever met. There were hundreds and hundreds of entries in her cell phone directory. They suggested I steal her cell phone, and I did get it away from her for a couple of hours, reading off the contact names and numbers for the producers during a conference call.

They slowly built out the names for the show, starting with our older sister, Linda, who lived in Denver. They wanted her hairdresser, friends, the local diner owners, and even teachers from high school. A wide variety of people were contacted. The producers even secured Mr. Met, the New York Mets mascot.

It was all very nerve-wracking, and the producers of the show had to organize everyone getting out to California for the taping. Most were from New York. The idea was to put them all on a New York City transit bus and, in the middle of the show, drive the bus onto the set. Her three chosen helpers to start the show were me, our cousin Jimmy Guerri, and our lifelong friend, who we consider family, Louis Esposito.

The show started normally, and then the host, Howie Mandel, picked up the phone and went, "What do you mean the banker's not here?" It turned out there was a guest banker, and it was Donald Trump—and Donna went bananas. She has always loved Donald Trump, both as a New Yorker and from his time on TV on the *Celebrity Apprentice*. But as the banker, Trump was supposed to be the opposition, and my sister was just gushing over him. If anything, he played a tougher game against her because of it, making some unfair offers.

Donna made some strategic mistakes on the show, one of which cost her a million dollars. Her lucky number is 11, she was born on June 11, our father's apartment number was 111, and so on. The producers ask these questions in pre-interviews. I later found out that her friend, the hair stylist, who ironically could not make it to California for the taping, strongly suggested to the show's organizers, "Put that million in suitcase 11!" Donna chose suitcase 26, and it collapsed from there. Dominic was 10 at the time and was in the audience crying when she didn't get the money. She walked away with 25 dollars, making her one of the biggest losers ever on that show.

The producers manipulate you during this hour because they want you to go all the way, they want you to fill the entire hour. It's hard to explain unless you were there experiencing it.

They didn't bring out the bus of people when they had said they were going to, which was near the beginning of the show. They brought the bus out after Donna had collapsed after seeing what was in suitcase 11, and not the one she picked. The bus with her friends and family was then a way for Howie to try to make her feel better.

It was great television, though. Her lifelong friend and maid of honor, Lisa Esposito (Louis's sister), came jumping out of the bus, then my sister Linda, and so many friends from New York, including Mr. Met. It was an emotional moment, and there was not a dry eye in the house.

Through all this Trump was watching from his bunker on the show, and I felt that he gave her a bum rap with his offers. I interrupted Howie and asked to say a few words to Mr. Trump. I looked at him and I said, "You're fired!" I knew from my wrestling days that it would get a big "pop." The place went nuts and Donald just smiled. NBC thought it was good enough to put in its promos for the season premiere, which meant I was on NFL football saying, "You're fired!" to Trump. They played it over and over again. To my knowledge I was the second one to fire Trump on national television, after Vince McMahon of WWE. It's an even more surreal moment to look back on now, as he became the most divisive and horrific President of the United States in history.

They shot some B-roll at the end of the show, including Donna and Dominic meeting Trump. Backstage, Trump was taking photos with all the models. He saw my sister and nephew and called them over. He had made an offer of $93,000 when there was still big money on the table, and Donna had kept playing the game, which Jimmy, Louis, and I had all encouraged her to do. Hindsight being 20-20, I should have told her to stop the game. "You should have listened to me," he said, and then turned to Dominic, "Your mother should have listened to me. But there's something about you, I like you, and I'm going to do something that has nothing to with the show. I'm going to write Dominic a check for $25,000 for his college." Which he did.

It's not even the last time that Donald Trump came through for Dominic. When Donna and Dominic moved back to New York, Dominic was diagnosed with a disease called dystonia. In simple terms, it's a disorder where a person's muscles contract uncontrollably, and it can be a small muscle or the entire body. Donna looked at all the options to treat her son, from medication to, at the extreme, brain surgery. None of the choices were ones any of us wanted to put Dominic through. An unconventional method, which insurance didn't cover, was a hyperbaric oxygen chamber, and Dominic needed to use it three times a week. One of Donna's high-school friends started a GoFundMe campaign to pay for the treatments.

Another of Donna's friends in Tennessee, Megan Hull, contacted Trump's office in New York and told them about it, and he paid for a number of the treatments, several thousand dollars. Later, Dominic took it upon himself to raise money for a charity associated with Trump's hit TV show, *The Celebrity Apprentice*, and raised a good amount. Trump invited him and my sister to that season's live TV finale and the after-party, so they got to hang out there and met Melania.

When Trump decided to run for President in 2015, I thought it was a big publicity stunt. However, as he won primary after primary, then the Republican nomination, and finally the Presidency, we all realized it was no stunt. I didn't vote for Trump in 2016 nor in 2020, despite the good deeds he did for my nephew. His character alarmed me, and I couldn't vote for him and keep my self respect. And, as he proceeded to divide America, and spew hate during his term, it caused tension with me and some family members and a few of my closest friends. I debated removing all Trump references from this book, but it is part of my story.

The end result of *Deal or No Deal*, though, was that I was recognized, and it was reported that I had surfaced in Dave Meltzer's *Wrestling Observer Newsletter* and other wrestling outlets. People even recognized Donna from my conventions. It reconnected me to the pro wrestling world, these people who had not seen me in 10 years. People were wondering if this was a shoot or a work—believe me, it was a shoot!

★ ★ ★ ★ ★

From that point on, I had a little bit more to do with pro wrestling. Wade Keller at the *Torch* reached out and I let him share my old radio shows with his online subscribers. I have done a number of podcasts in recent years, especially with "The Great" Brian Last, who had me on to talk about AAA and Ron Skoler, about Vince Russo, and about photographer Mike Lano. I didn't really give pro wrestling a thought as a time-consuming side gig.

Russo had his book published in 2005, and there were allegations in it that I felt I needed to address but didn't at the time. Russo kept on telling tall tales about how our relationship worked, but I didn't pay attention. Dominic is a Russo follower and gets a kick out of him. At Thanksgiving 2018, he texted me and said, "Hey Genie, Russo is talking about you on this podcast." He sent me the link and I thought that enough was enough, because he was saying a lot of lies.

Russo challenged anyone who ever had a problem with him to reach out and settle things on his podcast *Truth with Consequences*. When I heard that, I got in touch with Matt Koon, who was his co-host and producer, and said that I wanted to take him up on the opportunity. Russo agreed, and I agreed to do it as long as it wasn't an ambush, as long as it wasn't him screaming and yelling. It needed to be a conversation between two gentlemen to talk out our history and our differences. The end result is a fascinating YouTube video where we talk about everything, our entire history, at least to the best of both our recollections.

Naturally, anything that Russo does gets a lot of attention in the pro wrestling world, and that YouTube video reignited whatever pro wrestling fire that I had buried deep within myself. So, just as I got him into the business originally, he brought me back in—is that irony, or what? (Russo and I have made up and communicate now, and even got together during Christmas 2018 in Colorado.)

REUNITING WITH THE POWER TWINS AT THE 2019 CAULIFLOWER ALLEY CLUB REUNION IN LAS VEGAS.

Now that the fire was rekindled, what to do with it? I went through all my wrestling archives, dating back to the early 1970s, and started Twitter, Instagram, and Facebook profiles under John Arezzi. They immediately caught fire, and people were shocked to see me back. Friends like Cactus Jack, Sean Waltman, Konnan, Sabu, and others contacted me and welcomed me back into the fold. I found a market for those who love wrestling history. I had become a "historian."

★ ★ ★ ★ ★

Brian Last was a listener to *Pro Wrestling Spotlight* back in the day, when he was 13 years old, living on Long Island. He's a key player to everything that has brought me to this point, with a book in your hands.

After having me on some of the other podcasts that he co-hosted, Brian and I spoke about doing something together. Given my background, I was intrigued and decided to explore potential shows with him. He demonstrated how even the playing field was online, and how a podcast could generate a little revenue, especially with a member-only section chock full of exclusive content.

The result is *John Arezzi's Pro Wrestling Spotlight Then & Now*, which has been running since May 2019. It's been a blast, because it's reminiscing. At its core, we're just revisiting the old shows, playing segments and talking about not just what was on the air, but also what was happening in pro wrestling at the time, and even the chaos in the radio control room. If someone wants to listen to the entire original program, they pay a small monthly fee. It has developed a growing following with thousands of listeners weekly, and unlike my regional show, can be heard around the world with today's distribution methods. But the real fun now is making fun of who I was back then, and the characters who were part of the show 30 years ago.

★ ★ ★ ★ ★ ★ ★ ★ ★ ★ ★ ★

THE STORY OF ANTONIO PENA WANTING ME TO PORTRAY PUPUCHO FOUND NEW LIFE IN THE PODCAST WORLD IN 2019.

Through Brian and the people who listen, many of whom were original listeners of *Pro Wrestling Spotlight*, I have found that there's a market for my other wrestling-related goodies too, such as my ringside photography and, perhaps most impressively, my 8mm films shot at Madison Square Garden of WWWF in the 1970s. The *Dark Side of the Ring* show on VICE is just one of the places that has not only licensed my photos and footage, but has also had me on the show to talk about my experiences. This has led to my reviving the old *Pro Wrestling Spotlight* show as a live-streaming weekly broadcast on Facebook and YouTube. I also am developing a new website called MatMemories.com, which will be a place for wrestling historians to share their archives. It ties into an association with Greg Oliver's SlamWrestling.net.

I am trying my best to keep my expectations realistic and my time commitment to this wrestling resurgence under control, but as each month now passes, I have found myself devoting more and more time to it.

THE TRAGOS/THESZ PRO WRESTLING HALL OF FAME IN IOWA, WHERE I ACCEPTED BRUNO SAMMARTINO'S POSTHUMOUS INDUCTION. LEFT TO RIGHT: THUNDERBOLT PATTERSON, JERRY BRISCO, SGT. SLAUGHTER, DAN GABLE, WADE KELLER, BETH PHOENIX, BARON VON RASCHKE, BRIAN BLAIR, ME, AND BRIAN SHIELDS.

The more I've come back to wrestling, and as much as I dislike most of its current presentation, I love the history of it. And I genuinely enjoy my role as a historian and sharing my memories to what has become a growing, robust fan base.

There's limited opportunity to make income in this business. As with most entertainment endeavors, there are the haves and the have-nots. I certainly don't want to be a have-not again. But making a living in this business is a long shot. So what am I doing approaching 65 and trying to make a go of it, *again*? Am I trying to go back in time? Even back then I couldn't make a freakin' living in it! And now I'm back in it? I guess I've always rolled the dice and hoped for the best. It's the only way I've done things in my roller-coaster, multi-personality/identity life I've led. I've never been afraid to blow the house up and start again . . . and again . . . and again. It does make it hard waking up in the morning and wondering if today I am John Alexander or John Arezzi.

20.

WHAT IF?

As I sit here at my computer, thinking about my past "lives," pondering how this book should end, and how I will finish my career before retirement, I can't help but wonder, "What if?"

What if Uncle Sonny took me to a Yankees game instead in 1966? Or if he never took me to a game at all? Would I have followed my dad's footsteps and worked with the likes of Uncle Fritzy?

What if I did not walk into the Stardust Lounge in 1981, hear the band Straight Up, and fall in love with their lead singer, Patty Lovelace? Would I have had a career in baseball and with the New York Mets? Would Patty have become a country music legend?

What if Andrew Goldberger didn't see the Will the Thrill Video store on a walk home? Would Vince Russo have been unleashed to help spearhead wrestling's Attitude Era? Would Dwayne Johnson have become The Rock? Would WCW still be around?

What if I decided not to have lunch at the Mellow Mushroom in July of 2012? Would Kelsea Ballerini have become the number-one hitmaking artist she is today? Would Black River Entertainment have gone out of business?

What if my nephew Dominic did not hear Vince Russo's podcast talking smack about me? What if my media company took off or there was no COVID-19 pandemic? Would I be here writing these words to conclude my memoir?

While I don't know what the future holds in these uncertain times, what I do know is that my life has been filled with adventures, and misadventures. I've seen people who have been a major part of my life, and I in theirs, go to the top of their industries and achieve great financial rewards. But for me, as I write this, I do not know if I will have to survive off social security when I retire.

TO STEAL A LINE FROM TERENCE MANN IN *FIELD OF DREAMS*, WHICH CERTAINLY APPLIES TO MY LIFE, "THE ONE CONSTANT THROUGH ALL THE YEARS, RAY, HAS BEEN BASEBALL." HERE I'M AT COORS FIELD IN DENVER IN 2006 ENJOYING A GAME WITH MY NIECE, MELISSA, AND HER KIDS, JOHNNY AND GABBY.

It all comes back to baseball for me. I consider myself akin to a minor-league baseball manager. I coached and mentored some diamonds in the rough in the music business and then watched them hit home runs in that industry. I gave opportunity to a brash, ambitious video store owner who wanted a gig in the wrestling business and saw him help change the face of pro wrestling, for good and bad. I opened doors for many with aspirations to achieve greatness. I watched them excel and waved goodbye to them without reaping the benefits of their success.

As I enter the late innings of this life, my happiness comes from taking my nephew on our annual spring training sabbaticals to watch our beloved Mets, sitting at Citi Field with him on Opening Day, at the Subway Series games versus the hated Yankees, and hoping this year will be the one that the Amazin's win the World Series. Simple? Yes, but fulfilling.

I've worked in the entertainment business all my life, having spent years in the circus-like world of pro wrestling and in the have-or-have-not world of country music. I only had, as they say, a "cup of coffee" in baseball, having worked for a season in the minor leagues and spent a few additional months with MLB in video production. But that cup of coffee still tastes the best to me.

ACKNOWLEDGMENTS

John: First, thank you to Greg Oliver, who took on this project and held my hand through the process. I could not have asked for a better partner. At times I felt like I was working with a psychologist, to whom I was telling my innermost revelations. I hope that honesty is transparent in this book. I want to also give thanks to Michael Holmes, who not only gave me the opportunity to write my story but suggested Greg as the writer for the project.

Thank you to my attorney, my consigliere, my friend, Wayne Halper, for help through the good and bad times. Thanks to Donny Laible, who's been a lifelong cheerleader and friend. George Napolitano was instrumental in opening so many doors for me in the pro wrestling world. Thanks to Brian Last, who gave me the chance to relive my Mat Memories with him each week on our podcast.

To my family who all left us way too early, I pay tribute to you. My mom, Snooky, and older sister, Linda, you battled with mental health all your lives, and still loved and fought for your family with unrelenting strength. My dad, Sam, I wish we had been closer. I understand the challenges you faced, and the reasons you were not there as much as you wanted to be. I know you were proud of my accomplishments. I

VALUE YOUR FAMILY TIME. AT CHRISTMAS 2018, MY SISTER
DONNA, NEPHEW DOMINIC, AND I WENT OUT TO COLORADO FOR
THE HOLIDAYS. THESE ARE THE KIDS OF MY LATE SISTER, LINDA:
MICHAEL, MELISSA, AND EDDIE WITH THEIR FATHER, EDDIE SR.-WHO
DIED JUST THREE DAYS LATER, AND WE ALL FLEW RIGHT BACK FOR
HIS MILITARY FUNERAL.

wish you were here today to hold this book in your hands, and show
it off to your friends and Italian "associates." To my Uncle Sonny, you
were the man I looked up to all my life, and I owe you for giving me the
gift of the Mets, by taking me to that first game in 1966. To my Uncle
Tom, you were always encouraging me to be the best I could be, and I
am grateful for that. To Grandma Fanny and Aunt Nana, you loved me
and my sisters, protected us, and watched over us during the times my
mom could not. Grandma Dorothy, thank you for allowing me to go to
college; that gift changed my life forever. I don't know where I would be
today if you didn't come through!

And finally, to my incredibly resilient small family who are all
still here, sister Donna, nephew and godson Dominic, brother-in-law
Thomas, niece Melissa, her husband John, nephew and godson Eddie
Boy, nephew Michael and his wife Sarah, great niece Gabby, her
husband Danny, great nephew Johnny, great-great nieces Gia and little
Ellie, cousin Jimmy, my goddaughter Jessica, cousin Judy, Anthony, and

cousin Kathy, who've all faced struggle and challenges, your fighting spirit has always inspired me. I love you all.

Greg: Thanks to Michael Holmes for suggesting that John and I work together. John approached me at the Cauliflower Alley Club reunion in 2019, and we had a deal not long after. Personally, I was excited by the music industry side of things rather than the pro wrestling, but it was all pretty damn interesting; the baseball was a bonus. His candor and honesty is what makes this book what it is. There were a few times he was exhausted and emotionally drained after talking about a particular subject. Thanks to his family and friends who shared thoughts on his life and times. Bob Kapur proved to be a great research assistant/drinking buddy on our memorable trip to Nashville, and has been a valued friend for a long time now. And, as always, thanks to my wife, Meredith, and son, Quinn, for letting me do this writing thing.

★ ★ ★ ★ ★ ★ ★ ★ ★ ★

GREG OLIVER AND JOHN AREZZI IN FEBRUARY 2020.